ISLAM AND
HUMAN RIGHTS

ISLAM AND HUMAN RIGHTS

Tradition and Politics

THIRD EDITION

Ann Elizabeth Mayer

UNIVERSITY OF PENNSYLVANIA

Westview Press
A Member of the Perseus Books Group

Published in 1999 in the United States of America by Westview Press, 5500 Central Avenue, Boulder, Colorado 80301-2877, and in the United Kingdom by Westview Press, 12 Hid's Copse Road, Cumnor Hill, Oxford OX2 9JJ

Library of Congress Cataloging-in-Publication Data
Mayer, Ann Elizabeth.
  Islam and human rights : tradition and politics / Ann Elizabeth
Mayer. — 3rd ed.
     p.   cm.
  Includes bibliographical references and index.
  ISBN 0-8133-3564-7 (hardcover). — ISBN 0-8133-3504-3 (pbk.)
  1. Human rights—Religious aspects—Islam.   I. Title.
LAW
342'.085'0917671—dc21   98-20762
                                                                            CIP

The paper used in this publication meets the requirements of the American National Standard for Permanence of Paper for Printed Library Materials Z39.48-1984.

10   9   8   7   6   5   4   3   2   1

*To my mother
and her mother*

Contents

Preface

Perspicacious readers will note that the title of this book is a misnomer. A more accurate title might be "A Comparison of Selected Civil and Political Rights Formulations in International Law and in Actual and Proposed Rights Schemes Purporting to Embody Islamic Principles, with a Critical Appraisal of the Latter in Terms of International Law and Islamic Jurisprudence and Relevant State Practice." The actual title stands as it is simply because it is the kind of rubric that people tend to consult when looking for material on human rights in Muslim milieus. That is, it has been selected for purely practical reasons despite its not being very informative.

The reference to "Islam" in the book title is potentially misleading, since I repudiate the commonly held view that Islam by itself determines the attitudes one finds in the Muslim world on human rights issues. In fact, I see Islam as only one factor in the reception of human rights in the Middle East. The reason this book focuses on Islamic human rights schemes is that my own research interests happen to center on the role of Islamic law in contemporary Middle Eastern societies.

A central thesis of this book is that one should not speak of "Islam" and human rights as if Islam were a monolith or as if there existed one established Islamic human rights philosophy that caused all Muslims to look at rights in a particular way. The precepts of Islam, like those of Christianity, Hinduism, Judaism, and other major religions possessed of long and complex traditions, are susceptible to interpretations that can and do create conflicts between religious doctrine and human rights or that reconcile the two. In reality, one cannot predict the position that a person will take on a human rights problem simply on the basis of the person's religious affiliation—and this is as true of Muslims as of members of other faiths. Even where the discussion is limited, as it is here, to Muslims living in the area stretching from North Africa to Pakistan, Muslims' attitudes toward human rights run the gamut from total rejection to wholehearted embrace. Indeed, since the publication of the last edition of this book, events provoking controversies about where Islam stands on rights have so proliferated that this third edition has had to be substantially revised, with much material cut and reorganized to accommodate the coverage of recent developments.

What currently differentiates Muslims' approaches to rights from discussions of rights in secularized Western milieus is the tendency of the former to rely heavily on religious principles and interpretations of Islamic sources to develop their positions supporting or condemning rights. Under present conditions, questions of human rights, like other great political issues facing Muslim societies, cannot easily be severed from disputes that are raging about the implications of Islamic theology and law for contemporary problems. "Islam" has become the vehicle both for political protest against undemocratic regimes and for the repression meted out by such regimes, simultaneously expressing aspirations for democracy and equality and providing rationales for campaigns to crush democratic freedoms and perpetuate old patterns of discrimination.

At a time when Islamic themes and terminology dominate political discourse, it can be difficult for persons both inside and outside Muslim societies to distinguish neatly between political and religious issues. Nonetheless, when the substantive issues being contested are compared with matters in dispute in non-Muslim societies, one can discern that under the surface of the debates about "Islam," political struggles are going on that have much in common with the history of campaigns for democracy and equality in non-Muslim countries. In the West, analogous debates on civil and political rights have been carried out in secular terms—as indeed they were for decades in many Muslim milieus before the onset of the Islamic resurgence after 1967. In this connection, it is noteworthy that results of the rights policies associated with upholding the supremacy of Islamic law at the expense of rights and freedoms have simply replicated patterns of rights violations already familiar under repressive and undemocratic regimes outside the Muslim world. Dissent is silenced, opponents are imprisoned or killed, free elections are barred, and other familiar ills are engendered. The patterns of discrimination against women and religious minorities that proponents of Islamization currently insist are mandated by rules of Islamic law likewise mimic patterns of discrimination found elsewhere, as will be apparent to anyone who reviews the historical record of treatment of women and religious minorities in Western societies.

In this book I analyze the political use of Islamic law since World War II in formulations of distinctive Islamic human rights schemes—meaning combinations of elements connected by design. As I point out, these schemes embody highly selective and often less-than-coherent views of applicable Islamic principles. I critically appraise these schemes. The problems that I discuss include a refusal to abandon philosophies inimical to rights and freedom, misrepresentations of comparative legal history, failures to address actual patterns of rights abuses, insufficient grasp of international rights principles, imprecise legal methodologies, evasive and ambiguous formulations, and misleading rhetoric. All these flaws should be ascribed to the failings of the human authors, not to Islam.

The emphasis placed here on the problems of interpreting and applying the Islamic sources, problems central to the production of Islamic human rights schemes, resembles the emphasis placed on issues of methodology by the premodern jurists of Islam. Islam has historically been a very decentralized religion encompassing a wide range of dissimilar opinions and competing schools of law, and one could say that the Islamic legal tradition has historically been a culture of argument. Critical appraisals of divergent interpretations of the Islamic sources preoccupied the jurists, who argued endlessly in their treatises about the right techniques for deriving rules of law. This disagreement among the jurists was accepted as an integral feature of the Islamic tradition.

Unfortunately, this tradition of tolerance of debate and argument about the meanings of the Islamic sources has been repudiated in many quarters today. Ideologues who imagine that Islam is a unitary utopian scheme for governing society may condemn any criticisms of their interpretations or official religious policies, confusing these with attempts to malign Islam or with a lack of respect for the views of its adherents. The unfair and often grotesque demonization of Islam in the West has also prompted some Western academics to attribute any critical perspectives on political Islam in the Middle East to prejudice. Due to the inhibiting effect of such attitudes, much of the secondary literature currently available in the West on the relationship between Islam and human rights is informed by an uncritical approach and contributes little to an understanding of the subject. In many ways, the approach taken in this book has been inspired by the defects in the secondary literature and is intended to compensate for its gaps and its prevailing uncritical quality. Since I am consciously endeavoring to respond to what I see as defects in the secondary literature, these defects should be summarized.

The authors of many of the works in the secondary literature on Islam and human rights fail to analyze and explain the criteria that are being employed to decide what qualifies as "Islamic law." They seem not to perceive the need to distinguish between principles set forth in the Islamic sources and the historical patterns of interpreting these sources. Treating Islamic law as static, they do not address evolutions and reforms in interpretations of the Islamic sources that have taken place over time—or they dismiss evolving contemporary understandings of the sources as if these necessarily fell outside the bounds of the Islamic tradition. The disparities in views among contemporary Muslims on rights questions are rarely given their due. Generally, these authors seem to miss the significance of the fact that human rights ideas are recent legal transplants in the Middle East, which cannot be accommodated within the framework of premodern juristic doctrines without substantial adjustments. They likewise neglect to differentiate between moral values or ideal prescriptive norms of Islam and the actual laws, legal institutions, and policies in Muslim countries. In particular, there is a disinclination to take into account the skewed balance of power between the government and the governed in the political systems of the contemporary Middle East and the implications of that situation for rights issues. Their work often reveals an unfamiliarity with international human rights law. Comparisons of Islamic rights standards with their international counterparts, if undertaken at all, tend to be careless and underdeveloped. Specific analyses of how Islamic versions of rights relate to actual rights abuses in the Middle East are usually wanting, so that discussions remain at the level of vague, decontextualized generalizations.

The weaknesses in the secondary literature correlate with the tendency one finds in the work of the average Western student of the Middle East and Islam to accept at face value Islamic rationales for denying human rights. A curious assumption underlying this attitude seems to be that the proper empathy for Muslims and their beliefs requires uncritically accepting the "Islamic" rubrics for legal rules and policies that deny human rights to Muslims. In contrast, among Muslims, skeptical scrutiny of official rhetoric and of Islamic rationales for policies that disregard international human rights is common. Thus, although governments may claim that their opposition to international human rights is justified by Islamic culture, the Muslims whom they govern may dismiss such claims as cynical appeals to religion, made with an intent to legitimize the vices of corrupt and undemocratic political systems.

Western academics may dismiss the opinions of those Muslims who call for democracy and human rights as "inauthentic." Academics in the West often seem to be committed to irrebuttable presumptions about the distinctive mind-sets of peoples from non-Western cultures and the absolute nontransferability of Western institutions like democratic government and human rights. Thus, at an academic conclave in 1996 during which I was speaking on international human rights law in the Middle East, a senior scholar of the Middle East urgently advised me that Muslims could not have democracy. This was because, in his view, certain verses in the Qur'an precluded Muslims from having political parties, a view that is also promoted by some Islamic ideologues. To this scholar, the aspirations of Muslims for democracy and the real-world experiences of Muslim countries with democracy were immaterial in deciding what could be; according to him, the Muslim world was a place where all attitudes and actions necessarily had to flow from a sacred text, a text that he treated as having univocal, unchanging meaning. The cultural order mandated by Islam was self-contained and impervious to "alien" concepts. Political contestation could not exist within this monolithic tradition, where religious culture was the be-all and end-all. Such rigid, stereotypical preconceptions about how Islamic universals predetermine the mind-sets and concrete practices in Muslim societies are far from uncommon, and their purveyors remain unresponsive to the insightful critiques of such preconceptions that Muslims have published.

I am critical of governments' claims that unimpeachable Islamic authority warrants their violations of human rights, even though I understand that individual Muslims may freely decide to accept the authority of interpretations of Islamic sources that place Islamic law at odds with international human rights law. Muslims may have the sincere conviction that their religious tradition requires deviations from international law, and such private beliefs must be respected. However, the situation becomes different when beliefs that Islamic rules should supersede human rights are marshaled to promote campaigns or measures for stripping others of rights to which they are entitled under international law or when such beliefs are cited to buttress governmental policies and laws that violate the International Bill of Human Rights. The resulting curbs on rights and freedoms go well beyond the realm of protected private beliefs and enter the domains of politics and law. Projected or actual programs based on distinctive Islamic versions of human rights can engender conflicts with international law, and it is these conflicts that will be examined in this book.

Any Islamic rationales offered by governments for violating international human rights law must be open to scrutiny. Since contemporary governments only adhere to Islamic law very selectively and only to the extent that local politics dictate that they do so, it is legitimate to investigate what reasons other than religion may lie behind policies that are officially grounded in Islamic law.

In assessing Islamic human rights schemes I have endeavored to treat all sources and arguments objectively, but that does not mean that I feel obligated to withhold judgment or to suppress my own opinions. My own views—with supporting reasoning—are expressed at various points in this book. On human rights questions, I do not consider that it is possible or even advisable to withhold all judgment on the moral rightness of positions. In clarification, I would say that one can write on questions of slavery in a serious and fair manner without withholding all judgment about whether slavery is a benign or an evil institution. Similarly, one should be able to offer scholarly assessments of the practice of torture without having to adopt the attitude that torture is a morally neutral phenomenon. On the same grounds, I also believe that it is possible to give a fair appraisal of conflicts on rights issues without being obliged to deny all philosophical convictions about whether human beings possess rights that deserve respect or whether governmental rights violations are blameworthy.

I believe in the normative character of the human rights principles set forth in international law and in their universality. Believing that these are universal, I naturally also believe that Muslims are entitled to the full measure of human rights protections accorded under international law. This inclines me to be critical of any actual or proposed governmental rights policies that violate international human rights law, regardless of whether they employ secular rationales or Islamic doctrines as justifications. Conversely, I welcome the emergence of serious human rights movements in Middle Eastern countries and the growing tendency to interpret Islamic sources in ways that harmonize Islamic law and international human rights.

As a supporter of international law and an advocate of respect for human rights, I readily concede that I regard liberal reformist trends in Islamic thought as positive developments. Since the ideas of liberal reformist Muslims are under constant attack by powerful and extremely well-financed conservative forces determined to discredit them and delegitimize their programs, their beleaguered positions cannot escape being subjected to the harshest possible critical scrutiny. Middle Eastern governments have found it expedient to invest large sums in polishing their images and have discovered that is all too easy to win influence and to buy apologists in Western institutions and academia as well as governmental circles. Western hirelings assiduously work to discredit critics of governmental wrongdoing and are prepared to employ every trick in the public relations artist's portfolio to rationalize and cover up governmental delinquencies in the human rights domain. In reaction to this imbalance, I think it appropriate to focus on critical examinations of the use of Islam by governments and institutions to legitimize policies antithetical to rights, a use of Islam that people in Middle Eastern countries can assail only at great risk to their personal safety and freedom.

International human rights standards have won a wide following among Muslims. It is worth pointing out that international human rights assume far greater importance for the inhabitants of Muslim societies than they do for citizens of Western liberal democracies, who rarely try to secure protections for their rights by appeals to international law. In the West, average persons, when deprived of rights, tend to think in terms of vindicating claims under domestic legal standards of civil or constitutional rights. Thus, an American with a rights claim would normally seek relief exclusively under domestic laws like provisions of the Bill of Rights in the U.S. Constitution, discounting the utility of any appeal to international law. In contrast, a Muslim in the Middle East may well know that there is no realistic possibility of obtaining redress for rights violations by appeals to domestic legal standards and may use international rights concepts set forth in instruments like the Universal Declaration of Human Rights to try to pressure the local government to recognize the legitimacy of a rights claim.

I have learned about Muslims' growing involvement in international human rights through discussions with Muslim friends, who have drawn me into human rights networks. I have participated in a variety of efforts to try to secure greater respect for human rights in Middle Eastern countries—and not just in those countries pursuing Islamization. Even without studying the question of how Islam relates to human rights issues, my experience in work on behalf of the cause of human rights would have sufficed to convince me that Islam is not the cause of the human rights problems endemic to the Middle East. Human rights activists quickly discover that rights abuses may be every bit as prevalent and just as severe in countries where Islamic law is in abeyance or consciously violated as in countries where it figures, at least officially, as the legal norm. One must recognize that, depending on the political context, supporters of Islamization may easily turn out to be the victims of rights violations committed by secular regimes, and the violations of their human rights must be taken as seriously as any other rights violations. However, rights violations by secular regimes do not take place under the rubric of applying Islamic law, and they lie outside the scope of this volume.

This study focuses on the legal dimensions of human rights problems, examining the questions within the framework of comparative law and comparative legal history. Given the centrality of law in the Islamic tradition, the legal emphasis is warranted. However, there is no intention to imply that Islam is exclusively a legal tradition or that comparative legal history is the only legitimate way to approach this topic. In a more comprehensive study on the relationship of Islam to human rights, one would ideally want to include analysis of how principles of Islamic theology, philosophy, and ethics tie in with the treatment of human rights. One would also want to link the analysis to an examination of problems of the cultural accommodation of new rights concepts and the relationship between human rights protections and economic development. This would carry one into areas beyond the comparative legal analysis of civil and political rights that is the sole concern of this study. The reader who conscientiously attempts to follow all the arguments and the specific comparisons of legal provisions that I shall be making will probably concur that the task of sorting out the existing material is sufficiently arduous.

Ann Elizabeth Mayer

Acknowledgments

The genesis of this book was my experience during three decades of study of Middle Eastern history and law. My interest in the subject of human rights in the Middle East emerged only belatedly, stimulated by talks with Middle Easterners. The attitudes that Middle Easterners of many backgrounds expressed on human rights struck me as being different from what my academic training in the West had led me to expect and were often hard to reconcile with the descriptions of Middle Eastern culture and Islamic political thought in scholarly literature written by Westerners. I became intrigued by the comments that my interlocutors made about their aspirations for democratic freedoms. I noticed a common—though not unanimous—tendency to demand the same kinds of democratic institutions that exist in liberal democracies in the West and a general impatience with all official rationales that governments exploited to justify repression and discrimination. I was ultimately brought to the conclusion that Muslims' ideas of human rights deserved more systematic investigation, and I reoriented my research accordingly.

There are so many Middle Eastern friends and colleagues to whom I owe debts of gratitude for their generous efforts to enlighten me about their political attitudes, their understanding of the Islamic tradition, and their ideas of human rights that it would be impossible to list them all here. It might also be inadvisable to mention names in a book on this sensitive topic at a time like the present, when human rights issues are so bitterly contested and when speaking out on these issues can involve such terrible risks. I hope the many friends and colleagues who have enlightened me appreciate that I acknowledge owing them a great debt.

I also wish to thank Oceana for kindly granting me permission to reprint excerpts from the translation of the Iranian Constitution published in their collection.

A.E.M.

CHAPTER 1

Comparisons of Rights Across Cultures

In the Muslim Middle East there has been a strong but mixed response to the ideals of human rights. Formulations of human rights have often been made in Islamic terms, suggesting that Islam is a critical factor affecting Muslims' receptivity to human rights concepts. This Islamic dimension is analyzed here.

The Islamic religion was a deeply ingrained feature of the culture of the traditional Middle East. In the course of the difficult modernization process to which all Muslim countries have been subjected, societies in the Middle East have been transformed and their Islamic institutions have faced new challenges. Islam is responding on both the theological and ideological levels to new situations in the Middle East.[1]

International human rights concepts have percolated through Middle Eastern societies at a time when new formulations of Islamic doctrine are emerging. Responsive to the changing realities in the Muslim world, these new formulations may seek to accommodate the evolving attitudes and aspirations of Islam's followers, which include hopes for greater freedom at a time when governments have enormously increased their power at the expense of those whom they govern. Muslims' resentment of unaccountable, despotic governments has prompted a surge in activism supporting democratization and human rights.[2]

The relationship between the Islamic legal tradition and human rights, which is of great theoretical interest, has gained in practical significance in the wake of the Islamic resurgence that began after the Arab-Israeli war of 1967. Prior to that time, this issue seemed to be academic, because the movement toward secularization of legal systems had been very consistent, leaving only small islands of Islamic substantive rules in what were basically modern, secularized legal systems. In a dramatic turnabout, the survival of imported Western legal systems was threatened as the Islamic resurgence led to calls for rejecting Western legal models and for the Islamization of laws. Proliferating Islamization programs have made the topic of Islamic law and human rights a matter of great controversy. This study is limited to the controversies over international provisions on civil and political rights, which have been particularly vigorously contested.

Despite the features that they share in common, Islamic human rights schemes turn out to serve a variety of political agendas and to reflect the influences of local contexts in which they have arisen. Therefore, what will be examined here is not how Islam per se pertains to human rights, but rather how Islamic doctrines and concepts are being interpreted by contemporary Muslims to apply to rights issues.

In their writings on the relationship between Islamic and international law, Muslims have espoused a wide range of opinions on rights—from the assertion that international human rights are fully compatible with Islam to the claim that international human rights are products of alien, Western culture and represent values that are repugnant to Islam. In between these extremes, one finds compromise positions that in effect maintain that Islam accepts many but not all aspects of international human rights or that it endorses human rights with certain reservations and qualifications.

Views that are representative of this middle ground will constitute the focus of this study. In this connection, I shall present analyses of specific aspects of selected Islamic human rights schemes. These schemes, not one of which has been ratified by a universal consensus, have been promoted by members of educated elites and by certain governments. They purport to represent definitive Islamic countermodels of human rights that Muslims should follow in lieu of the international formulas. The fact that the middle-ground positions are being emphasized in this study does not mean that they are deemed more authentically Islamic than the others. They are simply more attractive subjects for investigation because they reveal the conflicting trends presently at work in shaping distinctive Islamic provisions on human rights. Middle-ground positions illustrate the problems of transplanting legal institutions from a culture in which they originally grew to another culture. Such positions are also of great practical importance because they relate to how human rights have been treated under governments that are officially committed to according overriding priority to upholding Islamic law.

Muslims who oppose international human rights and demand their replacement by Islamic law have not to date conceived of Islam affording more extensive protections for human rights than are provided by international law. As will be shown in the discussion of Islamic human rights schemes, distinctive Islamic criteria have consistently been used to cut back on the rights and freedoms guaranteed by international law, as if the latter were deemed excessive. The literature arguing that Muslims may have human rights, but only according to Islamic principles, provides the theoretical rationales for many recent government policies that have been harmful for rights.

Cross-comparisons between what has been or is being implemented in several countries under the rubric of Islamization and relevant Islamic human rights formulations will be presented here. The latter, in turn, will be compared with international human rights standards to elucidate where they coincide with or diverge from the Islamic formulations.

Comparative legal history is an academic field where major political controversies are rarely encountered. As an eminent comparatist has stated, comparative law looks at the relationships among legal systems and their rules, and ultimately it is concerned with similarities and differences in legal systems and rules in the context of historical relationships.[3] In the main, scholars can expect such studies to be of interest to specialists and will be justified in assuming that any controversies they may provoke will center on issues of scholarship. If scholars are comparing, say, German law and Japanese law or Spanish law and community property rules in California, they do not expect the mere undertaking of such comparisons to be condemned by their academic peers. Nor do they expect that their work will be denounced as politically unsound if they objectively record the similarities and differences that they have uncovered or state whether aspects of one system were historically derived from the other. Those writing on comparative legal history are used to working in a discipline free from ideologically inspired precensorship. Thus, their scholarly inquiry is unimpeded by political constraints, and they may express their conclusions without having to adjust them to fit the canons of a prevailing orthodoxy.

There should be no bar to evaluating Islamic human rights schemes and Islamization measures, along with their theoretical underpinnings, by the standards of international human rights. Since the study of the relationship between contemporary Islamic rights formulations and their counterparts in contemporary international human rights law is a proper and even conventional topic in the field of comparative legal history, one would not expect that researching and commenting on it would resemble stepping into an ideological minefield. In actuality, a Western scholar discovers that undertaking a critical assessment of Islamic approaches to rights will be widely denounced as a venture necessarily motivated by ethnocentric biases and designed to promote political objectives associated with Orientalism and Western imperialism. It is therefore essential both to offer a preliminary response to the kinds of objections that can be anticipated and to establish the nature and goals of a comparative legal study like the one being attempted here.

The pressures to censor discussions of this topic may in part account for the fact that until recently there has been a paucity of literature available in the West offering critical comparisons of Islamic and international human rights.[4] Much of what has been written in this area is characterized by superficiality and an unwillingness to tackle real problems using tools of comparative legal analysis. Western scholars who perceive this gap and venture to undertake such analysis will quickly discover why it is a path that others have feared to tread. If they persist, they will find their work seriously misunderstood and often deliberately distorted by critics who have ruled such analysis off-limits.[5]

Obstacles to Comparison

What are the reasons why this topic has been effectively ruled off-limits for any critical scholarly inquiry? The impetus behind this informal but effective censorship does not come from scholars in the fields of international and comparative law. It comes, instead, from specialists in area studies like the study of the Middle East, where Islamology is a major subject.[6] Islamologists and other students of the Middle East tend to become acculturated by their academic milieus in ways that lead them to conclude that such comparisons are objectionable. Because many Third World spokespersons reject the idea of the universality of human rights and defend culture-based resistance to international rights standards, these perspectives may be uncritically assimilated by scholars studying areas like the Middle East. Scholars who are conscientiously seeking to understand the cultural background of Third World attitudes toward Western institutions may assimilate these attitudes. A critical perspective that might be suspected of reflecting Western biases will tend to be discarded as a possible impediment to understanding the societies under study. In contrast, the present study will try to demonstrate that a critical and even skeptical perspective should be maintained in the face of assertions that human rights norms do not apply outside Western countries.

A factor underlying objections to Western critiques of human rights in the Middle East is that the criticism is seen as inevitably tinged with hypocrisy and double standards. The West does have its own history of egregious human rights violations—including an extensive record of patterns of torture, genocide, religious persecution, racism, sexism, and centuries of slavery. It also has a record of disregarding the rights of the inhabitants of the Middle Eastern societies that it ruled in the past and of wielding gross double standards in deciding which nations currently deserve condemnation for rights abuses. This history prompts arguments that Westerners are in no position to pass judgment on human rights issues in Middle Eastern countries.

The most frequently cited example of contemporary Western hypocrisy in judging the rights records of Middle Eastern countries is the Western reaction to rights violations in Iran. Current Western criticism of Iran's rights record is rejected because of the disparity between the Western response to human rights abuses under the shah of Iran and under the regimes of Ayatollah Khomeini and his successors. The inference is drawn that the West condones or ignores human rights abuses by allied pro-Western regimes and brings up human rights issues only to discredit regimes that defy Western hegemony and reject Western cultural values.

In the case of Iran, there is no disputing the fact that the West generally and the United States in particular played a major role in propping up the shah's brutal regime and that, while paying lip service to human rights ideals, the West demonstrated a lack of determination to end the shah's human rights violations. U.S. apologists for the shah's regime were notorious for their rationalizations of rights abuses. To such apologists, practices that were ingrained under the Pahlavis suddenly became reprehensible after the Khomeini regime came to power and adopted an anti-Western stance. Their expressions of concern for human rights after the revolution obviously have little credibility.

However, having conceded this, one does not see why the U.S. government's record of hypocrisy and double standards in the human rights area should bar independent scholars in the West from looking at human rights issues in Middle Eastern countries. In fact, if the hypocrisy of the foreign policy of a scholar's home government disqualified that scholar from pursuing study of other societies and cultures, most such study would be barred. The evidence is that all governments, whether in the West or in the East, in the conduct of their foreign relations, are much more critical of their foes than of their allies or client states. The priority that they accord to political advantage renders most governments unfit as arbiters of morality.

The argument that private criticisms of the treatment of rights in Muslim milieus are of a piece with hypocritical governmental policy is especially weak in the case of this study, which includes Pakistan under President Muhammad Zia ul-Haq and his successors, Saudi Arabia, and the Sudan under Ja'far Nimeiri. With respect to these, the United States was hypocritical not in the sense of judging them particularly harshly but, rather, the reverse—it glossed over human rights abuses committed by strategically important friendly governments. Related strategic concerns seem to have inhibited U.S. criticisms of rights abuses by Afghan leaders until 1997. Only the rights abuses in postrevolutionary Iran, the Sudan under Omar al-Bashir, and Afghanistan after the 1996 Taleban takeover have been harshly excoriated.

The United States provided the strongest military and economic support for President Zia's regime in Pakistan from his 1977 coup until his death in 1988 and was relatively tolerant of the rights violations perpetrated under his Islamization program. Washington has been reluctant publicly to denounce rights abuses in Saudi Arabia, one of the most valued of U.S. allies.

In the case of the Sudan, the United States was the staunch mainstay of the Nimeiri government in 1983–1985, when Nimeiri was pursuing his Islamization campaign, and accommodated its abuses. The Reagan administration even gave President Nimeiri a cordial reception in the White House in spring 1985 after Nimeiri had ordered the execution of a seventy-six-year-old Sudanese religious leader as a "heretic." When Afghan factions fighting the Soviets and aiming to establish Afghanistan as an Islamic state showed disregard for human rights, the United States remained willing to underwrite their campaign. Such treatment indicated that the United States acquiesced in Islamization programs that grossly violated human rights— as long as the regimes served U.S. policies. It also illustrated how the lives of Muslims and non-Western peoples may be devalued in the calculations of Washington officialdom in charge of U.S. human rights policy. Thus, consistent critical appraisals of the human rights records in these countries hardly correlate with hypocritical U.S. policies, which have focused on human rights abuses in a selective and politicized manner.

Another reason why people have been inclined to condemn critical comparisons of Islamic and international human rights is that they see sinister political objectives in Western criticisms of rights violations related to Islamic institutions. Some consider such criticisms as part of an effort to tarnish the image of Islam and to portray Islamic culture as primitive and cruel. The ultimate goal in this regard is thought to be the celebration of Western culture as advanced and inherently superior, and a demonstration that Western political, economic, and cultural hegemony was and is a natural and beneficial phenomenon for humankind. Such critiques may be understood as an effort to prove that Western domination of Muslim countries in the past was justified and also to legitimize neocolonialist designs by retroactively rehabilitating the imperialist enterprise. Their sensibilities in this regard have been exacerbated by the pervasive influence of Edward Said's seminal book, *Orientalism*.[7] In this book, Said argued that much of Western scholarship on the Orient, meaning the Islamic Middle East, is not conducted in a spirit of scientific research but is based on a racist assumption of fundamental Western superiority and Oriental inferiority. By positing ineradicable distinctions between the West and the Orient, Orientalist scholarship, in Said's view, obscures the common humanity of people in the West and the Orient and thereby dehumanizes Orientals in a way that serves the goals of Western imperialism.

Although Said is not a lawyer and did not analyze legal scholarship, people influenced by his arguments tend to expand them to include legal scholarship, and although Said did not assert that all critical examination of Islamic institutions is infected by Orientalist biases, his disciples seem inclined to draw this inference from his book. In consequence, they may perceive all projects involving a comparative legal analysis of Islamic law and international law—the latter being identified with the West—as Orientalist in a pejorative sense, particularly in cases where they anticipate that the analysis will show that Islamic law falls short of meeting the standards of international law. This perception is unjustified.

The use of international rights standards as norms in critical examinations of Islamic human rights schemes and restrictions on human rights imposed by governments in the Muslim world does not necessarily reflect a racist assumption of Western superiority. Rather, such use may rest on the premise that peoples in the West and the East share a common humanity, which means that they are equally deserving of rights and freedoms. To maintain that human rights do not apply to Muslim societies is to accept the quintessentially Orientalist notion that the concepts and categories employed in the West to understand societies and cultures are irrelevant and inapplicable in the East. To believe that Islam precludes Orientals from claiming the same rights and freedoms as people in the West is to commit oneself to perpetuating the Orientalist tenet that Islam is a static, uniform system that dominates Oriental society, the coherence and continuity of which should not be imperiled by foreign intrusions such as democratic ideas and human rights.[8] Those who charge that comparisons of international and Islamic law as these affect human rights are Orientalist implicitly endorse the same elitist stance as the cultural relativists, discussed below—that international human rights are the sole prerogative of members of Western societies. Therefore, they are distorting Said's message, which was, ultimately, that categories like "Islam" and "Oriental" should not be allowed to obscure the common humanity of peoples in the East and in the West.

Cultural Relativism

At the core of most efforts to delegitimize comparisons of Islamic and international law is the conviction that such comparisons violate the principles of cultural relativism. Not all cultural relativists approach questions in an identical fashion, but in general they are inclined to endorse the idea that all values and principles are culture-bound and that there are no universal standards by which cultures may be judged. Similarly, they deny the legitimacy of using alien values to judge a culture and reject using ideas taken from Western culture to judge the institutions of non-Western cultures. They also tend to oppose the idea that human rights norms are universal.[9] To impose on Third World societies norms taken from the Universal Declaration of Human Rights involves, according to this perspective, "moral chauvinism and ethnocentric bias."[10] For strong cultural relativists, evaluative comparisons of Islamic rights concepts and international ones are impermissible because such comparisons are believed to involve judging Islamic institutions by the criteria of international law, which the relativists view as an alien, Western system.

Cultural relativists seeking support for their position might take comfort from statements like that of Iran's UN representative, Said Raja'i-Khorasani, defending Iran from charges that it was violating human rights. His argument that international standards could not be used to judge Iran's human rights record was paraphrased as follows:

> The new political order was . . . in full accordance and harmony with the deepest moral and religious convictions of the people and therefore most representative of the traditional, cultural, moral and religious beliefs of Iranian society. It recognized no authority . . . apart from Islamic law . . . conventions, declarations and resolutions or decisions of international organizations, which were contrary to Islam, had no validity in the Islamic Republic of Iran. . . . The Universal Declaration of Human Rights, which represented secular understanding of the Judaeo-Christian tradition, could not be implemented by Muslims and did not accord with the system of values recognized by the Islamic Republic of Iran; his country would therefore not hesitate to violate its provisions.[11]

Raja'i-Khorasani identified the official position of the Iranian government with the Islamic religion and traditional culture. Similar assertions that governmental resistance to international human rights represents a defense of traditional culture and morality have been made by other governmental spokespersons in international conferences in attempts to defend governmental records of human rights violations, thereby demonstrating the political usefulness of the cultural relativist stance.[12]

Employing a cultural relativist stance to deny the universality of human rights and to challenge the validity of comparative examination of international and Islamic versions of rights is problematic for several reasons. An initial point that needs to be made is that cultural relativism, like Said's idea of Orientalism, is not a concept developed for application in the field of law or for evaluating whether national governments are adhering to international legal norms. Instead, it is a term that was developed for use in anthropology and moral philosophy.[13] There are several reasons why cultural relativism should not be invoked to delegitimize criticisms of rights violations or challenges to the cultural defenses offered by governments for disregarding international rights norms.

As Jack Donnelly has noted, the interesting issue for cultural relativists is when there are practices that are internally defensible within the cultural system but unacceptable by external standards.[14] The opposition of cultural relativists to critical comparisons of Islamic and international rights concepts rests on an assumption that the curbs on human rights that Islamic rights schemes entail constitute authentic products of Islamic culture.

They imagine that the authority of Islamic versions of rights are accepted by Muslims—with the corollaries that Muslims do not think as Westerners do about rights and do not aspire to have them on the same terms. That is, cultural relativists assume that there is a single authoritative, identifiably "Islamic" cultural position on rights issues and that the internal Islamic position entails practices that are violative of external international norms but defensible within the framework of Islamic culture. In so doing, they tend to devote insufficient critical attention to what "culture" means in the context of modern state societies, wrongly equating Islamic culture with governmental representations of culture, and also to discount the complexity and diversity of non-Western cultures.[15] A priori generalizations about an Islam necessarily opposed to human rights are relied on when what is needed are assessments based on empirical investigation of how Muslims actually think about rights and whether Muslims truly care to be governed by versions of rights that render them even more vulnerable to mistreatment and oppression.

Muslim Responses to Human Rights

Muslims in the 1980s produced a large literature trying to define where Islam stands on human rights and comparing Islamic and international human rights. The very existence of this literature demonstrates that Muslims believe that such comparisons are both timely and legitimate. The frequent references to international human rights even by Muslims who quarrel with these show that international human rights concepts exist not only outside Islamic culture; the evidence shows that they are already percolating through that culture and becoming part of the apparatus that Muslims use internally to determine what practices are or are not acceptable and to judge the adequacy of positive laws. A survey of this literature will quickly disabuse anyone of the assumption that Muslims adhere to a monolithic Islamic cultural standard on rights issues. On the contrary, Muslims have taken many differing positions on human rights, including the unqualified endorsement of international human rights as fully compatible with their culture and religion.

It is natural that rights concepts should have become a preoccupation of contemporary Islamic thought because they are intimately related to the actual political and legal problems facing all Muslim societies. Concepts of human rights are just one part of a cluster of institutions transplanted since the nineteenth century from the West, the foremost of which was the model of the modern nation-state. This institution, with its great centralized power over society and its monopoly of control over resources, had never before existed in Islamic history and had not been contemplated in Islamic jurisprudence. The nation-state is now ubiquitous in the Muslim world, and it was inevitable that the legal institutions associated with it should also be transplanted. These legal institutions included constitutionalism and rules for the protection of the rights of citizens, which imposed legal constraints on the power of the modern nation-state and which constitute precursors of modern civil and political rights. Contemporary human rights formulations have at least some counterparts in the principles long ingrained in the domestic legal systems and constitutional provisions of almost all Muslim countries.

Thus, when one compares Islamic human rights concepts with international law, one is not judging an institution of an intact traditional culture by alien Western standards but examining Muslims' reactions to concepts already influencing their national legal systems. It should be borne in mind that elements of Western rights adopted in these national legal systems are institutions that independent Muslim countries have freely chosen. Thus, to maintain at this stage in history that rights are somehow external to Islamic culture entails accepting the notion that Islamic culture froze in its premodern formulations and taking the position that Islam rejects both the political changes wrought by modernization and the adoption of the new political ideas and legal institutions that accompanied the process. To maintain that Islam requires turning back the clock to the early nineteenth century entails adopting a fringe view that would be acceptable to only a few extremist groups in the Muslim world.

The efforts by governments to justify their rejection of international human rights on the basis of their alleged concern for Islamic principles are paradoxical, because those same governments have already indicated in various ways their acceptance of international law. Since Muslim countries have, without exception, joined the international community of nations formed under UN auspices, they have agreed to be bound by international law. Muslim nations, like other nations, contribute to the formulation of public international law in such capacities as working with other countries in the United Nations and its affiliated organizations and in drawing up and ratifying treaties and conventions.

It is difficult to maintain that Muslim countries are outsiders to the present system of international law. Several Muslim countries were among the founding members of the United Nations and participated in deciding on the terms of the UN Charter, which in Article 1 affirms the members' commitment to promote and encourage respect for human rights. Muslim countries also worked on the drafting of the Universal Declaration of Human Rights (UDHR) of 1948. Fereydoun Hoveida, an Iranian man of letters who later became Iran's ambassador to the United Nations, served on the committee that drafted the UDHR along with his French law professor, René Cassin, who was perhaps the most influential of all the drafters.

The Saudi UN representative at the time the UDHR was submitted for a vote condemned the declaration on the grounds that it reflected Western culture and was "at variance with patterns of culture of Eastern States" and on the grounds that the provisions for religious liberty violated Islamic law.[16] On the latter point, his comments provoked sharp dissent from the representative of Pakistan, who took the position that Islam unequivocally endorsed freedom of conscience.[17] This debate on whether Muslim countries could approve the UDHR thus presaged decades of subsequent disputes in the Muslim world about whether in endorsing international human rights Muslims were betraying Islamic law and submitting to Western cultural domination. In the end, when it came time to vote on the UDHR, Saudi Arabia was alone among Muslim countries in abstaining, being joined only by South Africa and various East Bloc countries.

In the main there has been little to distinguish the responses of the governments of Muslim countries to international human rights principles from those of non-Muslim nations, although some Muslim countries have recently earned notoriety for joining together with other conservative states to mount resistance to new proposals for advancing the rights of women. Muslim countries have uneven records of ratifying the major human rights conventions, with some countries having ratified most conventions and others, few, but the very unevenness and dissimilarities in the patterns of ratification and nonratification indicate that, from the governmental perspective, there is no single, definitive interpretation of Islamic rights principles standing in the way of accepting international human rights. It is worth noting that various non-Muslim countries, including Angola, Belize, China, Japan, Liechtenstein, Luxembourg, Singapore, and the United States, as well as the Vatican, have had relatively poor records of ratifying these conventions. Muslim countries can hardly be said to be less likely to ratify than non-Muslim countries when the ratification records of Algeria, Egypt, Iran, Iraq, Jordan, Mali, Morocco, Niger, Syria, and Tunisia compare favorably with that of the United States. Even Saudi Arabia, which found itself unable to endorse the UDHR, has subsequently ratified many of the specific conventions.

The 1972 Charter of the Organization of the Islamic Conference (OIC), the international organization to which all Muslim countries belong, expressly endorses international law and fundamental human rights, treating them as compatible with Islamic values. In the Preamble of the charter, two adjacent paragraphs assert that the members are

RESOLVED to preserve Islamic spiritual, ethical, social and economic values, which will remain one of the important factors of achieving progress for mankind;

REAFFIRMING their commitment to the UN Charter and fundamental Human Rights, the purposes and principles of which provide the basis for fruitful co-operation amongst all people.

That is, the formal position of OIC members indicates that the international human rights standards developed in the United Nations are regarded as compatible with Islamic law by the very actors—governments—whose conduct is subject to regulation by international human rights law.

Having formally accepted international human rights, governments of Muslim countries are bound by these norms and are also subject to being judged under them. Furthermore, support is growing for the notion that at least some principles of international human rights have been subsumed over time as features of customary international law and hence are binding on all states regardless of their ratification of individual conventions. International human rights law does not cease to bind states when their representatives formally comment, as Saudi Arabia's and Iran's have done, that adherence to Islamic law justifies diverging from the standards of international law. Countries are not permitted to opt out of their international legal obligations at will or on pretexts of their own devising. As is discussed in Chapter 4, derogation from international human rights standards is permitted only under specific, narrow conditions, which do not include denying people human rights by appeal to the standards of any particular religion.

Since Muslim governments have chosen to join the international system and to commit themselves in various ways to the observance of international human rights, it is surprising that cultural relativists seem to be so easily impressed when governmental spokespersons invoke "Islam" and "Eastern culture" to justify their violations of the human rights that they have voluntarily chosen to endorse. Instead of questioning whether nation-states can speak with authority on matters of Islamic doctrine and culture, cultural relativists seem disposed to accord more deference to governmental assertions that their fidelity to Islam precludes the acceptance of "Western" international human rights than to the positions of the individual Muslims who protest the use of Islam to deny rights or who join independent human rights organizations. The latter have vigorously rejected the Islamic rationales offered by governments for oppressing them.[18] Muslims who enthusiastically support international human rights risk being dismissively treated by cultural relativists on the grounds that advocates of human rights must be Westernized or, even worse, traitors to their own culture. In this the cultural relativists betray their Orientalist proclivities, which, as discussed above, dispose them to view the peoples of the Orient and Occident as having inherently different natures and to consider the adoption of Occidental ideas and institutions by Orientals as somehow incongruous and unnatural.[19]

The attitude of cultural relativists may affect Western approaches to rights issues in Third World settings generally. As an Argentinean observer of the attitudes of American cultural relativists has noted, their position implies that countries that do not spring from a Western tradition may somehow be excused from complying with the international law of human rights. This elitist theory of human rights holds that human rights are good for the West but not for much of the non-Western world. Surprisingly, the elitist theory of human rights is very popular in the democratic West, not only in conservative circles but also, and even more often, among liberal and radical groups. The right-wing version of elitism embodies the position, closely associated with colonialism, that backward peoples cannot govern themselves and that democracy only works for superior cultures. The left-wing version, often articulated by liberals who stand for civil rights in Western countries but support leftist dictatorships abroad, reflects a belief that we should be tolerant of and respect the cultural identity and political self-determination of Third World countries (although, of course, it is seldom the people who choose to have dictators; more often the dictators decide for them).

The position of relativist scholars who are human rights advocates illustrates an eloquent example of concealed elitism.

Such persons find themselves in an impossible dilemma. On the one hand they are anxious to articulate an international human rights standard, while on the other they wish to respect the autonomy of individual cultures. The result is a vague warning against "ethnocentrism," and well-intentioned proposals that are deferential to tyrannical governments and insufficiently concerned with human suffering. Because the consequence of either version of elitism is that certain national or ethnic groups are somehow less entitled than others to the enjoyment of human rights, the theory is fundamentally immoral and replete with racist overtones.[20]

The elitist approach underlying the cultural relativist position vis-à-vis the Muslim world implies that Muslims, because of their non-Western cultural identity, are outside the realm where international human rights should be applied. This is hard to reconcile with the endorsement of international human rights by Muslim governments and the evidence that many Muslims find the observance of international human rights standards perfectly compatible with their tradition and enthusiastically embrace these standards.

Western cultural relativists, when dealing with rights in Muslim countries, do seem to mistake official, ideologized representations of Islamic culture for authentic manifestations of indigenous culture and tradition. The currently voguish romantic communitarianism may dispose persons in Western academia to accept uncritically arguments on behalf of preserving cultural identity at the expense of human rights.[21] However, there are reasons to doubt that present governmental policies of denying human rights in the name of upholding Islamic law stem from what may be accurately called culture and tradition. States like Iran, in order to enforce their Islamization policies, have to resort to measures like threats, beatings, jailings, torture, and executions. Where such coercive measures are routinely used to enforce compliance with official codifications of Islamic tradition, those policies cannot embody an authentic tradition. Authentic tradition imposes itself on its own authority and is normative because it has authority.[22] Thus, authentic living tradition is automatically accepted as such and does not have to be imposed with police-state tactics on a resisting population. What Islamization policies involve is more like "traditionalism," or the ideology of tradition.

As Donnelly has noted, there is irony in the largely Westernized elites in the Third World warning against the values and practices that they themselves espouse. He warns that it may be necessary for today's supposedly "traditional" models—like Tanzania's "villagization"—to be imposed by force over the intense objections of the supposedly "traditional" population.[23] He has pointed out the hypocrisy of Third World elites in praising traditional communities and values, which they themselves have long since escaped, while asserting their prerogatives to "wield arbitrary power antithetical to traditional values, pursue development policies that systematically undermine traditional communities, and replace traditional leaders with corrupt cronies."[24] Such remarks apply with great force to Muslim countries, where governments eager to impose an ideologized, uniform version of national culture have shown little inclination to respect cultural diversity and distinct local traditions.

If supposedly traditional Islamic values are in fact being manipulated for political ends by governments, this should be seen as part of a broader recent phenomenon in the Third World. Donnelly's remarks are worth citing in this connection. He warned that "while recognizing the legitimate claims of self-determination and cultural relativism, we must be alert to cynical manipulations of a dying, lost, or mythical cultural past," and commented: "In the Third World today, more often than not we see dual societies and patchwork practices that seek to accommodate seemingly irreconcilable old and new ways. Rather than the persistence of traditional culture in the face of modern intrusions, or even the development of syncretic cultures and values, we usually see instead a disruptive and incomplete westernization, cultural confusion, or the enthusiastic embrace of 'modern' practices and values."[25]

Muslims impatient with the lack of progress toward democracy are clearly unimpressed by the explanations of governments that their aspirations for human rights cannot be reconciled with respect for their culture. Cultural relativists may fail to perceive how rapid urbanization, industrialization, and factors like the growing power of the repressive state apparatus are creating conditions that foster awareness of the need for human rights among people in the Middle East. Organizations committed to the furtherance and protection of human rights according to international standards have proliferated throughout the Muslim world, sometimes in very hostile political environments and under extremely dangerous conditions. Many Muslims have risked imprisonment, torture, and even death to stand up for the same human rights principles that cultural relativists would maintain are not suited for application in the Muslim world because of its dissimilar culture. As a scholar familiar with Arab human rights activism has stated:

> There are thousands of militants of the cause of human rights across the Arab world, people who subscribe to the notion of universal human rights. Who has the authority to decree that their belief in the ideal of universal human rights is a betrayal of their culture? They have achieved a synthesis of the culture they were raised in on the one hand, and of values that promote equality and non-discrimination among all citizens on the other hand. The fact that there are thousands of them, in many areas of the Arab world, shows that this synthesis is not alien to our most fundamental values, those that are embedded in the traditional culture. Who has the right to declare them to be cultural apostates?"[26]

Governments in the Muslim world have recently taken steps that indicate their awareness of the mounting popularity that human rights enjoy. Concerned about their legitimacy, several have found it prudent to make concessions to their citizens' demands for the observance of international human rights. For example, in June 1988, after years of trampling on the human rights of Libyans, Mu'ammar al-Qadhafi, assuming the posture of an advocate of human rights, issued a Libyan human rights charter, released hundreds of political prisoners, and denounced the human rights abuses that had previously been carried out under his regime.[27]

Increasingly, human rights groups and Islamic movements compete for the loyalties of disaffected Muslims, and, sometimes, their appeals to the disaffected are combined.[28] In many Muslim countries Islam has become the most potent language of political protest against oppressive dictatorships and military regimes. Popular support for groups calling for "Islamization" in situations where undemocratic and corrupt secular governments stubbornly cling to power may signal more a repudiation of governmental policies than the intent to support the specifics of the Islamization programs that are pursued by these groups once they come to power and, as in Iran, prove unwilling to tolerate the democratic freedoms that they clamored for while still in the opposition. Whether there is a popular mandate for Islamization at the expense of democratic freedoms is doubtful. What Islamization programs will mean in practice becomes clear only once their proponents have the chance to implement them. Once in power, their proponents have not been prepared to allow fully free and democratic elections to test whether the voting public approves of actual Islamization measures.

In Iran since the Islamic Revolution the population has not been permitted to vote to reject the official version of Islamization, because candidates have not been allowed to run for office unless they supported the official Islamic ideology and were acceptable to Iran's clerical leadership. The Iranian secular, liberal, and leftist opposition organizations have meanwhile been eliminated as significant political forces, having been systematically decimated by government measures including censorship, harassment, jailings, torture, and executions. The disillusionment of Iranians with almost two decades of Islamization was indicated in 1997 by the 69 percent of votes that were cast for presidential candidate Mohammed Khatami, a known proponent of expanded rights and freedoms. Although Khatami was himself a member of the clerical establishment, he amounted to the closest approximation to an opposition candidate that Iranian voters had seen since the revolution.

If there were regular free elections in the Muslim world, one would have a better basis for saying exactly what rights policies do enjoy popular support and to what degree. Unfortunately, even semifree elections are infrequent in Muslim countries, so one does not have an accurate record of how people would vote about governmental Islamization programs. However, one can conclude from the patterns of holding and not holding elections in Pakistan and the Sudan that the official Islamization programs were undertaken by military fiat, not on the basis of any electoral mandate, and that they were effectively repudiated by a majority of voters once the military dictators imposing them were removed from power. The fact that democratization has been consistently seen as a threat by regimes committed to Islamization suggests that cultural relativists who assume that official Islamization measures necessarily express popular mandates or embody the local culture are mistaken.

Although there is little evidence of a popular mandate behind the diluted Islamic versions of rights that Middle Eastern governments have sponsored, the possibility remains open that, if Muslims were allowed to vote freely, segments of Muslim opinion would endorse some of the features in these programs. Moreover, there is no reason to assume that most Muslims would call for precisely the same human rights formulations that one finds in Western legal systems. Their priorities could well diverge, even as the views of the United States and Canada diverge on many rights issues, despite the fact that the two countries are closely linked in terms of their history and legal heritage. Westerners tend to overlook the significant differences in concepts of rights and rights protections that one can find in the West. Respect for international human rights law does not require that every culture take an identical approach, but it does require that human rights be defined and protected in a manner consonant with international principles. One Muslim scholar who has offered a thoughtful critique of typical misuses of cultural relativism in the rights sphere suggested that a proper respect for cultural relativism means that we should accept "the right of all people to choose among alternatives equally respectful of human rights," and that the latter must include the rights of life, liberty, and dignity for every person or group of people.[29]

The kind of cultural relativism that demands tolerance for dissimilar ways of resolving rights problems in different cultures seems legitimate. Likewise, the cultural relativism that calls for the West to forbear condemning intact traditional societies as defective because they fail to protect human rights according to modern international standards seems justifiable. There is little reason to disturb the already jeopardized equilibrium of the occasional community that has so far managed to resist the inroads of modern civilization. The social orders in isolated mountain villages, the hierarchy in a remote oasis settlement, or the mores of a nomadic clan struggling to preserve its traditional way of life may not conform to UDHR ideals, but these may offer their members a more humane environment than the larger state societies surrounding them. What does not seem defensible is that cultural relativism should insulate the conduct and ideological apparatus of modern nation-states from critical scrutiny simply because the states claim to be following the dictates of a religion or a culture that exempts them from the duty to abide by the standards of international human rights. The most serious and pervasive human rights problems afflicting the Middle East are not ones created by the increasingly rare survival of intact traditional cultures: They are ones created by governmental policies and laws inimical to rights and democratic freedoms—and, in the case of Islamic human rights schemes examined here, by policies and laws that are designed by elites for implementation by modern state systems at the expense of the rights and freedoms of the individual. The way governments treat those they govern should not be ruled off-limits to critical scholarly inquiry, and judging Islamic schemes of human rights by the standards of the international human rights law that they seek to replace is entirely appropriate.

CHAPTER 2

Laws on Human Rights: Sources and Contexts

International Human Rights: Sources

Even with a focus narrowed to civil and political rights, the range of potential sources is too vast to be covered in this study. For the comparisons undertaken here, the International Bill of Human Rights will be used to exemplify the position of public international law on civil and political rights. The International Bill of Human Rights consists of the Universal Declaration of Human Rights (UDHR) of 1948, the International Covenant on Economic, Social, and Cultural Rights (ICESCR) of 1966, and the International Covenant on Civil and Political Rights (ICCPR), also of 1966, along with the ICCPR's Optional Protocol. The 1966 covenants entered into force in 1976. The universal declaration has, since its adoption by the UN General Assembly, achieved great international renown as an authoritative statement of the modern standards of human rights protections and is the single most influential international human rights document.

Acknowledging that there is not full academic or political consensus regarding the authority of aspects of the International Bill of Human Rights, one can nonetheless maintain that they are representative, if perhaps not ultimately definitive, statements of what a broad segment of international opinion believes that human rights entail. In addition, because of the general recognition of their validity in state practice—in which they are commonly treated as governing legal standards—many provisions of the bill have achieved the stature of customary international law and, as such, are binding on states regardless of whether they have ratified the individual conventions.

Many countries have refused to ratify one or more of the conventions involved. Among the Middle Eastern Muslim countries that did not ratify the ICCPR and the ICESCR, one finds Pakistan, Saudi Arabia, Turkey, and the

United Arab Emirates (UAE). On the other hand, such diverse countries as Afghanistan, Algeria, Egypt, Iran (here it is undoubtedly significant that the issue of Iran's ratification came up prior to the Islamic Revolution), Iraq, Jordan, Kuwait, Libya, Morocco, the Sudan (during 1985–1989, the brief period of democracy between two military regimes committed to Islamization), Syria, and Tunisia have ratified the same covenants.[1]

Another reason for relying on these international human rights documents is that their formulations of human rights principles are succinct enough to allow easy comparisons with principles in Islamic human rights documents. The broad outlines of the Islamic documents in many instances are clearly inspired by provisions in the International Bill of Human Rights, even though they may differ from the latter in important respects.

Islamic Human Rights: Sources

The materials authored by Muslims on Islam and human rights are extensive, and only a small fraction of the literature can be covered here. Selected provisions on civil and political rights in several Islamic human rights schemes and in Islamic constitutions will be evaluated. By "Islamic constitutions," I mean constitutions that purportedly adhere to Islamic principles, not merely constitutions of countries where the inhabitants are predominantly Muslim. The treatment of human rights in constitutions is critical, because international human rights law relies for its implementation on national laws and institutions. The international standards are meant to serve as models for the rights protected under the constitutions and other domestic laws in individual countries.[2]

The works to be examined have been composed by Muslims from both the Sunni and Shi'i traditions, from inside and outside governments, and from several important countries. All are from the Middle East and North Africa, and the comparisons will not go beyond these regions. In selecting the material to be surveyed, I have emphasized Islamic approaches to human rights that have been presented by major Islamic institutions and influential figures as well as ones adopted by governments. The exception is the work of Sultanhussein Tabandeh, who is a relatively minor figure but who is interesting because of his candor and his detailed responses to various UDHR provisions. The range of material surveyed is, therefore, broad enough to permit some generalizations to be made.

A word needs to be said at this point about the way different rights positions will be characterized. It will be necessary to distinguish between the views of Muslims who favor and those who oppose adherence to international human rights standards. Since the aim is to contrast the views of Muslims who fall on one or the other side of the line in this dispute, for the purposes of this study, only two categories need to be designated. Here and throughout, the terms *liberal* and *conservative* will be used in their dictionary senses, "liberal" denoting views favoring reform and progress toward democracy, and "conservative" denoting views calling for the preservation of established institutions and opposing any changes in these. Here, liberal Muslims are those who favor adherence to democratic principles and human rights, and conservative Muslims are those who oppose democratization, resisting human rights insofar as they appear to threaten established Islamic institutions. Obviously, many finer distinctions could be drawn, but they would only burden a work that is already heavily weighted down by discussions of very specific distinctions.

One of the documents assessed will be *A Muslim Commentary on the Universal Declaration of Human Rights* by Sultanhussein Tabandeh (Sultan Hussain Tabanda). This pamphlet was originally published in Persian in 1966 and appeared in an English translation in 1970. Tabandeh, who was born in northeastern Iran in 1914, inherited the leadership of the Ni'matullahi Sufi order, a mystical brotherhood affiliated with Twelver Shi'i Islam. He was educated at Tehran University and Tehran Teachers' Training College and traveled widely in the Muslim world and also in Europe. He presented his commentary on human rights to the representatives of Muslim countries who attended the 1968 Tehran International Conference on Human Rights. His purpose was to advise them of the positions they should adopt vis-à-vis various provisions in the UDHR, which he had analyzed in terms of the requirements of Islamic law. In his comments, one sees the reactions of an Iranian Shi'i leader of a religious order. He is much more outspoken in his criticisms of international human rights and his defenses of premodern doctrines than are many of his fellow conservatives.

A pamphlet entitled *Human Rights in Islam,* by the internationally prominent Sunni religious leader from the subcontinent, Abu'l A'la Mawdudi, will also be covered. The centerpiece of the pamphlet, first published in 1976, is an English translation of a talk presented by Mawdudi in 1975 in Lahore, Pakistan. In 1941 Mawdudi founded a political group, Jama'at-i-Islami, whose members are committed to the reinstatement of Islamic law and the establishment of an Islamic state in Pakistan; the group has been active in Pakistani politics. In addition to leading political campaigns on behalf of Islamization, before his death in 1979, Mawdudi wrote extensively on the application of Islam to contemporary problems, and his work was widely disseminated in translations. In recognition of what were said to be his outstanding services to Islam, he was accorded the King Faisal Prize. Lacking the traditional religious education enjoyed by highly trained religious scholars, Mawdudi had been able to present his ideas in a way that could reach a popular audience, reaching Muslims who shared his bitter resentment of Western power and the West's dismissal of Islamic civilization as backward. He adopted a combative stance vis-à-vis the West, castigating Western society and culture for decadence and materialism and arguing that Islamic civilization was far superior to its Western counterpart. His human rights pamphlet embodies the attitudes that informed his work generally.

The 1981 Universal Islamic Declaration of Human Rights (UIDHR) will be discussed as well. This document was prepared by representatives from Egypt, Pakistan, Saudi Arabia, and other countries under the auspices of the Islamic Council, a private, London-based organization affiliated with the Muslim World League, an international, nongovernmental organization headquartered in Saudi Arabia that tends to represent the interests and views of conservative Muslims. The declaration was presented with great public fanfare to the United Nations Educational, Scientific and Cultural Organization (UNESCO) in Paris. In a casual reading, the English version of the UIDHR seems to be closely modeled after the UDHR, but upon closer examination many of the similarities turn out to be misleading. In addition, the English version diverges from the Arabic version at many points. Both versions of the UIDHR will be examined here. As will be shown, many of the formulations in the UIDHR are obscure or ambiguous. Although the UIDHR is generally representative of conservative Muslim opinion, the inconsistencies and equivocations in the UIDHR suggest that its authors may not have been able to achieve a consensus among themselves about how Islamic human rights should be formulated.

The rights provisions in the "Draft of the Islamic Constitution" are reviewed. These provisions were devised by the Islamic Research Academy of Cairo, which is affiliated with al-Azhar University, the most prestigious institution of higher education in Sunni Islam and a center of conservative Islamic thought. This draft constitution, published in 1979 in Volume 51 of the Azhar journal *Majallat al-Azhar,* appears to represent an official position of that institution as to what rights should be recognized in a political system based on Sunni Islamic principles. Published at the time that the Iranian Constitution was receiving much attention and Iran's Shi'i leadership was attracting a following in the Sunni world, the Azhar draft may be seen as a Sunni response to the political repercussions of the Iranian Revolution and an effort to demonstrate that Sunni Islam was not bereft of resources to fashion a constitution for a modern government.

The rights provisions in the 1979 Iranian Constitution, which, according to its Preamble, "is based upon Islamic principles," will be assessed.[3] The Iranian Constitution represents one attempt to resolve the question of what rights belong in a constitution tied to Twelver Shi'i Islam, and it may be usefully contrasted with the Azhar draft.

The 1979 Iranian Constitution replaced Iran's first constitution, which was drawn up in 1906–1907. This first constitution had emerged out of a struggle between laypersons and clerics who supported the campaign to limit the powers of the shah by a constitution and laypersons and clerics who upheld a traditional autocratic system of government. That is, there were secular and clerical forces on both sides. The disputes were never resolved, and the constitution embodied compromises that left neither side satisfied.[4] The 1979 constitution did not signify a new beginning for constitutionalism but only an Islamic overlay resting on a constitutional tradition of many decades that was heavily indebted to French influences.

Although there were many elements in Iran's first constitution that seemed to recognize the supremacy of Islamic law, in actual practice, Iran's legal culture became increasingly secularized over subsequent decades. Objections by Iran's clerics to the displacement of *shari'a* law were largely ignored. After Iran's Islamic Revolution of 1978–1979, a draft constitution was prepared in spring 1979. Like the 1906–1907 constitution, this draft contained both secular and Islamic principles, but it showed far less deference to the ideas and wishes of conservative clerics than the constitution that was subsequently adopted. The first draft was discarded, and in August 1979 a constituent assembly with a majority consisting of conservative Shi'i clerics was chosen to draft a new constitution in elections that were denounced as unfair by secular political groups. The new constitution, approved by a referendum in December 1979, retained some features of the earlier draft but gave much greater scope for the application of Islamic law and significantly enhanced the power of the Shi'i clergy over the government and the legal system. Given the hostility of Ayatollah Khomeini to human rights, it is not surprising that the final text of the constitution, though referring to human rights in Article 20, did not include any endorsement of the UDHR, which secular groups had called for incorporating in the constitution.[5] The current Iranian constitution is, therefore, a product of a long history of struggle to define what role Islamic law and the clergy should play in the legal system and government. It perpetuates rather than resolves old tensions in this regard. Significant revisions were made in July 1989 in an attempt to find a mechanism for resolving these tensions—without much prospect of ending them.[6]

Two recent documents are also considered. The Cairo Declaration on Human Rights in Islam[7] was presented at the 1993 World Conference on Human Rights in Vienna by the Saudi foreign minister, who asserted that it embodied the consensus of the world's Muslims on rights issues.[8] The declaration has assumed special importance because it continued the trends already established in previous Islamic human rights schemes and because it was endorsed in August 1990 by the foreign ministers of the Organization of the Islamic Conference (OIC). It thus appeared, at least superficially, to embody a more general consensus—albeit only at the governmental level—on how Islam should affect rights. However, the appearance of consensus was belied by the actual stances on rights taken by OIC member states, which continued to diverge as widely after the issuance of the declaration as they had before.

The 1993 World Conference on Human Rights in Vienna provided impetus for Muslim countries to define their stance on human rights. The conflicts over whether human rights were inextricably linked to Western culture and whether they could or should be universal were central preoccupations of the conference.[9] In the period leading up to the conference, Saudi Arabia and Iran remained strong supporters of the 1990 Cairo Declaration. At one point, Iraq joined Iran in pressing the UN Commission on Human Rights for the acceptance of the Cairo Declaration as the Islamic alternative to international human rights.[10] That these regimes with their vastly diverging philosophies would promote any document on the basis of a commitment to shared Islamic values was highly improbable. Saudi Arabia's official Wahhabi Islam, which upheld the rule of an absolute monarchy and had a strong anti-Shi'i bias, was denounced by Iran. Saddam Hussain, Iraq's dictator, had been excoriated by Ayatollah Khomeini. A member of Iraq's Sunni minority, Hussain adhered to a secular Arab nationalist ideology and repressed and persecuted Iraq's restive Shi'i majority. However dissimilar their religious policies, all three regimes had a common practice of denying rights and freedoms to their citizens and resorting to drastic measures to repress and eliminate their opponents and critics, and all three apparently calculated that they stood to benefit from promoting an alternative to international human rights law that was supposedly based on Islam. On the occasion of the OIC meeting in Tehran in December 1997, Iran and various other OIC members continued to press the idea that the existing UN human rights system was excessively Western and needed to be adjusted to accommodate the culture and religious values of Muslim countries, a view rejected by UN Secretary General Kofi Annan, who insisted that human rights were universal.[11]

Also reviewed is the Basic Law of Saudi Arabia, which was issued on March 1, 1992.[12] Unlike Iran, Pakistan, or the Sudan, Saudi Arabia was not pursuing Islamization, having elected instead to retain premodern Islamic law as set forth in juristic treatises as the law of the land. Instead, Saudi Arabia was belatedly embarking on a program of tentative reforms of a kind that most nations had already undertaken by the early twentieth century. The 1992 Basic Law, although very rudimentary, was the closest thing to a constitution that Saudi Arabia had ever possessed. The provisions of the Basic Law purported to derive from Islam and to establish a government that likewise derived from Islam.[13] The disparity between the rights that the Basic Law affords and those in the Cairo Declaration, which Saudi Arabia had also publicly espoused, is yet another sign of the difficulties that Muslim states have in articulating a coherent policy on rights.

Aspects of a number of other publications dealing with how Islam relates to human rights will also be discussed for the purpose of comparison. It will be stressed throughout this study that the fact that the Islamic human rights schemes presented here are referred to as "Islamic" does not imply that the principles involved represent definitive statements of where Islamic doctrine stands on rights issues or that all or even a majority of the world's more than 1 billion Muslims would endorse them. Human rights and the question of how human rights protections relate to the Islamic tradition remain intensely contested issues throughout the Muslim world.

The Islamic human rights documents reviewed here represent a middle ground between two sharply opposed positions, to which I will also occasionally refer. Muslims in the middle tend to advocate compromise positions asserting that Islam does accept human rights—as long as the necessary Islamic rules and concepts are integrated in the rights to bring them in conformity with Islamic standards. The result is a mélange—and often a very awkward one—of international law principles with rules and concepts that are taken from the Islamic legal heritage or that are presented as having Islamic pedigrees.

The literature corresponding to the compromise position offers the most interesting material for comparison with international legal standards. It provides a fascinating illustration of what happens when two very dissimilar legacies combine, producing a blend of legal principles that has no historic antecedent. As it happens, the compromise view that Islam tolerates human rights in some form but imposes conditions and restrictions on them is also one that has enormous political significance. Over the last two decades, regimes undertaking Islamization programs and states that derive their legitimacy from their application of Islamic law have increasingly exploited the notion that unfettered rights are incompatible with Islam to justify restrictions that they impose on rights and freedoms.

Controversies over Islam and Human Rights

The burgeoning human rights movement in the Muslim world has already been mentioned. As the enthusiastic response to human rights principles at the grassroots level has demonstrated, many Muslims are convinced that Islam constitutes no barrier to their insisting on respect for international human rights. This may be due to the belief now shared by many that Islamic law is not designed to deal with the governance issues facing contemporary Middle Eastern societies.[14] Muslims have also offered schemes for harmonizing international human rights norms with Islam, taking the position that Islam requires scrupulous respect for human rights.[15] Muslims have energetically condemned the human rights abuses perpetrated in the name of Islam in countries such as Afghanistan, Iran, Pakistan, Saudi Arabia, and the Sudan. Even Muslims who do not use the terminology of modern human rights often display attitudes revealing their belief that justice and respect for human life and dignity are such central principles of Islam that a legal system that fails to honor these cannot be in conformity with Islamic requirements. Muslims who are appalled by the rights violations perpetrated in the course of Islamization programs include prominent Islamic clerics who have denounced oppressive governmental measures and curbs on rights undertaken in the name of Islam.

For example, viewing the deteriorating rights situation in the Sudan in the wake of Omar al-Bashir's harsh Islamization measures and despite the great dangers of speaking out, in 1997 an imam in his Friday sermon denounced governmental repression, publicly asserting: "Islam does not accept oppression and confiscation of the rights of the people and suppression of the freedom of expression."[16]

The denials of rights by the postrevolutionary Iranian government in 1980 were vigorously condemned by the late Ayatollah Taleghani, one of Iran's most distinguished clerics and a religious leader whose ideas were particularly popular among younger, left-leaning Iranians. He was obviously deeply troubled by the Khomeini regime's constantly invoking Islam as it sought to cut down on freedoms, when, in his view, the protection of freedom was a central concern of Islam. He argued:

> The most dangerous of all forms of oppression are laws and restrictions forcibly imposed on people in the name of religion. This is what the Monks, through collaboration with the ruling classes, did with all the people in the name of religion. This is the most dangerous of all impositions, because that which is not from God is thrust upon the people to enslave and suppress them and prevent them from evolving, depriving them of the right to protest, criticise and be free. These very chains and shackles are the ones which the Prophet [Muhammad] came to destroy. Islam is an invitation to peace and freedom. Let us keep aside opportunism, group interests, forcible imposition of ideas and, God forbid, dictatorships under the cover of religion. [Let us] raise our voices with the toiling, oppressed, the deprived masses. Islam as we know it, the Islam which originates from the Quran and the traditions of Prophet, does not restrict freedom. Any group that wants to restrict people's freedom, [the freedom] to criticise, protest, discuss and debate, does not comprehend Islam.
>
> Islam is the religion of freedom. Its goal is people's liberation. If a religion aims at liberating people from all forms of bondage, it cannot itself be made a chain for keeping people in bondage. The reactionaries are trying to distort the concept of freedom by equating it with a decadent version [used by] the bourgeoisie in the West, in order to enslave the masses. In the name of religion [they wish to] further the interest of their own class by enslaving people in exploitative chains.[17]

Ayatollah Taleghani saw Islam as a vehicle of liberation that was inherently inimical to restrictions on personal freedoms. He characterized the use of religion under the Khomeini regime to stifle freedoms as very dangerous, associating such use not with Islamic tradition but with the Christian church ("the Monks"). According to Taleghani, the mission of Islam is one of freeing people from the enslavement that results from the alliance of religion and the ruling classes. Far from concurring with the official view that the pursuit of Islamization justified curbs on freedom, Taleghani charged that the ruling classes in Iran were attempting to further their own interests by using a self-serving definition of "Islam" to justify enslaving and exploiting the poor. That is, in the view of this eminent Shi'i cleric, Iran's postrevolutionary ruling elite was distorting Islamic doctrine for its own advantage by pretending that Islam denies people freedom, whereas, in reality, Islam should be recognized as the guarantor of freedoms. Although Taleghani did not use the language of human rights or appeal to international law in his denunciation of oppression, his understanding of Islam is one that could encompass guarantees of civil and political freedoms like those in international law. In appealing for observance of the values of Islam, he was effectively calling for respect for human rights and treating Islam and human rights as natural allies.

After long restricting who could run for office and excluding any candidates who might pose a real challenge to the establishment, Iran's clerical elite miscalculated in 1997 and permitted Mohammed Khatami, a cleric known for his relatively liberal views and his advocacy of expanded freedoms, to run for president. Khatami's speeches, although often cautious and equivocal, suggested that he believed that liberalization and openness were essential if Islam were to continue to have influence.[18] Khatami was meant to be only one of the token candidates running against the officially approved candidate, Majles Speaker Nateq Nuri, a clerical hard-liner known for his zeal in enforcing retrograde notions of Islamic morality. Despite having to campaign in disadvantageous circumstances, Khatami was able to garner 69 percent of the votes, indicating that Iranians responded positively to his promises of protections for rights and the rule of law and were hoping for relief from the endless rationalizations for repression.[19] After his election, he called for freedom of expression of opposition views and condemned "the imposition of viewpoints and violation of law even under the pretext of religion."[20] Threatened by the popularity of his policy of democratization and openness, the conservative establishment and forces allied with the supreme jurist Ali Khamene'i rallied after Khatami's electoral victory to try to block reforms and to discredit Khatami.

One sees that skeptical, critical assessments of the Islamic rationales for rights violations perpetrated in the course of Islamization programs have come not only from Western observers but also from Islamic clerics and Muslims immersed in the Islamic tradition and committed to honoring it. At the other end of the spectrum, one finds Muslims who disparage human rights as reflecting alien, Western values. In their view, international human rights are incompatible with Islam, and Muslims must reject them. Thus, some Iranian clerics have offered scornful denunciations of human rights. Ayatollah Khomeini asserted: "What they call human rights is nothing but a collection of corrupt rules worked out by Zionists to destroy all true religions"; and Khamene'i, then president of Iran, stated: "When we want to find out what is right and what is wrong, we do not go to the United Nations; we go to the Holy Koran. For us the Universal Declaration of Human Rights is nothing but a collection of mumbo-jumbo by disciples of Satan."[21]

In summary, contemporary Muslim opinion is far too divided to allow an outside observer to make general pronouncements regarding where Islam stands on rights. It is not appropriate for an outsider to interfere in an internal doctrinal debate among Muslims. It is, however, legitimate for an outside observer to investigate what the range of opinion among contemporary Muslims is, to present critical comparative appraisals of various Islamic versions of human rights and to evaluate the significance of positions that Muslims have been taking on the relationship of Islam and human rights. I undertake these tasks in the following chapters.

The Impact on Rights of Islamization Programs in Pakistan, Iran, and the Sudan

A brief review of some patterns of governmental responses to demands for Islamization and governmental Islamization measures is in order. People outside the Muslim world tend to lose sight of the fact that measures to implement Islamic law and ideology in given countries cannot in the nature of things be severed from local politics. Thus, for example, the specifics of the Islamization programs in Iran and Pakistan differ considerably, and these two models in turn differ from the version of Islamization pursued by the Taleban in their common neighbor, Afghanistan.

The autocratic regime of the late shah of Iran, a secular monarch who had little support outside military circles, belatedly confronted the political potency of Islam as a means of mobilizing political protest and was ultimately destroyed in Iran's Islamic Revolution. A clerical faction ultimately wrested control over the government and crushed secular and liberal forces. Iran's Islamization program, coming in the wake of a major revolutionary upheaval and being masterminded by conservative clerics, was naturally more far-reaching and more representative of clerical attitudes than the Islamization offered by more secular governments. Although the Iranian model of Islamization is criticized and rejected by many Muslims, the Iranian experience of a popular Islamic Revolution being captured by a conservative Islamic faction has implications for other countries.

Strong countermeasures by undemocratic regimes in countries such as Algeria, Egypt, Iraq, Syria, Libya, and Tunisia have at least temporarily crushed opposition groups calling for Islamization. Other regimes have tried to co-opt Islamization movements by making concessions to demands for reviving Islamic law. In 1979, two years after his coup overthrowing Pakistan's elected government, General Muhammad Zia ul-Haq launched an official Islamization campaign, which he pursued until his death in 1988. The aftereffects of his Islamization measures continued to be felt after his demise. Islamization was inaugurated in the Sudan in 1983–1985, during the last years of Ja'far Nimeiri's dictatorship, and again after the military coup of June 1989 by Omar al-Bashir.[22]

In these countries Islamization was theoretically designed to bring the law and the administration of justice into conformity with the standards of the *shari'a*, or Islamic law. Many rules taken from the premodern *shari'a*, or at least ostensibly inspired by *shari'a* principles, were enacted into law, and the previous, Western standards were abandoned. Not only substantive laws but also courts and enforcement practices were altered to reflect what were officially described as Islamic requirements. The Western-influenced bar and judiciary were regarded as roadblocks in the way of implementation of Islamic law. In all three countries there was a pattern of replacing judges who had Western-style legal training with Islamic clerics or persons with a traditional Islamic education. Members of the bar in these countries, who had the outlook of highly trained professionals and who were influenced by liberal values that supported human rights, found it difficult, if not impossible, to fulfill their professional responsibilities in the changed circumstances. In Iran and the Sudan, Islamization had the most drastic impact on the legal profession. After sharply curtailing the powers of lawyers in reaction to their criticisms of mounting political repression and the increasingly arbitrary regime of justice, the Iranian authorities finally took measures in 1981–1982 to dismantle and altogether destroy Iran's bar association, and the Sudan followed suit under the Bashir regime.[23]

All in all, the systemic changes made under the rubric of Islamization in Pakistan, Iran, and the Sudan did much to erode due process and inject arbitrariness in the administration of justice, as well as compromising judicial independence and politicizing legal proceedings. Thus, in all three countries Islamization became associated with setbacks to the rule of law. The deterioration was particularly noticeable in Pakistan and the Sudan, where the legal systems had previously upheld a higher standard of justice than was common in developing societies. The pursuit of Islamization in Iran, Pakistan, and the Sudan also coincided with the emergence of shifts in patterns of human rights violations, such as aggravated discrimination against women, an upswing in religious intolerance, and more aggressive persecution of religious minorities. The seriousness of the patterns of human rights violations that accompanied the Islamization programs has been extensively documented by many reputable observers and by international organizations and institutions concerned with the protection of human rights.[24]

How Islamization programs in Iran, Pakistan, and the Sudan correlated with policies of crushing freedoms will be considered. One might ask whether the dismantling of rights protections that occurred in the course of these programs is attributable to factors inherent in the Islamic tradition or to other causes. There seems to be much merit in the analysis of a prominent Moroccan human rights leader, who treats Islamic law as a mere epiphenomenon and points to the dominant political culture as the cause of human rights problems in the Arab world.[25] Both in Arab and other Middle Eastern countries, Islamization may be opportunistically exploited by cynical elites who are predisposed to crush freedom and who resort to appeals to divine authority as the rationale for oppressive, exploitative rule and systems of inequality and discrimination. Thus, official Islamization policies may tie in with strategies for trumping demands for democratization and human rights, which are growing throughout the Muslim world. Rationalizations for policies should be distinguished from causation.

In general, regimes pursuing Islamization have reacted defensively and angrily when accused of violating human rights. This suggests that, by and large, despite their assertions that Islamic law justifies breaching human rights, states regard international human rights as normative and fear criticism for violating them. In a few cases, however, information on egregious human rights violations was proudly disseminated by the governments involved as an indication of the seriousness of their commitment to applying Islamic law. This was, for example, the case in January 1985 when the Nimeiri regime convicted Mahmud Muhammad Taha of apostasy and chose to publicize both the trial and his subsequent execution by hanging, and in February 1989 when Khomeini called for the murder of author Salman Rushdie. Such instances were exceptional.

The governments of Iran, Pakistan, and the Sudan were conscious that the denials of rights under their Islamization programs would not only earn them criticism from outsiders for violating international law but also could lead to embarrassing charges by domestic critics that they were not even abiding by locally applicable constitutional principles. Therefore, the governments involved had to devise strategies for obviating constitutional challenges that could undermine the authority of their Islamization measures. Whereas all three regimes seem to have been anxious to avoid direct challenges to their Islamization measures based on domestic constitutional rights provisions, they took different tacks in dealing with this potential problem, either rewriting constitutional rights provisions or suspending them. In all three countries, Islamization has meant in practice the victory of philosophies antithetical to constitutionalism.

In Iran, the basic approach was to discard the old constitution and to rewrite constitutional rights provisions, inserting a number of vague Islamic qualifications. Simply by invoking the latter, the government had ready-made pretexts for overriding rights. These Islamic qualifications will be discussed in greater detail in Chapters 4–8. Although the addition of qualifications to rights provisions did not entirely eliminate problems of conflicts between the government's conduct and certain provisions of the Iranian Constitution, it provided sweeping justifications for infringing on rights. Article 4 of the Iranian Constitution set the stage for using Islamization as a pretext for diluting rights. It provides: "All civil, penal, financial, economic, administrative, cultural, military, political laws and other laws or regulations, must be based on Islamic criteria. This principle applies absolutely and generally to all articles of the Constitution as well as to all other laws and regulations, and the *fuqaha* [Islamic jurists] of the Guardian Council are judges in this matter." The clerics on the council may rule that laws are not in conformity with Islamic principles; the latter not only override ordinary laws but also provisions in the constitution itself. As this article shows, it will be Islamic principles as determined by Islamic clerics (who, according to Article 110, are to be appointed by Iran's religious leader in his capacity as the leading jurist) that constitute the supreme law in Iran.

In consequence, even constitutional rights guarantees cannot have force should clerics decide that those guarantees are not compatible with Islamic principles. Significantly, what these Islamic principles mean for rights has never been set forth with any precision. The clerical elite has dismantled many elements of Iran's largely French-based legal order, but it did not replace these by constructing a firm framework of legality using Islamic standards, leaving Iran instead in a kind of legal limbo. As a recent report on Iran asserts, by monopolizing the interpretation of core ideological precepts, Iran's clerics have seriously undermined the rule of law in the country.[26] An example of the mindset of clerical officialdom was presented in 1997 when Ayatollah Yazdi, the head of Iran's judiciary, reacted to Ayatollah Montazeri's challenging the authority of supreme jurist Khamene'i. To chasten Montazeri for questioning a pillar of Iran's system of clerical rule, supporters of the regime had already launched violent attacks on his home and staged menacing demonstrations, but, not being sure that the mayhem and threats had been sufficiently intimidating, Ayatollah Yazdi thought it well to warn publicly that the people would give Montazeri "an even stronger response" if he did not desist from speaking out.[27] That is, in responding to critical remarks from a senior cleric, the head of Iran's judiciary spoke like the head of a criminal syndicate accustomed to using threats of violence on the part of his henchmen to instill fear and acquiescence—hardly like a judicial official charged with upholding the law.

In the Sudan and Pakistan, the approach taken was different. Constitutions were effectively suspended for most of the respective Islamization programs. A few aspects of the connection between Islamization and the human rights violations perpetrated by the Sudanese and Pakistani regimes are catalogued here.

President Ja'far Nimeiri, who had ruled the Sudan after seizing power in May 1969, decided in 1983 to try to consolidate his increasingly unpopular regime by cementing an alliance with the Sudanese contingent of the fundamentalist Muslim Brothers. He inaugurated an ambitious but haphazard Islamization program, which led to a renewed outbreak of civil war between the Arab and Muslim north and the mostly animist or Christian Africans in the south. In 1984, Nimeiri sought to rewrite the Sudanese Constitution to make himself the supreme political and religious leader but was thwarted by determined opposition. Instead, in order to press ahead with his Islamization program while avoiding charges that he was violating the constitution, he declared a state of emergency on April 29, 1984, which allowed him to suspend all constitutional rights provisions and to grant extraordinary powers to the police and the military.[28] Nimeiri asserted: "Plots have increased our faith. We shall be more determined and strong-willed. In view of this faith, in order to protect our faith and our homeland from the plotters and from the tampering of Satan and in view of my commitment to my constitutional responsibilities, I have issued Republican Decree No. 258 for the year of 1984 proclaiming a state of emergency in all parts of the country."[29] Angered by the resistance of judges and lawyers, Nimeiri gave judicial appointments to compliant judges who would be prepared to ignore constitutional constraints. The state of emergency was officially lifted in autumn 1984 under U.S. diplomatic pressure. Thus, there was a period from late 1984 to early 1985 during which constitutional guarantees were theoretically again in force. In practice, constitutional rights remained suspended until Nimeiri's overthrow.

It was Nimeiri himself who associated the state of emergency with the protection of Islam. He claimed that it had been declared "not to fight an incoming enemy or to resist an external military attack but to protect a believing society against those who infiltrate it and transgress against its values, morals and security,"[30] insisting that it was needed to preserve Islam from its enemies and identifying his foes as "Satan and his supporters."[31] He tried to portray himself as a deeply pious Muslim whose decision to declare the state of emergency had been motivated by a concern for protecting the Islamic religion from its enemies, corrupt persons who "exploited the situation by challenging the law and attacking the Islamic Shari'ah."[32]

Despite Nimeiri's invocation of his "constitutional responsibilities" in connection with the state of emergency, he could not point to anything in the Sudanese Constitution that justified the suspension of rights protections to facilitate the dictatorial imposition of a religious law on a resisting population. The reference to the constitution suggests, however, a residual concern on Nimeiri's part lest he be accused of violating constitutional tenets. Obviously, Sudanese Islamization was intimately associated with the suspension of human rights protections guaranteed in the Sudanese Constitution.

Upon Nimeiri's overthrow by a popular revolution in 1985, there was a period of rule by a caretaker military regime, during which the 1973 Sudanese Constitution was replaced by an interim constitution with provisions designed to cure some of the evils fostered by Nimeiri's Islamization campaign.[33] The Sudan reverted to a free, democratic system in April 1986. After moves in spring 1989 to abrogate Nimeiri's Islamic laws, military leaders allied with Hassan al-Turabi's National Islamic Front (NIF) staged a coup, which resulted in the installation in July 1989 of a military dictatorship under General Omar al-Bashir, in which Turabi played the role of an éminence grise. With this coup, prospects for ending the ravages of the civil war collapsed, with devastating consequences for southern Sudan.[34] Zealously committed to Islamization, the new government promptly abrogated the interim constitution and suspended all the rights and freedoms that the Sudanese had enjoyed in the brief period of democracy. Mass arrests of politically active Sudanese ensued, political parties were suppressed, harsh censorship was imposed, and critics of Islamic fundamentalism in government employment found themselves dismissed from their jobs. Laws sharply curbing women's freedoms were enacted, and ethnic and religious minorities were mistreated and abused. Southerners suffered from episodes of genocide and enslavement. The criminal justice system utilized harsh physical punishment, protracted incarceration without trial, and torture. Again, oppressive military government and systematic denials of rights and freedoms were associated with the pursuit of Islamization.[35]

Bashir's regime promptly disbanded the independent Sudan Human Rights Organization, replacing it in 1991 with a docile, government-controlled organization by the same name with a mission to defend Khartoum from charges of human rights violations.[36] As it continued dismantling the institutions of civil society, the regime undertook various initiatives designed to erect a facade of constitutionalism, such as staging elections to enable Bashir to claim the title of "president" and issuing the Sudan Document of Human Rights, which indicated that the Sudan protected human rights according to Islamic standards, both in 1993.[37] However, it was not until 1997 that the regime finally announced that a constitution would be promulgated and set up a committee to draft it.[38] That for eight years this regime did not bother to start the process of establishing a formal constitutional basis for government was indicative of the low priority it accorded to the values of constitutionalism.

Responses by Sudanese officialdom to independent human rights monitors, who continued to decry the level of rights abuses, were revealing. Reacting to the critical 1994 UN Commission on Human Rights report by Gaspar Biro finding that Sudanese law, including its Islamic laws, clashed with international law, the Sudanese delegate to the commission lashed out with charges that the findings constituted an attack on Islam and a flagrant violation of the sovereignty of the Sudan and the freedom of religion of its people.[39] The attorney general of the Sudan charged that Biro's report was "satanic"—his adjective recalling Khomeini's death edict for Salman Rushdie. He castigated Biro as "an enemy of Islam" guilty of "blasphemy" for criticizing the Sudan's Islamic laws.[40] That is, in attempting to deflect the aspersions cast on the Sudan's human rights performance, he resorted to Islamic categories that amounted to thinly veiled death threats against the UN rapporteur—apparently assuming that the kind of terror employed by the regime to silence its domestic critics could be appropriately employed to intimidate critics in the international arena.

There are intriguing similarities between the Sudan under Nimeiri and Pakistan in the period 1977–1988. President Muhammad Zia ul-Haq, after overthrowing the elected government of President Zulfikar Ali Bhutto, ruled Pakistan as a military dictator until his death in a plane crash in August 1988. President Zia declared martial law after seizing power, and it remained in force until December 1985. However, the formal termination of martial law in 1985 did not mean an end to the dominance of the military over Pakistan's political life, nor did it mean in practice a full restoration of constitutional guarantees of fundamental rights, even though these were officially revived when martial law ended.

President Zia's reliance on a suspension of constitutional rights may be connected to the fact that in Pakistan, as in Nimeiri's Sudan, a project for drafting an Islamic constitution, which was to replace the existing 1973 constitution, eventually came to naught. It appears that Zia found the question of what constitutes an Islamic constitution to be so contentious and divisive that he decided to abandon the project. Had it been pursued, given President Zia's dictatorial style, it is probable that Islamic qualifications would have been placed on constitutional rights provisions, substantially reducing the protections that they afforded. It would then have ceased to be necessary to suspend constitutional rights, since the rights themselves would have become eviscerated, as they were in the rewritten Iranian Constitution.

Zia used his commitment to pursue Islamization as the justification for his retention of dictatorial powers and the suspension of constitutional rights. As in Nimeiri's Sudan, under Zia the major thrust of Islamization was in the area of criminal law and procedure, which means that many of the developments in Pakistan lie outside the scope of this study. In a major address given in 1983, while all fundamental constitutional rights were formally suspended, Zia analogized his position as chief martial law administrator to that of a traditional prince, or emir.[41] Like Nimeiri, Zia indicated that opposition would not be tolerated:

One basic point that emerges from a study of the Quranic verses and the Prophet's sayings is that as long as the Amir or the head of State abides by the injunctions of Allah and his Prophet (PBUH) ["peace and blessings upon him"] his obedience becomes mandatory for his subjects or the people, irrespective of the personal dislike that someone may harbour for the Amir or any of his actions. Not only in my opinion but also in the opinion of legal experts and scholars, my Government, too, is a constitutional Government, which has been acting upon the tenets of Islam. We are devout Muslims. I concede, and I am proud of it, that the present Government is a military Government.[42]

Here one sees Zia's dedication to Islam offered as the rationale for a military dictatorship. In fact, Zia's ideas come from premodern Islamic thought, in which there was considerable support for the proposition that Muslims should obey persons in authority as long as they were not being commanded to engage in conduct that was sinful. One also finds support among contemporary Muslims for the idea that a government that follows and applies Islamic law must be obeyed. Still, for all his appeals to Islamic loyalties, Zia seems to have been concerned about possible charges that his overthrowing the previous, elected government and his rule by martial law violated the Pakistani Constitution—hence his surprising assertion that his was a "constitutional" government. In this assertion, Zia relied on the fact that his government was acting "upon the tenets of Islam," which, apparently, justified to his way of thinking a military seizure of power and a subsequent military dictatorship. Notwithstanding this claim, "legal experts and scholars" would be hard-pressed to cite a constitutional provision that supported Zia's position. In fact, later events proved that Zia was apprehensive lest, should he lose political control, he and his associates could be prosecuted for acts committed during the period of martial law. In 1985 he had the constitution amended to validate and affirm all the acts and rules of the martial law regime. His efforts to shield himself from prosecutions via a constitutional amendment suggests that he thought that he would need special immunity to escape civil and criminal liability once martial law had ended.

Zia tried to consolidate his alliance with Islamic clerics who supported his program by giving them the chance to serve as judges. As a result of his policy, many persons deficient in conventional professional qualifications but with religious educations were appointed to the judiciary, leading to changes that compromised the integrity and independence of Pakistan's formerly distinguished judiciary.

Through legal initiatives and court rulings such as the *Zaheeruddin* decision, discussed in Chapter 8, Islamization continued to have impact well after Zia's demise.[43] Pakistan's leading politicians were locked in a bitter rivalry that precluded much benefit ensuing from the return to democracy. Benazir Bhutto, Zia's most determined opponent, and Nawaz Sharif alternated terms as prime minister, using their office to pursue partisan agendas rather than working to advance the national welfare or shore up the foundations of the rule of law in the country. In late 1997, Prime Minister Nawaz Sharif emerged victorious from a fierce political contest involving his office, the president, and the supreme court, a victory that seemed likely to impair the separation of powers as well as the independence of the judiciary. Although he had been Zia's protégé and had occasionally spoken in favor of Islamization, Sharif seemed preoccupied with political infighting and relatively uninterested in pursuing Islamization, especially when compared with Pakistan's right-wing religious parties, which continued to demand strict application of Islamic law and also to fare badly at the polls. An indication of Sharif's true attitude came in December 1997 when he nominated Rafiq Tarar for the presidency, which ensured his election by Sharif's majority faction. Since Tarar was notorious for deprecating human rights in general and for denigrating the rights of women and minorities in particular, his nomination at a time when the rights situation was becoming desperate seemed to betoken Sharif's own antipathy toward human rights. Zia's onslaught on constitutionalism was turning out to have far-reaching, poisonous consequences.

The Impact on Rights of the Taleban Takeover in Afghanistan

It is impossible in a short space to catalogue the tragic vicissitudes of the turbulent history of Afghanistan since the 1989 Russian pullout, and it is too soon to predict whether the country's current leaders can long hold onto the reins of power.[44] In terms of Islamization, the most recent developments matter most—the 1996 conquest of most of the country by the Taleban, a Pashtun faction zealously committed to the implementation of an extraordinarily harsh and repressive version of Islamic law, which, for example, bans music, flying kites, keeping pigeons, and taking photographs. In October 1997 the Taleban renamed the country the Islamic Emirate of Afghanistan.[45] The emir was the Sunni cleric Mullah Mohammed Omar. Since the Taleban takeover, human rights violations have assumed epidemic proportions. As is often the case when countries say they are discarding Western-style laws to return to the *shari'a,* the actual result seems to be a total collapse of the rule of law. Taleban abuses reportedly have included the deliberate and arbitrary murder of thousands of men, women, and children; unacknowledged detention of several thousand people after being abducted by various armed political groups; torture of civilians; rape of women; and routine beatings and ill treatment of persons suspected of belonging to rival political groups or having a non-Pashtun ethnic identity.[46] Under the rubric of applying Islamic law, drastic curbs have been imposed on women's freedoms, as is discussed in Chapter 6.

Most of the Taleban abuses have little or no connection to Islamic law as understood elsewhere. Instead, Afghanistan has emerged as another example of how distinctive the local versions of Islam can be, the Taleban's official Islam reflecting the attitudes of a brutish Pashtun rabble whose members are determined to impose by force and terror their dominion over Afghanistan's culturally and ethnically diverse population and to eliminate all signs of resistance to their reactionary policies.

The Impact on Rights of the 1992 Saudi Reforms

As has already been indicated, Saudi Arabia embarked on a different course, being engaged not in Islamization but in adopting some modest modernizing reforms. Unlike other countries, which were resorting to Islam to take away rights that had previously been afforded under their modern constitutions, in Saudi Arabia, where medieval Islamic law and institutions had remained largely intact, the problem was seeing whether the existing system of Islamic law would incorporate human rights and other elements of constitutionalism. The reforms included promulgating the 1992 Basic Law.[47] The tentative moves to accommodate internal pressures for change came after both liberal and conservative sectors of Saudi society had indicated their impatience with the Saudi family's autocratic rule, the deficiencies of the legal system, and the failure to respect basic rights and freedoms.[48] To date, however, the adoption of the Basic Law does not appear to have led to an improvement in the human rights situation, which, even in the relatively charitable assessment of allied governments like the United States, has continued to be marked by pervasive violations of international human rights.[49]

The Basic Law affirmed the absolute monarchy, treating it as if it were grounded in the Islamic sources. King Fahd appealed to "Islamic beliefs" to defend the failure to guarantee Saudis any of the rights that constitutionalism normally affords citizens. He asserted:

> The democratic system that is predominant in the world is not a suitable system for the peoples of our region. Our people's makeup and unique qualities are different from those of the rest of the world. We cannot import the methods used by people in other countries and apply them to our people. We have our Islamic beliefs that constitute a complete and fully integrated system. In my view, Western democracies may be suitable in their own countries but they do not suit other countries.[50]

In May 1993, the first independent human rights organization on Saudi soil was launched, the Committee for the Defense of Legitimate Rights (CDLR). Its stated objectives included fighting oppression and injustice and securing the release of political prisoners, and it called for human rights and democracy. This committee had emerged out of conservative

Wahhabi circles and claimed to be inspired by tenets of Islamic law.[51] Although its spokespersons often referred to "human rights" in communications, the CDLR was not appealing to international human rights but proposing its own eccentric version of Islamic rights.

The committee was officially banned and condemned for alleged ties to "terrorist" and "extremist" groups, and its members were arrested, dismissed from their jobs, and incarcerated. The official position was that, in a society like Saudi Arabia's that adhered to Islamic law, there could be no need for a human rights organization. The government tried to discredit the CDLR by securing a ruling from the council of senior ulama saying that the CDLR was heretical and that its criticisms were illegitimate and unacceptable, because the kingdom followed Islamic law.[52] After being harshly repressed, members of the CDLR were able to escape to London in 1994, from where they continued their oppositional activities. In 1995 they published a sizable report.[53] Members of the CDLR split into rival factions in Spring 1996. In response to CDLR accusations and other attacks, the Saudi Interior Minister Prince Nayif asserted that human rights were fully respected in Saudi Arabia.[54]

Thus, in the 1990s in Saudi Arabia, a country that had never been colonized by the West and that had stayed closer to the juristic tradition than any of its neighbors, the government and an opposition group whose real sympathies were with a purified form of archconservative Islam both felt obliged to adopt the pose of supporters of human rights when neither possessed a trace of real sympathy for human rights. This is emblematic of how human rights concepts have won influence in contemporary Muslim societies. The CDLR in phrasing its attacks on the Saudi rulers in terms of rights, and the Saudi rulers in phrasing their defense of their regime in terms of human rights, both paid tribute to the potency and prestige that human rights ideas had acquired, recognizing that these had become the criteria for legitimacy of governments and opposition movements. True, both sides also sought to buttress their causes by recourse to Islamic rhetoric, but it seemed that both effectively had conceded that preaching fidelity to Islamic law without claiming a commitment to human rights would no longer suffice in appealing to fellow Saudis. It remained for the latter to disentangle the actual rights policies of the regime and its Islamist opponents from the rhetoric supportive of human rights adopted by both sides.

Summary

The consequences of Islamization programs for human rights in these countries deserve to be carefully considered. The pursuit of Islamization—or in the Saudi case, the retention of premodern jurisprudence—have correlated with patterns of disregard for human rights and also the pursuit of policies inimical to the rule of law. To date one cannot point out a single government purporting to accord supremacy to Islamic law that has shown any real solicitude for protecting human rights as embodied in the local constitution, much less human rights as established in international law. On the contrary, the adoption of the principle that Islamic law overrides human rights seems to correlate with policies inimical to constitutionalism.

CHAPTER 3

Islamic Tradition and Muslim Reactions to Human Rights

The Contribution of Western Civilization

To understand the problems of accommodating human rights within an Islamic framework, it is necessary to review the development of international human rights concepts. The human rights principles utilized in international law are of relatively recent vintage. Although one can find ideas that anticipate human rights concepts in ancient Greek thought, the articulation of human rights principles—though not necessarily labeled as such—came much later. Certainly, the development of the intellectual foundations of human rights was given an impetus by the Renaissance in Europe and by the associated growth of rationalist and humanistic thought, which led to an important turning point in Western intellectual history. This was the abandonment of premodern doctrines of the duties of man and the adoption of the view that the rights of man should be central in political theory.[1] It was during the European Enlightenment that the rights of man became a preoccupation of political philosophy, and it was then that the intellectual groundwork for modern human rights theory was laid.

Eighteenth-century British and French thinkers put forward the precursors of modern human rights ideas and had great influence on the rights provisions in the American Declaration of Independence of 1776, the Virginia Declaration of Rights of 1776, and the Bill of Rights that was added to the U.S. Constitution in 1791. These, along with the Fourteenth Amendment of 1868, have in turn had great influence on subsequent rights formulations, as have the concepts of the 1789 Déclaration des droits de l'homme et du citoyen, developed at the time of the French Revolution.

Common to the British and French philosophies that prefigured modern human rights was the idea that the rights of the individual should be of paramount importance. In a survey of the historical evolution of rights concepts, one scholar has said that the significance of the shift from concern for law to concern for rights "derives from the fact that the concept of rights is individualistic in the sense that it is a from-the-bottom-up view of morality rather than one from the top down, and from the related fact that it generally expresses claims of a part against the whole."[2]

Long before international human rights law emerged, constitutionalism had been viewed as a means of placing legal limitations on the powers of governments, and the U.S. Constitution and later European constitutions became models that were widely copied elsewhere. Central to these constitutions are curbs on governmental power and safeguards for individual liberty, which is to be insulated from governmental intrusions. The rules establishing these curbs embody reactions to experiences of oppression and misrule and recipes for correcting these ills.

Recognizing that individual rights would sometimes need to be curtailed in the public interest or because of extraordinary circumstances, the drafters of constitutions sought to define and restrict the justifications that states could invoke to curtail rights, because it was appreciated that without such definitions and restrictions, states could unduly exploit various rationales for infringing rights.

It was on these Western traditions of individualism, humanism, and rationalism and on legal principles protecting individual rights that twentieth-century international law on civil and political rights ultimately rested. Rejecting individualism, humanism, and rationalism is tantamount to rejecting the premises of modern human rights.

The Role of the United Nations

Proponents of international human rights espoused the idea that rights should be guaranteed not just in constitutional rights provisions but also by an international law, binding on all nations. After World War II, the United Nations, as the preeminent international organization, took a leading role in formulating rights that had previously been left to domestic legislation. The UN Charter (1945) called for respect for human rights and fundamental freedoms but did not undertake the difficult task of specifying what these entailed. The Universal Declaration of Human Rights (UDHR), adopted by the General Assembly in 1948, in its Preamble called for members to seek to construct a new world order on a sounder basis, one in which "recognition of the inherent dignity and of the equal and inalienable rights of all members of the human family is the foundation of freedom, justice, and peace in the world."

One way of looking at this UN initiative is to see it as intimately bound to the particular situation facing the world community in the aftermath of World War II, when people around the globe contemplated the mayhem and horror of the war years and decided to rely on respect for human rights as the means to preclude a repetition of such horror. The wording of the Preamble can be interpreted as spelling out "a political, sociological, and historical interpretation of the historical circumstances of world society in the aftermath of World War II."[3] That is, the UDHR may constitute UN members' responses to a shared historical experience, meaning that it should be seen as independent of any particular theological or metaphysical framework. Viewed from this perspective, international human rights, even if they appropriate ideas from the Western tradition, have a different starting point, being grounded in a situated geopolitical moral rationality.[4] If one accepts this assessment, the fact that substantive UDHR provisions have antecedents in Western civilization does not mean that the new system inaugurated by the UDHR expresses principles that belong uniquely to the West.

Many rights instruments and conventions codifying international human rights norms were subsequently produced under the auspices of the United Nations. With input from countries around the world after UN membership expanded to encompass the Global South, doctrines have developed well beyond the negative rights referred to earlier, now encompassing many affirmative rights that require governments to take measures to meet people's needs, especially in the social and economic spheres. Although the patterns of ratification of international human rights conventions have been uneven and although there is much that remains controversial about international human rights law, on many issues there is sufficient consensus to justify the claim that human rights have come to be part of customary international law.

The Role of Islamic Law

The learned literature on international human rights produced by academic specialists shows an indifference to the Islamic tradition. The idea of consulting Islamic law as a means of better understanding human rights has clearly been dismissed by specialists. This is hardly surprising, given the current preeminence of the Western legal heritage, within which Islamic law has no normative value and enjoys little prestige. Serious treatises by recognized specialists on the development of international human rights law have not to date produced evidence of Islamic inspiration for international human rights law or its historical antecedents.

Questions of Islamic law are only occasionally mentioned in scholarly writing on international human rights—for the sake of comparison with international norms or to illustrate the problems of introducing international norms in areas of the developing world. Islamic law is treated, if at all, as a marginal, exotic phenomenon. The critiques offered by Muslims who object to international human rights law on religious grounds do not seem to have provoked much consternation or interest on the part of Western scholars of international law, for the latter do not feel that the legitimacy of international law is in any way jeopardized by assertions that it fails to conform to Islamic criteria. Underlying this framework is an emphatic presumption in favor of the superiority of international law and its associated institutions and a belief in the relative backwardness of any Islamic models with which they may conflict.

The perspectives of legal scholarship in the area of international human rights law are connected to the relative positions of the West and the Muslim world today. One should recall that Islam is overwhelmingly a religion of Third World countries. Centuries ago it was Islamic civilization that was more advanced than Western civilization, and a relatively backward Europe borrowed extensively from Islamic culture, but now it is the Western world that has attained the model of civilization that other societies generally seek to emulate. Islamic culture no longer beckons as something to be studied and copied; it seems at the moment to have little to teach the more economically developed and technologically advanced societies of the West.

To note that today the West has a legal tradition that seems more attuned to modern needs than its Islamic counterpart is not to say that Western law is by its nature superior and that Islamic law is by its nature inferior. Similarly, to indicate the historical lag in the development of human rights concepts in Islamic thought is also not the same as ascribing inadequacy to Islam. The lag in Islamic legal development vis-à-vis that of the West, leading to Muslims' belated attempts to construct Islamic versions of human rights, is the result of a complex interplay of political, economic, and cultural factors in which Islamic doctrines often were as much shaped by their environment as they were forces shaping that environment.

This study in no way aims to establish that human rights could not have developed in an Islamic milieu or to deny that one can find many concepts that prefigure human rights in the Islamic heritage. However, it relies on the evidence so far accumulated that, as a matter of comparative legal history, Islamic versions of human rights developed after Western and international human rights models had already been produced. The reasons for this lag must be taken into account. Without paying adequate attention to the historical circumstances that delayed the production of human rights in Islamic milieus, one cannot account for many of the peculiar features of Islamic human rights schemes. To understand what shaped the Islamic human rights schemes discussed here, it is essential to remember that aspects of Western rights concepts associated with a different level of political and legal development have been superficially imitated without their underlying tenets being fully examined or assimilated and that the authors have combined these rights concepts with features selected from a legal culture that is tied to non-Western values and experiences.

The Premodern Islamic Heritage

As we have seen, the individualism characteristic of Western civilization was a fundamental ingredient in the development of human rights concepts. Individualism, however, is not a characteristic feature of Muslim societies or of Islamic culture, even though Sufism, or mysticism, which is a major component of the Islamic tradition, does have elements of individualism.[5]

Islamic doctrines were historically produced in traditional societies, where one would not expect individualism to be prized. Nonindividualistic and even anti-individualistic attitudes are common in traditional societies, where individuals are situated in a given position in a social context and are seen as components of family or community structures rather than as autonomous, separate persons. Premodern Islamic thought naturally reflects these traditional values and communitarian priorities. When one says that Islamic doctrines formulated by Muslim thinkers in the past tend to be anti-individualistic, one is making an observation that relates more to the historical context in which these ideas were produced than to Islam as a religion. To describe such doctrines as anti-individualistic is not to say that Islam is inherently incapable of accommodating principles of individualism. However, as many examples in this book will illustrate, proponents of the Islamic human rights schemes examined here have tended to associate the defense of Islamic values with the rejection of individualism.

The connection of Islamic thought with the values of traditional societies has not, however, meant that Islamic culture lacks features that in the West contributed to the development of human rights. The Islamic heritage offers many philosophical concepts, humanistic values, and moral principles that are well adapted for use in constructing human rights principles. Such values and principles abound even in the premodern Islamic intellectual heritage. However, historical factors like the political ascendancy of an orthodox philosophy and theology that were hostile to humanism and rationalism—and, ultimately, hostile to the liberal ideals associated with human rights—kept the exponents of such values and principles in a generally weak and defensive position over much of the history of Islamic civilization. If the adherents of rationalist and humanistic currents had attained greater political power and influence, such thinkers might have oriented Islamic thought in ways that would have created a much more propitious climate for the early emergence of human rights ideas. As it is, despite their minority position, the views of rationalist and humanistic Muslim thinkers are definitely anchored in the Islamic tradition.

One of the most important rationalist currents in Islamic thought was that of the group known as the Mu'tazila, whose members' influence in the Sunni world reached its zenith in the ninth century, after which they were largely suppressed.[6] The Mu'tazilites called for rational interpretations of the Islamic sources and demanded justice in both the political and social spheres. The community was to control the government, not blindly to defer to authority, and it was free to revolt against governments that denied fundamental liberties.[7] Although, since the crushing of the Mu'tazila, rationalist thinkers have generally been on the defensive in Muslim milieus, rationalist currents were never entirely extirpated, and in Twelver Shi'i Islam such currents have remained influential. Islamic thinkers who adopted the Mu'tazilite approach, too openly espousing the idea of the supremacy of reason over Revelation and calling for laws to conform to human notions of justice, have always risked being branded heretical by staunch adherents of the view that neither Islam nor its divine law can be evaluated by reference to the tenets of human reason. The cases of Nasr Hamid Abu Zaid, discussed in Chapter 8, and of Abdolkarim Sorush illustrate the continuing relevance of the controversies set in motion by the Mu'tazilites' refusal to defer meekly to established orthodoxy. Sorush, a philosophy professor, offered visions of an Islam stripped of the restraints on freedoms that had characterized the reigning Islamic ideology.[8] Sorush has, among other things, dared publicly to maintain that justice preceded Islam and that Islamic law should conform to the criterion of justice.[9] Although Iran's ruling clerics attacked him for espousing heretical views, in articulating this position, Sorush was effectively endorsing a proposition that had been stressed by the ancient Mu'tazilites, whose rationalist philosophy had long roots in the Shi'i tradition. That is, his rationalist views were rooted in Iran's Shi'i heritage, which afforded grounds for challenging the idea that believers were to defer unquestioningly to the supposed dictates of Islamic theology and law regardless of whether these led to unjust consequences. For these and for other bold statements that challenged the official manipulation of Islam to circumscribe rights and freedoms, Sorush became a target of violent physical assaults and threats and was subjected to harsh censorship and restrictions designed to silence him.[10]

Some eminent Islamic philosophers, such as al-Farabi (d. 950) and Ibn Rushd ("Averroës") (d. 1198), came close to saying that it is reason that determines what is right and true and that religion must conform to reason's dictates.[11] However, orthodox theologians in Sunni Islam were generally suspicious of human reason, fearing that it would lead Muslims to stray from the truth of Revelation. There was an ongoing tension between the rationalist inclinations of Islamic philosophers, many of whom were influenced by Greek philosophy, and the tenets of the dominant philosophy of ethical voluntarism. The latter was the prevailing view in the Sunni world, one that the Mu'tazila unsuccessfully combated, holding that because of their divine inspiration, *shari'a* laws should supersede reason. They embodied God's will and were necessarily just. Human reason, in the orthodox Sunni view, was incapable of ascertaining what was just. Instead, the orthodox view was that Muslims should unquestioningly defer to the wisdom of God as expressed in Islamic doctrines that were taken to represent instructions from the Qur'an and the example of the Prophet.[12] Given the dominance of this mainstream Islamic view, it naturally became difficult to realize an Islamic version of the Age of Reason.

The ascendancy of ethical voluntarism and the relative weakness of rationalist currents in Sunni Islam had important consequences for Islamic thinkers' views of the relationship of ruler and ruled. Islamic thought tended to stress not the rights of human beings but, rather, their duties to obey God's perfect law, which, by its nature, would achieve the ideal balance in society. Since whatever God willed was ipso facto just, according to the orthodox Islamic view, perfect justice could be achieved if all God's creatures, both ruler and ruled, were obedient to God's commands as expressed in Islamic law. Still today one finds this emphasis on duties. For example, Ayatollah Khomeini insisted that man had no natural rights and that believers were to submit to God's commands.[13]

Since the pious Muslim was only supposed to understand and obey the divine law, which entailed abiding by the limits that God had decreed, demands for individual freedoms could sound distinctly subversive to the orthodox mind. Such demands might be taken to suggest that individuals did not consider themselves strictly bound to submit to the dictates of Islamic law and the commands of the authorities charged with its execution or that they were presuming to use their own fallible human reasoning powers to challenge the supremacy of religious teachings.[14]

The aim of Islamic law was generally conceived to be ensuring the well-being of the Islamic community, or *umma,* as a whole, in a situation where both the ruler and the ruled were presumed to be motivated to follow the law in order to win divine favor and avoid punishment in Hell. In consequence, *shari'a* doctrines remained highly idealistic and were not elaborated with a view to providing institutional mechanisms to deal with actual situations where governments disregarded Islamic law and oppressed and exploited their subjects.[15] Scholars of Islamic law did not traditionally address issues like what institutions and procedures were needed to constrain the ruler and curb oppression; rather, they tended to think of the relationship between ruler and ruled solely in terms of this idealized scheme, in which rulers were conceived of as pious Muslims eager to follow God's mandate.[16] Provisions to protect the rights of the individual vis-à-vis society or the government were wanting—with the single exception of the area of property rights, where the *shari'a* did provide remedies for the individual wrongfully deprived of property by official action.[17]

These characteristics of Islamic thought inhibited the growth of concepts of individual rights that could be asserted against infringements by governments, while never totally eclipsing other currents in Islamic thought that were hospitable to rights ideals. One can identify humanistic currents beginning in the early stages of Islamic thought and continuing to the present.[18] In addition, early Islamic thought includes precursors of the idea of political freedom.[19] Concepts of democracy very much like those in modern political systems can be found in the earliest period in Islamic history in the ideas of the Kharijite sect, which broke off from mainstream Islam in the seventh century over the latter's refusal to agree to the Kharijite tenet that the successors to the Prophet Muhammad had to be elected by the community.[20] Adherents of the Kharijite sect have been castigated for their unorthodox views, and their literature is not familiar to most other Muslims; but it still might be said that the Islamic tradition from the outset has included ideas that anticipated some of the democratic principles that underlie modern human rights norms.[21]

The premodern Islamic heritage was rich in ideas. The dominant currents did not provide a congenial setting for the early development of human rights concepts, but there were from the earliest stages of the Islamic tradition features that offered the potential for successful integration of the premises of modern human rights. Those who deploy Islam as a bulwark against democratization and human rights are therefore utilizing only one aspect of the multifaceted Islamic heritage. As a former member of the Egyptian Organization of Human Rights has observed: "Authoritarian and oppressive projects draw on the wealth of authoritarian traditions, images and symbols that are present in every human culture. Liberationist projects draw on the resistance and emancipatory traditions that are equally present in every human culture."[22] As this book argues, where interpretations of Islamic requirements constitute obstacles to human rights, these are likely to be tied to political preferences that lead to dismissing those elements in the Islamic heritage that have emancipatory potential.

Muslim Reactions to Western Constitutionalism

Just as there is no unitary Islamic position on the merits of philosophies like rationalism and humanism, so there is no unanimity on where Islam stands vis-à-vis constitutionalism, an institution closely tied to the development of legal protections for rights. The modern system of human rights, though set forth in international law, requires translation into rights provisions in national constitutions in order to afford effective legal guarantees for the rights involved. The reactions of Muslims to constitutionalism, which clearly came to the Middle East from the West, have historically run the gamut from enthusiastic endorsement to hostile rejection.[23]

The hold of Islamic doctrines, which tended to buttress the existing order and to stress the duties of the believer rather than individual rights, started to weaken as Muslim elites became familiar with Western ideas of law and governance in the nineteenth century. When Muslims began seeking legal means for curbing despotic and oppressive rulers, they turned not to the Islamic tradition but to Europe for models. Constitutionalist movements in the Middle East—typically inaugurated by adherents of secular nationalist movements and led by Westernized elites and often by Western-trained lawyers—were formed.[24] These groups perceived the inadequacies of traditional institutions of government in the Middle East. The relative weakness and backwardness of Middle Eastern countries, which proved incapable of standing up to European powers, became associated with the failure to establish and protect political freedoms. Early constitutionalists moved in the direction of dismantling legally imposed inequalities among citizens, and the nation rather than the religious community became the focus of political loyalty.[25]

Muslims who advocated constitutionalism frequently found that conservative ulama, or learned men of religion, were among their most determined foes. Often the ulama fought constitutionalism in the name of preserving Islam because they were convinced that constitutional principles conflicted with *shari'a* law.[26] The historical pattern of ulama resistance to constitutionalism endured longest in Saudi Arabia, the Muslim country where conservative ulama have retained the greatest political influence. Despite decades of efforts by liberal members of the Saudi elite to win acceptance for the notion of constitutionalism, a basic law was not adopted until 1992, and, even then, it fell short of meeting the standards of modern constitutionalism.[27]

However, there is no necessary opposition between Islam and constitutionalism, and there were many ulama who worked closely with liberal and reformist movements and who favored the adoption of Western-style constitutions. The famous and extremely influential Islamic reformer Muhammad 'Abduh (d. 1905), who served as grand mufti of Egypt, was one of the latter. An Azhar graduate and Islamic legal scholar, 'Abduh was a strong supporter of Egyptian nationalism and constitutionalism. He and other like-minded reformist clerics saw no fatal conflict between constitutionalism and fidelity to Islam or between political freedoms and the *shari'a*.

In sum, one can say that Islamic clerics were divided and have remained so on the merits of constitutionalism and whether the *shari'a* permits the adoption of constitutional restraints on governments and safeguards for individual rights and freedoms like those in the West. As current events show, Muslims continue to dispute whether elements of constitutionalism, an institution that is of central importance for the protection of human rights, are compatible with the *shari'a*.[28] Controversies in this area have been aggravated as contemporary Islamization programs have tended to correlate with the degradation of constitutionalism.

Muslim Ambivalence on Rights

As has been noted, there is demonstrable support among Muslims for international human rights. Obviously, these supporters find the values and priorities of international human rights congenial. If one may presume that the majority of Muslims who embrace human rights have attitudes that are influenced by Islamic teachings and Islamic culture, this phenomenon suggests that currents of Islamic thought must provide conditioning that is favorable for the reception of human rights. But what of those Muslims who accept human rights only warily and with substantial modifications and restrictions? What influences from the Islamic tradition or the associated value system account for their attitudes?

The best evidence of the attitudes of the authors of Islamic human rights schemes examined here lies in the texts of the schemes and in comments that they and other persons associated with the production of Islamic human rights documents have made. These sources will be analyzed in detail in Chapters 4–8. However, some general characterizations of the attitudes that have shaped the distinctive features of Islamic human rights schemes can be made. These attitudes are fundamentally at variance with the values of international human rights law. An attempt will be made to explain how the lack of awareness of the significance of these differences in perspectives has confused issues and has in turn affected features of Islamic human rights schemes.

Unlike Western scholars concerned with human rights, who regard the international rights model as normative and Islam as irrelevant, the authors of Islamic human rights schemes think in terms of two conflicting models simultaneously. Even while promoting Islamic versions of human rights, they seem to regard international human rights as the ultimate norm against which all rights schemes are inevitably measured and from which they fear to be caught deviating. This accounts for the defensive or apologetic tone that pervades much of the literature that puts forward distinctive Islamic schemes of human rights. On the evidence of the schemes analyzed here, the authors of Islamic human rights principles must feel torn between a desire to protect and perpetuate principles that they associate with their own tradition—in many respects a premodern one—and anxieties lest that tradition be assessed as backward and deficient if Islam is not shown to possess the kinds of "advanced" institutions that have been developed in the West. They thus seek to accentuate the formal resemblance between their schemes and the international ones even where that resemblance is misleading in terms of the actual level of rights protections that they intend to provide.

Proponents of Islamic human rights engage in strained attempts to blur distinctions between Islamic rules and their Western counterparts. They make special efforts to disguise features of the schemes that are most likely to provoke the opprobrium of the international community. As the following analysis of Islamic human rights schemes will show, where the intent is to deviate from the international standards, the discussion of rights protections is often kept at a level of idealistic abstraction, with individual provisions that are vague, equivocal, and evasive.

The desire to produce human rights schemes that appear to correspond to internationally accepted norms correlates with a lack of coherence in the thinking behind Islamic human rights schemes. This lack of coherence would not have arisen if the authors were deriving their rights schemes from Islamic models after having first identified the philosophical premises on which an Islamic approach to rights issues should be based and an appropriate methodology for interpreting the Islamic sources. Creating a human rights scheme in this fashion would entail genuine confidence in the viability of resources within the Islamic tradition on rights questions. These authors do not in fact possess that confidence.

As will be illustrated by the analyses of Islamic human rights schemes, the authors have not bothered to work out any clear theory of what rights should mean in an Islamic context or methods for deriving their content from the Islamic sources in a consistent and reasoned manner. Instead, they merely assemble pastiches of ideas and terminology drawn from two very different cultures without determining a rationale justifying these combinations or a way to reconcile the conflicting premises underlying them. That is, the deficiencies in the substantive Islamic human rights principles are the inevitable by-products of methodological confusion and weaknesses.

It must be emphasized that neither these methodological inadequacies nor the problematic results are necessary consequences of resorting to the Islamic tradition for inspiration. One can see, for example, in the work of Abdullahi An-Na'im the recognition that methodological questions are central to resolving the problem of where Islamic law stands on human rights. Offering a methodology that allows a fresh approach to the Islamic sources, an-Na'im has been able to develop a coherent scheme of human rights principles that is, for those who accept the validity of the proposed methodology, also one that rests on Islamic principles.[29]

The methodological failings that afflict Islamic human rights literature are just another manifestation of problems that typify contemporary Islamic thought generally and that have seriously hampered its ability to keep pace with modern intellectual and scientific developments. Valuable critiques of the deficient quality of contemporary Islamic thought have been provided by Mohammed Arkoun, a professor at the Sorbonne,[30] and also from a very different angle by Sadiq Jalal al-'Azm, a professor at the University of Damascus.[31] It is impossible in this study to do justice to these critiques, but one should note that the methodological defects decried here reflect a much bigger problem that presently preoccupies some of the most outstanding figures in the domain of Islamic thought.

Authors of Islamic human rights schemes, which emerged after those of international law had been firmly established, seem to worry that their creations will be perceived as basically derivative, as the schemes examined here obviously are. When they address the issue of what came first, the authors insist, against the weight of historical evidence, that Islam invented human rights and that the international standards are at best belated attempts to codify rules that Islam introduced in the seventh century.[32] Examples of such assertions can be found in the literature under consideration here and will be discussed also in Chapter 9.

In their attempts to support the contention that human rights originated in the Islamic tradition, the authors rely on strained readings of the Qur'an or the accounts of the custom, or *sunna,* of the Prophet Muhammad to establish the Islamic pedigrees of rights.[33] They cite passages that in their opinion demonstrate that the Islamic sources had established the equivalents of modern human rights. By concentrating on the era of the Prophet and projecting human rights principles back to the start of Islamic history and then jumping more than a millennium to the present, they largely avoid referring to the history of Islamic jurisprudence. However, if one is arguing that the Islamic tradition has a much older set of human rights principles than the West, it is important to show how Muslims have historically interpreted the Islamic sources.

Traditionally, the learned expositions of *shari'a* rules in the juristic treatises have been consulted as the definitive statements of how the Islamic sources should be interpreted. To answer the question of whether and when human rights concepts were produced in Islamic culture and to discover what Islamic jurists have traditionally believed Islam provided in the area of rights and freedoms, a legal historian would turn first to the great legal treatises and possibly also the writings on theology and philosophy that were produced in the premodern period of Islamic civilization—very approximately, from the ninth to the fourteenth century—and that are still widely consulted as the most prestigious statements of premodern Islamic doctrine. No documented Islamic authority dating from the premodern period has come to light that squarely addresses human rights issues as such or that anticipates the contemporary rights formulations.

The authors of these Islamic human rights schemes largely ignore the many centuries of juristic elaborations of the Qur'an and *sunna,* which one would expect them to examine and assess before asserting that Islam has a longer tradition of human rights than does Western culture. Even if the principles of Islamic human rights did inhere in the original sources, for purposes of legal history, one would want to know when Muslims first started perceiving the human rights implications of the sources. This, the record shows, did not happen until very recently. Thus, Islamic human rights principles are newly coined, much newer than rights principles in the West, which can be traced to the Enlightenment and to a certain extent even before that.

When one abandons the search for express treatments of human rights issues and looks instead in the writings of the premodern jurists, theologians, and philosophers for the elaboration of ideas that would either tend to accommodate human rights principles or to create obstacles to their reception in the Islamic tradition, one finds voluminous relevant material. The problem then becomes an overabundance of authority that has conflicting implications for rights. After one surveys premodern Islamic intellectual history, one realizes that there was no settled Islamic doctrine on rights or protorights in that period, only currents of thought that would create either a more or a less propitious foundation for the assimilation of modern human rights concepts within an Islamic framework.

Proponents of Islamization call for the extirpation of Western cultural influences and a return to Islamic models in the areas of government, law, social organization, and culture. A prominent feature of Islamization programs has been demands for decolonization in the legal sphere—a rejection of Western legal models that were imposed or borrowed in a period when Muslims were ruled or dominated by Western powers. This legal decolonization in theory should mean the reinstatement of indigenous Islamic models. However, the Islamization programs rest on a false premise: that there exist in all areas settled Islamic legal countermodels of the Western models that are being repudiated. It is an article of faith to proponents of Islamization that Islam is a comprehensive ideology and scheme of life; they do not acknowledge that it comprises a variety of competing strains or that there were major gaps in the *shari'a*.[34] Authors of Islamic human rights schemes want to promote the idea that Islam provides a uniform body of principles on rights. To concoct their Islamic human rights, they must simplify the Islamic tradition, paper over cracks, and deny evidence of disagreement.

Under these circumstances, provisions of Islamic human rights schemes, to serve the ends of Islamization programs, must be given Islamic pedigrees and enough distinctively Islamic characteristics to satisfy the demands for Islamic versions of rights. Simultaneously, the schemes must stick close enough to Western models in order to cover essentially the same terrain as the Western schemes that are being rejected. The pressure to avoid acknowledging a debt to the Western human rights tradition entails recourse to strained interpretations of the Islamic sources, which, in reality, provide little express guidance for drafting specific rights provisions.

It is natural, therefore, that some authors of Islamic human rights schemes who have not developed an adequate methodology for constructing human rights on an Islamic foundation should feel tempted to rewrite the historical record of the development of human rights in the Muslim world in an attempt to cancel out in advance the intellectual debt that they owe to Western culture and to defend their schemes against charges that they are derivative of Western human rights concepts.

The Persistence of Traditional Priorities and Values

For reasons already discussed, proponents of Islamic human rights may not comprehend the problems involved in integrating borrowed provisions on individual rights and freedoms in a matrix of values found in traditional Muslim societies and premodern Islamic thought. Although there are currents in premodern Islamic thought that would mesh readily with modern human rights theories, the authors of the Islamic human rights schemes reviewed here cling to the ideas and attitudes of traditional orthodoxy, such as ethical voluntarism, the supremacy of divine Revelation, and hostility toward rationalism and humanism. They have thus elected to adhere to the same intellectual framework that historically impeded the development of human rights concepts, with consequences that will be shown in analyses of rights provisions (Chapters 4–8).

Ideally, one would want complete expositions of the authors' philosophies of human rights appended to each of the schemes. Then those philosophies could be correlated with critical appraisals of the provisions of each scheme. Unfortunately, the authors have not provided such essays. In default of such, there are still some grounds for characterizing their values and priorities.

Insofar as the schemes expressly indicate their priorities, they uphold the primacy of Revelation over reason; none endorse reason as a source of law. For example, when one examines the Preamble to the English version of the Universal Islamic Declaration of Human Rights (UIDHR), one sees that it takes the position that divine Revelation has provided the "legal and moral framework within which to establish and regulate human institutions and relationships." This idea is implicit throughout the text of the Arabic version, as passages from the Qur'an, God's Revelation, and the *sunna* of the Prophet, the practice of the divinely inspired messenger, are extensively quoted. It is thus clear that for the authors of the UIDHR, divinely inspired texts enjoy primacy as the source of law. The status of reason is correspondingly demoted. In a later passage in the Preamble of the UIDHR, the authors proclaim in the Arabic version that they believe that human reason *(al-'aql al-bashari),* independent of God's guidance and inspiration, is insufficient to provide the best plan for human life. In the corresponding part of the English version, after stating that "rationality by itself" cannot be "a sure guide in the affairs of mankind," they express their conviction that "the teachings of Islam represent the quintessence of Divine guidance in its final and perfect form."

In such a scheme any challenges that might be made to Islamic law on the grounds that it denies basic rights guaranteed under constitutions or international law are ruled out ab initio; human reason is deemed inadequate to criticize what are treated as divine edicts. This affirms the traditional orthodox view that the tenets of the *shari'a* are perfect and just because they represent the will of the Creator, being derived from divinely inspired sources. In the Islamic human rights schemes proffered by Mawdudi and Tabandeh, there is also reliance on extensive quotations from the Islamic sources, which is an indication that they follow the traditional view that the texts of Revelation are the definitive guides for what law should be, not human reason.

The supremacy of Islamic law in Iran is confirmed in various provisions of the Iranian Constitution in addition to Article 4, which has already been quoted. The primacy of Revelation is confirmed in Article 1, which calls for a government based on truth and Qur'anic justice, and in Article 2, which states that the Iranian Republic is based on belief in the acceptance of God's rule and the necessity of obeying his commands, affirming belief in "divine Revelation and its fundamental role in setting forth the laws" and the "justice of God in creation and legislation." Also according to Article 2, these aims are to be achieved by "continuous *ijtihad* [interpretation] of the *fuqaha* possessing necessary qualifications, exercised on the basis of the Qur'an and the *Sunnah* [traditions] of the *Ma'sumun* [the divinely inspired imams of Twelver Shi'ism]." The Iranian Constitution thus professes to be anchored in principles derived from divine Revelation.

In a similar vein, according to the Preamble of the Cairo Declaration: "Fundamental rights and universal freedoms in Islam are an integral part of the Islamic religion"; they "are contained in the Revealed Books of God and were sent through the message of the last of His Prophets." That is, Revelation is theoretically central to this scheme of human rights, as well. Moreover, after speaking of "basic human dignity" in Article 1(a), the Declaration claims: "True faith is the guarantee for enhancing such dignity along the path to human perfection," indicating that faith—as opposed to reason—is to guide Muslims in this connection. In a similar vein, Article 7 of the Saudi Basic Law affirms that the Qur'an and the *sunna* of the Prophet reign supreme over the Basic Law and all other laws of the state, thereby clearly subordinating rights to Islamic Revelation and prophetic inspiration.

In the Azhar draft Islamic constitution, the evidence is less clear. One can, however, infer a similar emphasis on divine Revelation and conclude that a command of religious texts is deemed central to knowledge from individual provisions that incorporate Qur'anic language and concepts, the requirements in Articles 12 and 13 that call for the memorization of the

Qur'an in schools and the teaching of the prophetic traditions, and the provision in Article 11 stating that religious instruction should be a main subject in education.

In addition to according Revelation a central role in their Islamic human rights schemes, the authors do not seem to accept the shift from an emphasis on human duties to the emphasis on human rights that characterizes modern thought on rights. In a passage in the English version of the Preamble to the UIDHR that has no obvious counterpart in the Arabic version, the authors indicate "that by the terms of our primeval covenant with God our duties and obligations have priority over our rights," thereby coming close to reaffirming the traditional idea that Islam provides a scheme of duties, not a scheme of individual rights. It is therefore obvious from the outset that the UIDHR will have the effect of denying rights, including ones that are guaranteed under international human rights law, in the guise of establishing Islamic duties. Should there be complaints that this Islamic scheme strips away protections afforded the individual under international human rights law, the ready-made defense will be that the Islamic sources must be deferred to because they represent God's plan and that the purpose of Islam is not so much to secure rights as to ensure obedience to divine commands.

In the Azhar draft constitution, one sees a similar concern for the fulfillment of Islamic duties. In Article 12 the government is required to teach Muslims their duties *(al-fara'id)*. In contrast, in Chapter 4, which deals with the individual's rights and freedoms (which turn out to be highly circumscribed), there is no mention of any need to teach Muslims about freedoms.

The Cairo Declaration refers to duties and obligations and stresses the inferiority of humans vis-à-vis their Creator. For example, Article 1 provides in section (a) that all human beings "are united by submission to God" and "are equal in terms of basic human dignity and basic obligations and responsibilities," and states in section (b) that all human beings are God's children *('iyal)*. Similarly, having declared in Article 1 that the government is Islamic and in Article 5 that it is a monarchy in the Saudi family, the Saudi Basic Law in Article 6 treats the duty to obey the monarch as being religious in nature, asserting that citizens are to pay allegiance to the king, "in accordance with the Holy Qur'an and the *sunna* of the Prophet, in submission and obedience," thereby linking obedience to the king to obedience to God. Section 5, titled "rights and duties," contains precious few rights.

A. K. Brohi, a former minister of law and religious affairs in Pakistan, has written a number of pieces on human rights in Islam and puts forth a rights philosophy similar to the ones embodied in the schemes under discussion here. Brohi has been prominent enough in this field to be selected to give the keynote address at a major international conference on human rights in Islam held in Kuwait in 1980 under the sponsorship of the International Commission of Jurists, Kuwait University, and the Union of Arab Lawyers.[35] Brohi's speech recapitulated points made in an earlier piece on Islam and human rights, published in the official Pakistani case law reporter in 1976[36]—while Zulfikar Ali Bhutto, the prime minister whom Zia executed after his coup, was still in power. It is significant that the same points were incorporated in an article in the official Pakistani case law reporter in 1983, when President Zia's martial law regime and Islamization programs were in full force, showing that the regime found his perspective congenial.[37] Excerpts from the seminar and the article show how Brohi rejects the philosophical underpinnings of Western human rights:

Human duties and rights have been vigorously defined and their orderly enforcement is the duty of the whole of organized communities and the task is specifically entrusted to the law enforcement organs of the state. The individual if necessary has to be sacrificed in order that the life of the organism be saved. Collectivity has a special sanctity attached to it in Islam.[38]

The Western man's perspective may by and large be called anthropocentric in the sense that there man is regarded as constituting the measure of everything since he is to be regarded as the starting point of all thinking and action. The perspective of Islam, on the other hand, is theocentric, that is, God-consciousness, the Absolute here is paramount; man is here only to serve His Maker. . . . [In the West] rights of man are seen in a setting which has no reference to his relationship with God—they are somehow supposed to be his inalienable birthrights. . . . Each time the assertion of human rights is made, it is done only to secure their recognition from some secular authority such as the state or some such regal power.[39]

[In Islam] there are no "human rights" or "freedoms" admissible to man in the sense in which modern man's thought, belief, and practice understand them: in essence, the believer owes obligation or duties to God if only because he is called upon to obey the Divine Law and such Human Rights as he is made to acknowledge seem to stem from his primary duty to obey God.[40]

Thus, it would appear, there is a sense in which Man has no rights within a theocentric perspective; he has only duties to His Maker. But these duties in their turn, give rise to all the rights, Human Rights in the modern sense included. . . . There can, in the strict theory of the Islamic law, be no conflict between the State Authority and the individual—since both have to obey the Divine Law.[41]

Human Rights conceived from the anthropocentric perspective are treated by Western thinkers as though they were no more than an expedient mode of protecting the individual from the assaults that are likely to be made upon him by the authority of the State's coercive power—by the unjust law that may be imposed by that authority to deny man the possibility of self-development through the law-making power of the brute majorities. Islam, on the other hand, formulates, defines and protects these very rights by inducing in the believers the disposition to obey the law of God . . . and showing obedience to those "constituted authorities": within the realm who themselves are bound to obey the law of God. . . . Furthermore, affirmation of these rights is to enable man not only to secure the establishment of those conditions in terms of which the development of man as an individual on earth may be possible, but also to enable man so to conduct himself, inwardly as well as outwardly, as to be able to obey the Divine Law. . . . By accepting to live in Bondage to this Divine Law, man learns to be free.[42]

The tenets of Western individualism are unacceptable in Brohi's scheme, in which man is clearly not meant to be the measure of all things. The idea that individuals enjoy certain inalienable rights is dismissed. In Brohi's comments one sees again the emphasis on duties. The individual is expected to obey the duly constituted authorities, who, in their turn, should obey God. The idea that human rights standards would need to be fashioned to protect the individual from oppression by the government is rejected, as it was in the idealistic visions of premodern Islamic thinkers that precluded the development of modern concepts of individual rights. Like the premodern theorists of Islamic government, Brohi assumes that when Islamic law is in force, the government will necessarily obey the dictates of the *shari'a*.

In Brohi's treatment of rights one sees both a strong affirmation of the idea that the individual is bound by the duty of obedience and, withal, a carelessness regarding the issue of to whom or to what the individual owes obedience. One notes that Brohi is sometimes speaking of subordination to God and Islamic law, which is clearly required in the Islamic tradition, but that at other times he means the subordination of the individual to organized communities, a collectivity, political authorities, or the state. Regarding the latter, there is much less in the way of unequivocal Islamic authority justifying claims that obedience is owed. Brohi does not seem to perceive that the Islamic warrant establishing the duty of a believer to obey the commands of God should not necessarily be extended to cover the obligations of a citizen of a contemporary state.

Like many other Muslim conservatives who discuss rights, Brohi fails to appreciate that the model of communal solidarity that one finds in traditional societies in the Muslim world is in no way distinctively Islamic but reflects the features commonly found in societies that have not yet experienced the intrusions of industrialization and urbanization. Brohi does not analyze the significance of the original linkage between the lack of support for individualism in premodern Islamic thought and the situation of the individual in traditional societies, where the lack of individual rights and freedoms did not have the same nefarious consequences that the lack of protection for individual rights has had under the modern nation-state. From the fact that premodern Islamic thought was not anthropocentric, he leaps to the conclusion that in the twentieth century, the anthropocentric perspective should be treated as unacceptable by Islamic criteria. Brohi goes from a description of the subordination of the individual to group interests that was widely accepted in traditional societies—regardless of whether Islam was the dominant religion—to the unwarranted conclusion that Islamic doctrine calls for such subordination even in the drastically changed circumstances of contemporary states, where the power of the central government is immeasurably enhanced.[43]

The idea that in the modern state there will naturally be conflicts between the competing interests of individual citizens and the government is rejected by Brohi. His notion that in an Islamic system one cannot separate the individual and the government reflects adherence to the premodern jurists' views that the ruler and ruled stood together, united in their duties of obedience to the *shari'a*.[44] Where there is reliance on such anachronistic views, denials of individual rights and freedoms by governments are naturally not seen as a problem. It is conclusively presumed that in an Islamic setting, individual-state tensions do not arise.

Mawdudi's main political concern with regard to duties seemed to be how to preserve the power of the state. In his book *The Islamic Law and Constitution,* Mawdudi, who inaccurately quoted the Prophet as saying that "the state" (not referred to in the original) "shall have to be obeyed, in adversity and in prosperity, and whether it is pleasant or unpleasant to do so," opined:

> In other words, the order of the State, be it palatable or unpalatable, easy or arduous, shall have to be obeyed under all circumstances [save when this means disobedience to God]. . . . [A] person should, truly and faithfully and with all his heart, wish and work for the good, prosperity and the betterment of the State, and should not tolerate anything likely to harm its interests. . . . It is also obligatory on the citizens of the Islamic State to cooperate wholeheartedly with the government and to make sacrifices of life and property for it, so much so that if any danger threatens the State, he who willfully refrains from making a sacrifice of his life and property to ward off that danger has been called a hypocrite in the Qur'an.[45]

This is obviously an attempt to provide an Islamic rationale for total subjugation of the individual to the state—although assuming that the Prophet was referring to the modern nation-state involves a definite anachronism. One can see how similar Mawdudi's formulation of the individual's obligations to obey the government is to that offered by President Zia in justifying his military dictatorship in Pakistan (Chapter 2). The only excuse for disobeying the government is in cases where obeying the government would entail violating Islamic law, thereby constituting disobedience to a command of God. Of course, a government that purports to follow Islamic law, as President Zia's did, would not concede that it was giving the citizenry any grounds whatsoever for disobedience, so it is unlikely that such a government would tolerate any disobedience. In fact, many members of the political group that Mawdudi founded as well as others who shared his outlook were among the mainstays of support for President Zia's program of Islamization in Pakistan. They were clearly at ease with the loss of rights and freedoms under Zia's military dictatorship.

The authors just cited may take the position that there exists such a concept as Islamic human rights; their comments, however, reveal that they are hostile to individualism and the idea that individual rights and freedoms deserve strong protections against government infringement. Given their position, one would expect these authors to say that modern human rights concepts according primacy to individual rights and freedoms cannot be accommodated within an Islamic framework. Instead, many Muslims writing in this area have been inclined to try to preserve traditional anti-individualistic, communitarian values and priorities while paradoxically trying to insert human rights provisions in that unsuitable matrix.

In contrast, international human rights standards rest on the assumption that the rights of the individual are the primary concern of civil and political rights and that they must be protected against infringements, particularly by governments but also by society.[46] If one accepts Ronald Dworkin's definition of a "right" as a claim that it would be wrong for the government to deny an individual even though it would be in the general interest to do so, one could say that it would be impossible for authors with such attitudes to accept such rights, since they consistently accord priority to the interests of the collectivity, the community, or the state.

A person unfamiliar with Islamic history might assume that special circumstances or unique institutions in Islamic civilization may have compensated for the lack of formal legal safeguards for individual rights and freedoms and that this lack had less nefarious consequences in the Muslim world than it had in Western societies prior to the imposition of legal restraints on governments' ability to infringe human rights. One might speculate that special forms of social solidarity within the community meant that the relationship of the state and the individual was less adversarial than it was in the West, so that the authors of Islamic human rights were justified in downgrading the significance of protections for individual rights in terms of their own cultural experience.

In fact, in the Middle East the absence of legal protections for human rights has correlated with patterns of misrule, oppression, and denials of rights by despotic rulers that are very similar to those historically experienced in the West. The idealized schemes of Muslim ruler and Muslim ruled both acting in concert and in common obedience to the divine law that are invoked in the cited passages were not realized in practice. Although some Muslims would say that the feasibility of the Islamic model was illustrated by the harmonious collaboration of ruler and ruled in the era of the Prophet and under some of his immediate successors—to which the Shi'is would add the era in which they were ruled by divinely inspired imams—these reports of saintly rulers in the earliest period of Islamic history by no means signify that the dictates of Islamic piety have normally proved adequate to constrain the behavior of the despotic regimes that have dominated most societies in the Muslim world. The historical record shows that religious scruples rarely deterred Muslim rulers from oppressing their subjects. Although Muslim rulers had at their disposal the mechanisms to impose obedience on their subjects, individual subjects had few ways other than the risky course of overt rebellion to challenge cruel and tyrannical misrule.

In reality, the individual and the state in the Muslim world have had conflicting interests that have most often been resolved at the expense of individual rights and freedoms. The authors of these Islamic human rights schemes must be aware that this pattern has continued in the Muslim world today and now has more serious consequences, given the enormous increase in the repressive apparatus wielded by central governments. Nonetheless, such writers are disposed to ignore the significance of the vast disparity in power between the individual and the modern nation-state.

Consequences of Insecure Philosophical Foundations

As indicated, these rights schemes are not built on the foundations of a coherent rights philosophy. Instead, they have in some instances simply appropriated ideas from texts on Islamic law and ethics, treating them as if they offered authoritative statements on rights, irrespective of whether these ideas involve principles that could remedy actual rights abuses or deserve the status of rights. The consequence is the inclusion of many trivial or meaningless "rights" that in international law would not rise to the level of human rights. The Iranian Constitution is a noteworthy exception in this respect. It appears that Iran's established tradition of constitutionalism inhibited its drafters from abandoning most of the familiar categories that are normally used in formulations of rights.

Most current theorists of Islamic human rights persist in talking exclusively in terms of an idealized vision of Islamic social harmony, even though the evidence of centuries as well as the acts of current governments have manifestly demonstrated that this vision is unrealistic. Because of their otherworldly, idealistic focus, it is not surprising that the authors of

Islamic human rights schemes produce rights provisions that seem grossly inadequate by the standards of international human rights and that fail to call for human rights protections that could address actual human rights problems. The authors apparently have no concern for determining what rights and freedoms most need protection in light of the patterns of human rights abuses prevalent in contemporary Middle Eastern societies or for working out practical rules that deter rights violations.

Examples of the inadequate rights formulations show frivolous notions of entitlements. Some inadequate formulations seem to have resulted from an author gleaning from the Islamic sources the idea that certain conduct is censured and drawing the conclusion that human beings have "rights" not to be affected by such conduct. Thus, Islamic human rights include the "right" not to be made fun of or insulted by nicknames,[47] which is obviously taken from the Qur'an 44:11, "Let not a folk deride a folk who may be better than they ... neither defame one another, nor insult one another by nicknames." Other "rights" that have been derived from Islamic sources include the right of women not to be surprised by male family members of the household walking in on them unannounced[48] and the "right" not to be tied up before being killed.[49] In addition, one encounters a "right" not to have one's corpse mutilated,[50] which seems to envisage that human rights protections should be extended to corpses, even though human rights concerns ordinarily presuppose that the rights claimant be living, not dead.[51]

Indeed, when one thinks about the rights provision protecting women from surprise intrusions, one realizes that, far from affording protection for freedoms, it contains implicit restrictions on women's rights. There is an assumption that the world is sexually segregated and that women stay at home in seclusion from men. So strict is this segregation meant to be that male family members should never intrude on women's quarters without giving women warning so that they can cover themselves in a suitably modest manner. Thus, the provision implies that even in the home there will be female seclusion and veiling, which in turn is connected with the woman's duty to avoid indecency. There is really nothing linking this supposed right of women not to be surprised by men of the family coming in unannounced with any principle of international human rights, only with traditional notions that women's obligations under the *shari'a* include the duties to stay segregated, secluded, and veiled.

As a kind of corollary to the development of "rights" not to be subjected to behavior censured in the Islamic sources, behavior that is treated as good or proper in those sources may create a related right. "Rights" that fall within this category include "the obligation of believers to see that a deceased person's body is treated with due solemnity,"[52] affording yet another right to corpses, and the "right" to safety of life—meaning that people should come to the aid of a person in distress or danger.[53] It is hard to see how a conventional "right" can be involved, since the beneficiaries are either dead or in a state of peril where they are helpless to vindicate the "right" that is being afforded to them. Moreover, it seems here that rights are being confused with duties.

These and other "rights" provisions that are included in these Islamic human rights schemes do not belong in compilations of human rights because they concern offenses better dealt with by tort or criminal law, which involve the conduct of private actors. Generally, international human rights law, because it is concerned with governmental conduct, does not set rules for cases where injury or death is caused either by negligence or by the criminal conduct of a private individual.[54] Such cases are normally regulated through tort or criminal law, as most legal systems consider tort and criminal sanctions adequate for the purposes of compensation, retribution, and deterrence. In contrast, in Islamic human rights schemes, there are provisions that guarantee the "right" not to be burned alive,[55] the "right" to life—which turns out to be a right not to be murdered[56]—and a woman's "right" to have her chastity respected and protected at all times.[57] Although murder or rape does violate international human rights law if it is practiced as a matter of state policy, if no more than a criminal act by a private actor it is ordinarily left to domestic criminal legislation to impose a penalty. The Islamic "right" does not appear to be directed against state policy, only against the criminal. Furthermore, the woman's right to have her chastity respected is a very ambiguous one, since, in the context of the contemporary Middle East, the protection of women's chastity is often associated with regimes of sexual segregation and seclusion and female veiling, practices that can be justified on the grounds that they are necessary to protect women's chastity. So, the "rights" just discussed do not offer meaningful protections for individual freedoms, and at least one could be utilized to deprive women of freedoms.

A similarly insignificant "right" is the right of divorced individuals to strict confidentiality on the part of their former spouses with regard to information that the latter have obtained that could be detrimental to them.[58] This belongs to the realm of evidentiary privilege or private tort claims, which are not normally the concern of human rights law. Another "right" stipulated is that of unbelievers—this category itself being problematic—to recover the corpses of their fellows who have fallen in battle against the Muslims without having to pay for the privilege.[59] The question of whether a fee could be assessed from unbelievers in these circumstances is hardly one that any serious advocate of enhanced human rights protections in the Middle East would choose to place on an agenda of urgent human rights problems.

This category of rights that have no international counterparts also includes the "right" to cooperate (in the cause of virtue—presumably, Islamic virtue) and not to cooperate (in the cause of vice and aggression—presumably, as defined by Islam)[60] and the "right" to propagate Islam and its message.[61] These "rights" differ from international norms, where religious freedoms are protected regardless of one's religion; here it appears it is only Muslims who would benefit from these "rights."

After examining the vague and confused concepts that the authors of Islamic human rights include in their agendas, one sees that they have no sure grasp of what the concerns of human rights really are. They include provisions that would be totally out of place in a scheme that shared common philosophical premises with those of international human rights. In summary, the distinctive features of the Islamic human rights schemes do correlate in a general way with the authors' decisions to try to combine rights terminology with a body of concepts and values casually appropriated from certain strains in the premodern Islamic tradition without first rethinking that tradition in terms of its compatibility with modern human rights.

CHAPTER 4

Islamic Restrictions on Human Rights

One of the most striking and consistent features in all the Islamic human rights schemes is the use of Islamic criteria to restrict human rights. Provisions in the Islamic human rights schemes reflect the thesis that the rights afforded in international law are too generous and that these only become acceptable when Islamic restrictions are placed on rights to cut them down to size. There is, however, no explicit articulation of the thesis that Islamic rights mean reduced rights.

There are no historical antecedents that establish exactly what limits—if any—Islamic criteria impose on the range of civil and political rights afforded by international human rights law. The Islamic human rights schemes examined here avoid clarifying exactly what these restrictions on rights would entail. The resulting ambiguity in rights formulations, in which rights are qualified by reference to vague "Islamic" limitations, turns out to be one of their distinguishing characteristics. The significance of Islamic criteria circumscribing otherwise applicable international human rights is evaluated in this chapter.

Permissible Qualifications of Rights and Freedoms

International law recognizes that many rights protections are not absolute and may be suspended or qualified in exceptional circumstances such as wars or public emergencies or even in normal circumstances in the interests of certain overriding considerations.[1] In international law, one expects these overriding considerations to fall within one of several established categories. Qualifications may be placed on human rights in the aggregate common interest and to serve particular, specified policies.[2] The latter might include the preservation of national security, public safety, public order, morals, the rights and freedom of others, the interests of justice, and the public interest in a democratic society.[3] To ensure that accommoda-

tions and derogations are made within structures of authority and to prevent arbitrariness in decisions, the measures imposing these limitations
must be taken in accordance with or in conformity with the law.[4]

International law therefore tries to balance the need to protect human
rights against other needs with which rights protections may occasionally
come in conflict. It recognizes that unless the circumstances in which curbs
can be placed on human rights are sharply circumscribed, the rights would
become illusory. However, the extent to which curbs are permissible and
exactly what grounds justify restricting rights remain contested questions
in international human rights law.

Despite the unsettled nature of international law in this area, in the documents that make up the International Bill of Human Rights there are
some guidelines regarding the qualifications that may be imposed on civil
and political rights. These guidelines are relevant for evaluating the restrictions in Islamic rights provisions.

The Universal Declaration of Human Rights (UDHR) treats a number of
rights as absolute rights, meaning that there could be no justification for
curbing them. Among these are the right to freedom and equality in dignity
and rights; the right to equality before the law and to equal protection of
the law; the right in full equality to a fair and public hearing by an independent and impartial tribunal; the right to marry and the right to equal
rights in marriage and divorce;[5] freedom of thought, conscience, and religion, including the freedom to change one's religion;[6] and the right to work
and to free choice of employment.[7] The UDHR would not accept any criteria that would deny people the right to equality before the law, to a fair
hearing, to equal rights in marriage and divorce, to freedom of conscience,
to free choice of employment, and the like.

The UDHR includes a separate clause that defines the limits that may in
general be placed on human rights. In Article 29.2 one finds the following
provision: "In the exercise of his rights and freedoms, everyone shall be subject only to such limitations as are determined by law solely for the purpose
of securing due recognition and respect for the rights and freedoms of others
and of meeting the just requirements of morality, public order and the general welfare in a democratic society." In the drafting of the UDHR, the Soviet
delegation tried to impose a derogation clause that would nullify the new
rights being drafted by adding the words "and also [for the purpose of] the
corresponding requirements of the democratic state," but the Philippine delegate objected to this on the grounds that the definition of the "corresponding
requirements" would lie with the state and thereby potentially annul all the
rights and freedoms in the declaration. The Soviet proposal was rejected.[8]

The qualifications permitted in the general provision in Article 29.2 of
the UDHR should be taken to apply only to those rights that are not
among the absolute rights. They might apply to UDHR provisions regard-

ing freedom of opinion and expression; freedom of peaceful assembly and association; the right to take part in government; and the right to equal access to public service.[9] The absolute character accorded to certain rights correlates with the values and priorities of societies at an advanced state of development. In contrast, in traditional cultures, hierarchy, inequality, and systems of control over individual behavior and choices may be entrenched. In legal systems based on traditional values, considerations analogous to ones of morality, public order, and the general welfare invoked in Article 29.2 might be precisely the kinds of considerations that would be used to justify blanket denials of rights that international law would say should enjoy unqualified protection.

The limitations that could be applied to human rights were further clarified in subsequent international human rights documents, as specific qualifications were inserted in the texts of individual rights provisions. With the added qualifications, the new provisions guarantee rights as follows:

1. Freedom of expression: subject only to qualifications provided by law and necessary for respect of the rights and reputations of others and for the protection of national security or of public order *(ordre public),* or of public health and morals;
2. The right of peaceful assembly: subject only to restrictions "imposed in conformity with the law and which are necessary in a democratic society in the interests of national security or public safety, public order *(ordre public),* the protection of public health or morals or the protection of the rights and freedoms of others";
3. Freedom of association: subject to the same qualifications as the right of peaceful assembly, above; and
4. The right to take part in the conduct of public affairs, to vote and be elected, and to have access, on general terms of equality, to public service "without unreasonable conditions."[10]

A number of other fundamental rights are qualified, including the right to life, which is qualified by the state's ability to impose a death penalty, but only for the most serious crimes and subject to a number of other conditions; and the right to liberty and security of person, which is qualified by the state's ability to deprive the person of these "on such grounds and in accordance with such procedure as are established by law."[11]

The International Covenant on Economic, Social, and Cultural Rights (ICESCR) has a general provision on how rights may be qualified, providing in Article 4 that governments "may subject such rights only to such limitations as are determined by law only insofar as this may be compatible with the nature of these rights and solely for the purpose of promoting the general welfare in a democratic society."

Thus, international law offers definite standards regarding what constitutes permissible reasons for curbing human rights protections. The standards may not have been perfectly drafted, and the formulations of the qualifications are not so airtight as to preclude all efforts by states to manipulate them at the expense of the rights of the individual. However, they strive for formulations that carefully circumscribe the circumstances in which states will have justifications for cutting back on human rights. As will be indicated in the following examinations of Islamic human rights schemes, one of the most important ways in which the Islamic human rights differ from those in international law is that Islamic qualifications on rights have been deliberately left so vague that they allow states vast discretion in circumscribing rights.

Islamic Formulas Limiting Rights

A review of Islamic human rights schemes uncovers a pattern of borrowing substantive rights from international human rights documents while reducing the protections that they actually afford. This is accomplished by restricting the rights so that they can only be enjoyed within the limits of the *shari'a,* which are left unspecified. As a result, states decide what the scope of the affected rights should be. In this respect, the Islamic limitations on rights resemble the qualifications that have been placed on human rights in the African Charter on Human and Peoples' Rights, which have been decried as "claw-back clauses" that allow the state "almost unbounded discretion" in using domestic legal standards to restrict internationally guaranteed human rights.[12]

International law does not accept that fundamental human rights may be restricted—much less permanently curtailed—by reference to the requirements of any particular religion.[13] International law does not provide any warrant for depriving Muslims of human rights by according primacy to Islamic criteria. Thus, relying on the *shari'a* to limit or dilute human rights means that the rights that are established under international law are being qualified by standards that are not recognized in international law as legitimate bases for curtailing rights.

Limitations on rights that use terms like "the *shari'a,*" "Islamic precepts," or "the limits of Islam" to qualify human rights cannot be unambiguously defined by consulting the work of the premodern jurists, because this work is far too diverse. Premodern Islamic law included the doctrines of several sects and many law schools. Divergence of opinion among major law schools was historically tolerated in Islam, a situation acknowledged in the *shari'a* concept of *ikhtilaf al-madhahib,* or difference of law schools. In fact, even within one law school, doctrines and opinions could differ significantly as to what the interpretations of the Islamic sources should be.[14]

Furthermore, there were many individual jurists whose opinions differed from the views of the major schools, but whose works, nonetheless, are part of the premodern *shari'a* legacy.

In some areas, one might make tentative projections regarding what *shari'a* limitations would entail. Despite the great diversity in Islamic doctrine, on certain points of premodern jurisprudence there is sufficient consensus to allow speculation as to how the application of Islamic principles would affect rights. Reliance on rules of the premodern *shari'a* to determine the permissible scope of modern human rights could open the way to nullification of rights in areas where the *shari'a* calls for restrictions on rights and freedoms, such as the rules relegating women and non-Muslims to subordinate status or prohibiting conversions from Islam. Even on these topics, where there are extensive rules in the *shari'a,* there is enough complexity and nuance in the relevant legal doctrines to give the state considerable leeway in deciding what rules should be chosen as embodying the official Islamic norms.

On other topics relevant for civil rights and political freedoms, where the premodern jurisprudence is very underdeveloped and the *shari'a* standards are often uncertain and fraught with controversy, the reliance on the *shari'a* to qualify rights is also incompatible with the protection of the rights involved. Where the doctrines of premodern jurisprudence are disputed and no established Islamic authority is in evidence, states naturally are left free to invent what curbs on rights should be imposed in the name of "Islam." This deprives the affected rights of any substance.

Just as there is no definitive guidance in the premodern *shari'a* on the proper scope of human rights, there is no guidance in established doctrine in contemporary Islamic thought. The ambiguities that existed in the premodern tradition have been augmented by the multiplying and diverging interpretations of the requirements of Islamic law in the twentieth century. Understandings of Islamic law have changed under the impact of new intellectual currents. Reformist movements led to substantial departures from premodern models of Islamic thought around the turn of the century.[15] More recently, these changes have been augmented by the addition of new ideologized approaches to *shari'a* interpretation like those offered by Abu'l A'la Mawdudi and Ayatollah Khomeini, which contrast with sober rationalist interpretations like those offered by reform-minded intellectuals such as Nasr Hamid Abu Zaid, discussed in Chapter 8. Since vague "Islamic" qualifications that are used in Islamic human rights schemes do not specifically refer to the premodern *shari'a,* widely diverging contemporary versions of Islamic requirements could also be read into the qualifications. The differences in approaches to understanding Islam have been compounded by the absence of any generally recognized central authority for resolving disputed points of *shari'a* doctrine.

It is natural that in the prevailing circumstances in the contemporary Middle East, all such ambiguities in rights formulations will be exploited by the state and resolved at the expense of the individual rights and freedoms involved. Thus, vague "Islamic" limitations on human rights have ominous implications.

Restrictions in the Iranian Constitution

Before examining the 1979 Iranian Constitution to see how provisions qualified by Islamic principles laid the legal groundwork for the denial of basic freedoms, earlier Iranian formulations of civil and political rights provisions should be considered. Iranian constitutional history illustrates the difficulties in accommodating human rights within an Islamic framework.

Many of Iran's ulama were violently opposed to the adoption of Iran's 1906–1907 constitution, and one of the grounds for their objections was their opposition to the whole idea of freedom, which they considered dangerous and inimical to Islamic principles and values.[16] Clerical denunciations of freedom and constitutionalism as heretical were often vehement and uncompromising.[17] In many clerical interpretations, Islam was incompatible with constitutionalism.

However, Iranian nationalist sentiment and the popular determination to constrain the tyranny of Iran's Qajar shahs were ultimately strong enough to overcome clerical opposition to the proposed constitution. In addition, some clerics supported constitutionalism, believing that it was compatible with Islam. However, their support was in part attributable to the fact that they did not fully grasp the significance of constitutionalism and interpreted its concepts in ways that corresponded to *shari'a* categories and principles.[18] Thus, the first Iranian constitution emerged in an environment where the religious establishment was divided about the compatibility of constitutional freedoms and Islam.

The qualifications placed on civil and political rights provisions in the Supplementary Constitutional Law of 1907 were largely secular. However, religious criteria were also invoked as justifications for restricting constitutional rights.[19] Article 20 qualified freedom of publication by saying that this freedom did not cover heretical books or materials hurtful to Islam. Article 21 qualified the freedom to form societies and gatherings by saying that it applied where such societies or gatherings did not provoke religious disorder.[20]

After the 1978–1979 Iranian Revolution, the draft constitution of June 1979, devised before the clergy had fully asserted its dominance, likewise relied primarily on secular qualifications of civil and political rights, but there were exceptions. Article 25 of the proposed constitution included in the exceptions to freedom of the press the category of publications insulting to religious belief. In an ambiguous formulation, Article 26 included in the reasons for denying freedom of association the negation of "the basis of the Islamic Republic," which left room for religious qualifications on the freedom of association. Article 28 qualified the freedom to choose a profession by saying that the profession should not be opposed to Islam or the public interest.

The draft constitution was subjected to criticism from many quarters. Among others, a group that involved the Iranian Lawyers Association and the Iranian Committee for the Defense of Freedom and Human Rights offered proposals for rewriting the draft. The concerns of this group included ensuring the independence of the judiciary and protecting individual rights and the rights of women. It proposed that the UDHR be incorporated in the constitution and that international human rights organizations and lawyers be enabled to intervene in Iranian courts on behalf of Iranian nationals.[21] In other words, the proposals, had they been accepted, would have meant that international human rights law would have been treated as part of Iran's domestic law and that international human rights advocates would have had the capacity to defend Iranian nationals against their own government. This implied a mistrust of the ability of Iran's domestic legal institutions to afford adequate protection for human rights.

However, the draft constitution was also challenged by a coalition of clerics and Islamic organizations demanding that it be rewritten in a way that would give it a more Islamic character.[22] Ayatollah Khomeini said that he wanted the draft reviewed from an Islamic perspective, so that it would result in an Islamic constitution, not one made by foreign-influenced intellectuals who had no faith in Islam.[23] Ultimately, the rewriting of the draft was entrusted to an assembly of experts, in which clerics had a large majority; the assembly completed its task in December 1979. This was after the occupation of the U.S. embassy in November 1979 and the taking of U.S. diplomats as hostages had signaled the onset of a shift in power from moderate elements and liberal nationalists to conservative clerics and their followers.

The revision of the draft reflected this political shift. The proposals to adopt the UDHR as part of Iran's law were not only rejected, but the rights provisions in the draft constitution were also rewritten with Islamic qualifications added to reduce the strength of the protections involved. Nonetheless, it is a significant token of the prestige that human rights enjoy that, even with the ascendancy of a clerical faction opposed to human rights, references to human rights were not excised from the constitution. They appear in the Preamble and Articles 14 and 20, and individual rights are mentioned in Article 3.14. However, to make them palatable to conservative clerics, human rights had to be expressly subordinated to Islamic criteria. The most important provision in this connection was Article 4, quoted above, providing that Islamic principles should prevail over those in the constitution, and the text of Article 20, which provides: "All citizens of the country, both men and women, equally enjoy the protection of the law [*qanun,* or secular law] and enjoy human, political, economic, social and cultural rights, *in conformity with Islamic criteria [mavazin-e eslam].*"[24]

The equal protection clause will be discussed separately in greater detail, but here it should be noted that Article 20 constitutes a rejection of the position that international law determines human rights standards. Instead, this article expressly states that Islamic criteria govern human rights.

A brief clarification of the term *qanun* used in Article 20 and elsewhere needs to be offered at this point. In Islamic milieus, *qanun,* derived from the Greek *kanon,* is normally used to refer to secular laws as opposed to laws based on Islamic sources in the *shari'a.* However, given the principles set forth in Article 4 and the Article 20 provision that rights are enjoyed in Iran "in conformity with Islamic criteria," references to *qanun* in articles of the constitution to qualify rights do not seem to imply that the qualifications used must be secular but only that secular law will provide the legal framework for implementing principles taken from Islamic sources, which are ultimately controlling in this area.

Other rights provisions similarly provide that Islamic standards determine rights, using qualifications that in the following quotations are highlighted for emphasis.

Article 21

"The government must ensure the rights of women in all respects *in conformity with Islamic criteria [mavazin-e eslami].*"

Like Article 20, this article indicates that Islamic criteria are controlling, and, therefore, it might be considered redundant. However, the specification that women's rights are determined by Islamic standards is meaningful in the particular cultural context of modern Iran, where the application of secular law has been associated with women's emancipation and the application of *shari'a* law with the relegation of women to a subordinate status. Significantly, there is no provision subordinating men's rights to Islamic standards. By including a separate provision stipulating that women's rights would be determined by reference to Islamic standards, the government was indicating its intention to reinstate discriminatory *shari'a* rules. The consequences of this for women's rights will be addressed in Chapter 6.

Article 24

"Publications and the press have freedom of expression *except when it is detrimental to the fundamental principles of Islam [mabani-ye eslam] or the rights of the public.* The details of this exception will be specified by law *[qanun].*"

Article 26

"The formation of parties, societies, political or professional associations, as well as religious societies, whether Islamic or pertaining to one of the recognized religious minorities, is permitted, provided they do not violate principles of independence, freedom, and national unity, or *the criteria of Islam [mavazin-e eslami] or the basis of the Islamic Republic.*"

The status of minorities is discussed in greater detail in Chapters 7 and 8, but it is worth stating here that this provision not only waters down protection for freedom of association by making it subject to Islamic criteria, but it allows the government to deny minority religious groups even these fragile freedoms simply by refusing to accord them the status of "recognized" minority religious associations.

Article 27

"Public gatherings and marches may be freely held, provided arms are not carried and that *they are not detrimental to the fundamental principles of Islam [mabani-ye eslam].*"

Article 28

"Everyone has the right to choose any occupation he wishes, *if it is not contrary to Islam [mokhalef-e eslam . . . nist],* to the public interests, and does not infringe the rights of others."

Article 168

"Political and press offences will be tried openly and in the presence of a jury, in courts of justice. The manner of selection of the jury, its powers, and the definition of political offences, will be determined by law *[qanun] in accordance with Islamic criteria [bar asas-e qavanin-e eslami].*"[25]

Under Article 168 of the Iranian Constitution, it is Islamic criteria that determine what constitutes a political crime, thereby placing religious restraints on political freedom.

One can see that in the above provisions, concepts of fundamental rights have been taken from Western constitutions and international law. Some of the provisions include secular qualifications in addition to the Islamic ones, but others have only Islamic qualifications. As these demonstrate, in the Iranian Constitution, Islam is not conceived of as offering the basis for protecting rights but solely as the basis for limiting or denying the rights afforded by international human rights law and typically embodied in modern constitutions.

One might object to this conclusion by questioning the idea that the Islamic qualifications placed on these rights necessarily would restrict them more than secular qualifications would. Could it not be the case, one might ask, that the Islamic qualifications on rights might be narrower than those permitted under international law, that these clauses could be interpreted to mean that the government would have to produce much stronger justifications for curbing human rights than it would under secular criteria? In other words, perhaps the assumption that broad Islamic qualifications on rights imply the erosion of rights protections is only that—an assumption. Although in the abstract this question might seem justified, there are good reasons to conclude that these qualifications are designed to dilute rights.

First of all, one must consider the nature of the Iranian government itself. Liberal Muslims concerned with protecting human rights and clerics who disapproved curbs on freedoms were excluded from the circles of power. Both the regime's conduct and its statements show that the official version of Islam is seen as a pretext for suppressing dissent and censoring critics. It is also used as a tool of reverse social engineering for the purpose of combating social changes and expanded freedoms, which are identified with corrupting Western influences. Iran's ruling clerics have repeatedly lambasted Iranians who call for democratization and protection for human rights as minions of Western and Zionist conspiracies, "anti-Islamic," "enemies of God and the Prophet Muhammad," "Satanic," or "heretical." Iran's clerical government has demonstrated a consistent proclivity to utilize any rationales at its disposal that can be deployed to crush freedoms.

Second, there is the general nature of the relationship between the individual and the state in contemporary Middle Eastern societies, a relationship that predisposes governments in the region to be hostile to claims on behalf of individual liberties and the rights of the citizen. It is characterized by deeply ingrained patterns of authoritarian, if not totalitarian, government. Suppression of opposition, censorship of dissenting opinion, and intolerance of any kind of political or intellectual pluralism are prevalent. Favoritism on the part of the ruling elite for groups closely allied with it and corresponding discrimination against other groups are the rule. In a region where antidemocratic governments have the long-established habit of seeking to amass power at the expense of the rights of the individual and where the institutions that in other societies might protect the individual are weak or nonexistent, it is reasonable to expect that any vague qualifications of rights will tend to be exploited to enhance the power of the state at the expense of the freedoms of the individual.

Third, one must recall a point that has already been made: There is no developed tradition of Islamic human rights protections. This means that none of the various formulas that are used to set the Islamic qualifications of rights in the Iranian Constitution has any established legal content. One of the best illustrations of the arbitrariness that has resulted from relying on these vague Islamic qualifications is in the area of censorship, where subjective Islamic pretexts have been invoked to silence and punish Iranians in a harsh but often inconsistent manner.[26]

The problematic character of Islamic restrictions on rights might be contrasted with the vast number of precedents that exist limiting the qualifications that may be placed on rights in the U.S. Bill of Rights. For example, legal precedents establish that there are very few limits that the government may impose on freedom of speech in the United States. In the United States, when individuals assert that the government has unconstitutionally infringed First Amendment guarantees of freedom of speech, they can rely on an elaborate system of principles that has been developed by independent courts that sharply inhibits the ability of the government to curtail freedom of speech. The constraints on the government's ability to curb speech are so firmly entrenched that a heavy burden is placed on the government to justify conduct or laws restraining speech. If the government does not abide by the limits that the courts have set, it will be deemed to have acted in violation of the Constitution and the speech in question will be protected by measures such as injunctions or nullifications of relevant laws. U.S. freedom of speech guarantees are strong in part because of the framework of legal rules that define narrowly and specifically the grounds on which this right can be restricted or denied, but also because of the respect for laws and legal institutions that characterizes U.S. society.

In contrast, in Iran there are no firmly ingrained precedents set by an independent judiciary that narrowly limit the circumstances in which Islamic principles can be invoked to justify restrictions or denials of rights. On the contrary, the Iranian judiciary is politicized and subservient to the government, and thus the Islamic qualifications on rights provisions will have the content that the government chooses to ascribe to them. Those qualifications leave the Iranian government and its agents free to engage in any repressive, arbitrary, and discriminatory conduct they choose without fear that the injured citizens will be able to invoke Islamic criteria to challenge the legality of the governmental actions. Of course, the ability of the government to rely on Islam to insulate its conduct from effective judicial review is linked to the facts that Iran's bar was destroyed after the revolution, that rules of due process of law have been discarded in the wake of the revolution, and that judges do not stand up to the powers that be and use the law to curb the regime's rights abuses.[27] Iranian courts cannot offer a neutral forum that could build up a jurisprudence protective of human rights.

Iran's new president Mohammed Khatami, who during his campaign promised to shore up the rule of law, seems to appreciate that these serious deficiencies need to be dealt with. He articulates a modern vision of a constitution serving as an instrument for shoring up rights and freedoms. In December 1997 he announced the formation of a committee to ensure the implementation of the constitution, to present proposals "to pave the way for establishing the rule of law in society more than ever before." The committee's tasks included providing guidelines for ending violations of the provisions on the rights of the people and for ensuring the implementation of the constitution, "giving priority to the articles guaranteeing the protection of people's individual and social rights."[28] On Iranian television, he has asserted: "Under the constitution, no imposition of viewpoints is allowed, even if it is under the pretext of religion and Islam and no one is allowed to take the law into his own hands under such pretexts."[29] In other words, he appears to want to give substance to principles of constitutionalism and to curb the misuse of Islamic pretexts to nullify human rights and dismantle the rule of law.

Fourth among the reasons for fearing that Islamic restrictions will harm rights, there is the fact that Iran's Islam is not the Islamic religion but the state ideology, an ideology that purports to embody God's divine plan for running human society. Since the government professes to be carrying out this divine plan, there is a built-in tendency toward absolutism, intolerance, and harsh repression of dissent. A symptom of the inherent repressiveness of the official Islamic ideology can be seen in the scope and vigor of the persecutions and prosecutions of Shi'i clerics, many of whom have been martyred for failing to submit humbly to the official Islamic ideology.[30]

For example, Ayatollah Montazeri's liberal sympathies and comments evincing disagreement with the Iranian regime's policy of disregard for human rights prompted Khomeini to oust him as his designated successor in March 1989. Despite his disgrace and his being kept under virtual house arrest for a decade, Montazeri raised questions in 1997 about the undemocratic features of the system of rule by the supreme jurist that seemed threatening enough to prompt a harsh backlash by Iran's ruling elite. Montazeri questioned a cornerstone of the regime's Islamic ideology, the principle that Islam requires accepting rule by an unelected supreme jurist, and complained that this constituted an obstacle to the reform program for which the electorate had overwhelmingly voted in the 1997 presidential elections. After his criticism of political intervention by the supreme jurist Ali Khamene'i, a jurist with credentials inferior to his own, Ayatollah Montazeri was accused by the former of treason and threatened with prosecution for the capital offense of plotting against the regime.[31]

In November 1997 violent demonstrations orchestrated by the regime's supporters broke out denouncing Ayatollah Montazeri.[32] He was excoriated in official statements and the pro-establishment media. A senior cleric attacked Montazeri as a cultural bandit tied to the United States, with the admonishment: "All Iranians must be obedient to the orders by the leadership."[33] Another cleric close to the supreme jurist Khamene'i warned that anyone who took a political stand against Khamene'i would be dealt with "severely," and those who dared "the slightest affirmation of Montazeri's faction will face a bitter future."[34] This may have been an implied threat directed at the prominent dissident Abdolkarim Sorush, whose thinking followed lines similar to Montazeri's, for which he had been subjected to harsh sanctions.[35] As long as an entrenched clerical elite with such adamant hostility to any kind of pluralism fights to defend its increasingly discredited Islamic ideology, Islamic qualifications on rights will assuredly undermine rights.

In summary, constitutional civil and political rights have been denied in Iran under the rubric of following Islamic criteria and defending Islam and the official ideology. The evidence is overwhelming that Islamic qualifications of rights have stripped rights of their substance.

A clarification seems in order at this point: Showing the correlation between the Islamic qualifications on rights in the Iranian Constitution and the subsequent pattern of government conduct restricting and denying human rights is not the same as asserting that, but for the Islamic qualifications that were placed on rights in the Iranian Constitution, the rights would have been protected or that the regime in each instance when rights were being overridden relied formally on the Islamic qualifications in the constitution to justify its conduct. In other words, no attempt is being made to argue here that adding the Islamic qualifications to rights provisions in the constitution by itself caused the measures infringing human rights or that the regime always followed Islamic criteria when undertaking measures aimed at curbing or denying rights.

Instead, the connection appears to have been a more subtle one. The addition of the Islamic criteria qualifying rights signaled a general disposition not to be bound by the standards of the UDHR, which, as noted, its supporters had not been able to incorporate in the 1979 constitution. In addition, the Islamic qualifications were representative of the general philosophy of the associates of Ayatollah Khomeini, who eventually consolidated their hold over the country and according to whom the norms of "Islam," as embodied in the views of the ruling elite of clerics, could override all secular legal norms. However, the conduct of the regime revealed that it did not lay great store by principles of legality, irrespective of whether these were religious or secular, and that it was even quite prepared to engage in public violations of basic tenets of Islamic law where the latter stood in the way of its political objectives.[36] The council that was set up via the 1989 amendments in Article 112 to mediate when legislation in the public interest was deemed to be in conflict with Islamic law was a sign that the regime was looking for a mechanism to get out of the awkward situations that had been caused by the

Council of Guardians blocking desirable legislation on the grounds that it conflicted with Islamic law.[37] It soon became evident that this was not a regime that fastidiously adhered to Islamic law. Since the clerical takeover, the government acted out of its own notions of political expediency, as if it were unconstrained by Islamic law, resorting to whatever measures were deemed essential to defend its own interests. In this, of course, it acted just like the many secular regimes in the Middle East that pay lip service to official ideologies of nationalism or socialism, which on closer inspection turn out to be mere window dressing for policies dictated by the elites' desire to retain power to pursue their own selfish objectives.

Thus, one must be careful to avoid creating the impression that somehow the Islamic qualifications on rights that have been discussed created the human rights violations that ensued in Iran, but one should also not underplay the correlation between the rights violations and the official position that rights could be restricted or denied in the name of Islam.

Restrictions in the UIDHR

The Universal Islamic Declaration of Human Rights (UIDHR) relies more extensively and explicitly than the Iranian Constitution on Islamic criteria to limit rights. It must be emphasized that this pattern of pervasive reliance on the *shari'a* to qualify rights is less readily apparent in the English version than it is in the Arabic version of the UIDHR, which seems to be the authoritative text. The Explanatory Notes section accompanying the English version of the UIDHR states that the Arabic text is "the original," which suggests that it should be treated as more definitive than the English translation. However, the relationship between the Arabic and English versions is a very problematic one, as there are inconsistencies between the two as well as vagueness and ambiguities in the Arabic version.[38]

The Explanatory Notes section includes the assurance: "In the exercise and enjoyment of the rights referred to above every person shall be subject only to such limitations as are enjoined by the Law for the purpose of securing the due recognition of, and respect for, the rights and the freedom of others and of meeting the just requirements of morality, public order and the general welfare of the Community (Ummah)." Reading the English version, one could get the impression that many of the UIDHR provisions are subject to qualifications imposed by secular laws, since the wording of the qualifications is consistently "according to the Law." However, in reality there is no similarity between the qualifications placed on rights in the UIDHR and those found in international law. In the UIDHR the *shari'a* is the law that qualifies rights when the term "according to the Law" is used.

It is difficult but not impossible for the reader of the English version to discover that by "the Law" the UIDHR means the *shari'a*. The Explanatory Notes section states that the term *Law* in the text means the *shari‘a,* which is defined as "the totality of ordinances derived from the Qur'an and Sunnah [the reports of what the Prophet Muhammad said and did] and any other laws that are deduced from these two sources by methods considered valid in Islamic jurisprudence."[39] This definition does not by any means settle how this term should be understood or what qualifications would thereby be placed on rights. At a minimum, "the *shari‘a*" under this definition would seem to constitute the totality of premodern *shari‘a* jurisprudence, which means that "*shari‘a*" here is a term encompassing a vast range of diverging legal positions.[40] Depending on what methods are "considered valid in Islamic jurisprudence," this term might or might not also include many more recent interpretations as well. That is, given the enormous literature that this definition potentially covers, the standards that will be used are being left deliberately vague.

Some examples of how the *shari‘a* is used in the UIDHR to qualify basic rights will now be considered. In the English version of the declaration, Section 12 of the Preamble includes the guarantee that "no one shall be deprived of the rights assured to him by the Law except by its authority and to the extent permitted by it." Unless one bears in mind the fact that "Law" means the *shari‘a,* one might not appreciate the implications of this provision, that *shari‘a* requirements determine what rights people ultimately have. Essentially, this says that rights depend on the *shari‘a;* the *shari‘a* both ensures them and takes them away. The wording of Section 12 of the Preamble in the Arabic version confirms this. It provides that "each person is guaranteed security, freedom, dignity, and justice according to the dictates of what the *shari‘a* of God has decreed in the way of rights for people."

In the specific provisions of the UIDHR (English) one finds that the *shari‘a* (the Law) determines the scope of the following rights:

1. The right to inflict injury or death, in Article 1.a.
2. The right to liberty, in Article 2.a.
3. The right to justice, in Article 4.a.
4. The right to assume public office, in Article 11.a.
5. The right of expression, in Article 12.a.
6. The right "to protest and strive," in Article 12.c.
7. The right to disseminate information (also qualified by considerations of the security of the society or the state), in Article 12.d.
8. The right to earn a living, in Article 15.b.
9. The right to pursue given economic activities (also qualified by considerations of the interests of the community), in Article 15.g.
10. The rights of spouses in marriage, in Article 19.a.
11. A wife's right to divorce, in Article 20.c, and her right to inherit, in Article 20.d.

An example of a problematic article is Article 14. In English it appears to guarantee a right to freedom of association, with distinctive Islamic qualifications, but as will be discussed, it has no counterpart in the Arabic original, so its status is questionable.[41] Article 11 provides for a right to participate in public life, but the provision is qualified in a way that ensures that it will have discriminatory impact on non-Muslims, as will be discussed in Chapter 5.

To evaluate the strength of the human rights provisions in the UIDHR, one should put oneself in the position of a person being denied rights by the Iranian government in the name of Islam. Could one utilize the UIDHR to prove that Iran's rights violations constitute violations of Islamic human rights? It seems not. The UIDHR accepts the idea that all rights may be qualified by the *shari'a,* but it effectively leaves it to the authorities to determine the scope of Islamic qualifications of rights, because it defines the *shari'a* so broadly that governments can freely choose what "Islamic" principles to apply. Thus, if the UIDHR standards were applicable in Iran, they would permit the Iranian government to do exactly as it has done, consistently interpreting Islamic law to legitimize government curbs on rights. In contrast, a person being denied civil or political rights in Iran could utilize international human rights law to establish that the Iranian government was violating human rights.

Restrictions in Other Islamic Human Rights Schemes

Just as the Iranian Constitution and the UIDHR provide for the use of vague Islamic criteria to restrict basic rights and freedoms, so other Islamic human rights schemes impose Islamic limitations on basic rights and freedoms. Some examples are included in this section, while others that specifically affect women, minorities, and religious freedom will be treated in greater detail in later sections.

The Azhar draft Islamic constitution will be examined first in both the Arabic version, which one presumes was the original, and the often awkward English translation that accompanies it.

The Azhar draft constitution uses a variety of Islamic formulas to qualify rights. Article 29 guarantees freedom of religious and intellectual belief, freedom to work, freedom of expression, freedom to form and join associations and unions, personal freedom *(al-hurriya al-shakhsiya),* freedom to travel,[42] and freedom to hold meetings, all within *shari'a* limits *(hudud al-shari'a al-islamiya).* Article 37 guarantees the right to work and gain a living within *shari'a* precepts *(ahkam al-shari'a al-islamiya).* Article 43 says that rights are enjoyed according to the objectives of the *shari'a (wafqan li maqasid al-shari'a).* With the exception of Article 42, which places additional secular conditions on rights, Islamic law is treated as the sole basis for restricting or denying rights.

Although all of these qualifications are left very indefinite, one might be particularly curious as to what Islamic restrictions on the freedom of travel would entail. Article 13 of the UDHR guarantees everyone the freedom of movement within the borders of each state and the right to leave and return to one's own country without any qualifications, and it may not be immediately obvious why religious criteria would be relevant in the exercise of this freedom. However, Islamic conservatives tend to believe that women should not leave their homes save in case of necessity, and that, if they do leave their homes, they should be chaperoned.[43] Some conservative Muslims believe that it is "un-Islamic" for women to be allowed to drive, which is why Islam is invoked as the reason for not allowing women to drive cars in Saudi Arabia. The general treatment of women in the Azhar constitution, which will be examined later, warrants the inference that the "*shari'a* limits" on freedom of travel would be used to justify restrictions on women's freedom of movement.

One sees in the Azhar draft constitution a rights philosophy that is very similar to the one in the Iranian Constitution and the UIDHR. In all of these, rights are subject to vague *shari'a* criteria. The Azhar draft constitution relies especially heavily on these Islamic restrictions.

In the work of the Iranian Sufi Sultanhussein Tabandeh, one finds similar religious qualifications placed on human rights. However, Tabandeh coupled Islamic qualifications with others that indicate a bias in favor of preserving social order and harmony and enforcing respect for authority. The UDHR in Article 3 guarantees the general right to life, liberty, and security of person without qualification, but according to Tabandeh, those rights should be qualified by the requirement that they not be "contrary to the regulations of Islam [or] molest the peace of others."[44] It is striking to see that in Tabandeh's view, even the right to life itself is qualified by Islamic criteria. Apparently, he would allow the subjective reactions of persons who felt that their peace had been molested to deny another the right to live.[45] These standards deviate sharply from international norms, such as the principle in Article 6 of the International Covenant on Civil and Political Rights (ICCPR) that the right to life should be protected by law and that no one should be arbitrarily deprived of life. With regard to freedom of opinion and expression, Tabandeh said that freedom in these areas ceases to be a right where "it threatens public order or grows contumacious against government and religion."[46] Again, this view betokens a mentality light years removed from the philosophy of international human rights law, which would never accept such vague, subjective limitations.

As has already been noted, Mawdudi's discussion of Islamic human rights is sketchy and uneven and leaves the impression that he was avoiding a number of difficult problems. His presentation of Islamic qualifications on human rights is correspondingly short and incomplete. In his scheme he did limit freedom of expression and association by imposing the condition that such freedoms must conform to the Qur'anic command in 3:104 to order what is good and forbid that which is evil.[47] This indicates that Islamic standards of virtue would be used to determine what could be expressed and what associations would be allowed, but without giving the exact meaning of this qualification. On the basis of this example, one can say that Mawdudi was disposed to think of Islam as a curb on rights. However, there is much more evidence that he supported the use of Islamic law to deny rights, as discussed in Chapters 6–8.

The pattern of imposing vague Islamic limitations on rights continues in the Cairo Declaration, Article 24 of which provides that "[a]ll the rights and freedoms stipulated in this Declaration are subject to the Islamic *shari'a.*" Article 25 follows with a circular and unhelpful definition of what these limits would entail, providing that "[t]he Islamic *shari'a* is the only source of reference for the explanation or clarification of any of the articles of this Declaration."

In the Cairo Declaration one finds various vague Islamic restrictions placed on specific provisions. Several of the provisions relevant for civil and political rights are mentioned in this chapter, with others to be discussed subsequently. Article 16 establishes the right to enjoy the fruit of one's scientific, literary, artistic, or technical production and the right to the interests therefrom, except where such production is contrary to the principles of the *shari'a.* Article 22 invites censorship in accordance with Islamic criteria or on the grounds of Islamic morality. Article 22(a) provides that there is a right to express opinions freely—but only in a manner not contrary to the principles of the *shari'a.* Article 22(b), reflecting the directive in the Qur'an (3:104) to do good and prohibit evil, provides that everyone shall have the right to advocate what is right and propagate what is good and warn against what is wrong and evil according to the norms of the Islamic *shari'a.* In Article 22(c), the declaration provides that information "may not be exploited or misused in such a way as may violate the sanctities and the dignity of prophets, undermine moral and ethical values or disintegrate, corrupt, or harm society or weaken its faith."

In a similar vein, the Saudi Basic Law, which had already provided in Article 7 that the Qur'an and *sunna* of the Prophet were the supreme law, also provides in Article 26 that the state will protect human rights according to the Islamic *shari'a (wafqa 'l-shari'a al-islamiya),* with no further definition of what restraints this could entail. There is little chance of Islamic restraints being narrowly defined under the Basic Law, which provides in Article 6 that citizens are to submit to the rule of the King in accordance with the Qur'an and *sunna* and to obey him. Furthermore, Article 23 asserts that the state shall respect and apply the Islamic *shari'a,* ordering the good and forbidding the evil, thereby providing an additional basis for using Islamic law and Islamic values to shape the scope of rights and freedoms.

Under the Omar al-Bashir dictatorship, the Sudan likewise explicitly subordinated rights to Islamic principles. A document on human rights in the Sudan published in Khartoum on July 17, 1993, proclaimed that the principles of Sudanese philosophy protected the dignity and rights of individuals in accordance with Islamic law.[48]

In Pakistan and Egypt, rulings in two significant court cases involving constitutional freedom of religion issues indicated that the scope of rights was to be determined in accordance with Islamic criteria. In the course of decision in *Zaheeruddin v. State,* discussed in Chapter 7, the Pakistan Supreme Court effectively raised "the Injunctions of Islam" to a status above the constitution and also above the fundamental rights set forth in the constitution. According to the court, "the Injunctions of Islam" had become "the real and the effective law" of the country.[49] Speaking as if unqualified human rights would offend Islam, the court asserted that "even the Fundamental Rights as given in the Constitution must not violate the norms of Islam."[50]

In the notorious Nasr Hamid Abu Zaid case of 1994–1996, discussed in Chapter 8, the Egyptian Court of Appeals and Court of Cassation both purported to uphold the constitutional guarantee of freedom of religion, but in deciding that they were entitled to decree Abu Zaid an apostate and sever his marital tie, they treated freedom of religion as if it had been subsumed into the Islamic tradition and were subject to Islamic qualifications.[51] That is, even where there is no express constitutional provision or law explicitly stating that constitutional rights are subordinated to Islamic criteria, courts may act as if rights are qualified by Islamic restrictions. As one might expect, what these criteria will entail is left vague and open-ended

Summary

Imposing Islamic qualifications on rights sets the stage not just for the diminution of these rights but potentially for denying them altogether. As the foregoing discussion illustrates, those who impose vague Islamic criteria on rights do not see the relationship of the individual and the state as being an adversarial one in which the weaker party, the individual, needs ironclad guarantees of civil and political rights to offset the tendencies of modern governments to assert their powers at the expense of the freedoms of the individual. Furthermore, they seem to believe that where the freedom of the individual and religious rules are in conflict, it is the former that should give way. There is fear that the individual may attempt to assert excessive rights that could harm the authority of the state or undermine the moral order of society. Islam is viewed in these schemes as a device for restricting individual freedoms and keeping the individual in a sub-ordinate place vis-à-vis the government and society. However, the *shari'a* criteria that are employed to restrict rights are left so uncertain that they do not define any line beyond which the demands of the government and society for obedience and submission could be said to constitute an impermissible infringement of individual rights. That is, once qualified by these vague Islamic criteria, Islamic human rights can offer no means for protecting the individual against laws and policies violating international human rights law. That to date the Organization of the Islamic Conference as well as Egypt, Iran, Pakistan, Saudi Arabia, and the Sudan have adopted the position that Islamic criteria should override human rights indicates how this trend is eroding the guarantees theoretically afforded by international law.

CHAPTER 5

Discrimination Against Women and Non-Muslims

Equality in the Islamic Legal Tradition

Accommodating the principle of equality in an Islamic human rights scheme involves dealing with two aspects in the Islamic tradition, one egalitarian and the other hierarchical.[1] Much depends on which aspect of the Islamic heritage, the hierarchical or the egalitarian, is taken to be more truly representative of Islamic values.

There is much in the sources of Islamic law that bespeaks a fundamentally egalitarian philosophy. For example, it is an important tenet of Islam that the best person is the person who is most pious. The accounts of the earliest rulers of the community, including stories of the life of the Prophet, are full of incidents indicating the rulers' humility, their egalitarian spirit, and their humane concern for the rights and welfare of all of their subjects.

Other passages in the Islamic sources can provide a warrant for upholding privilege and discrimination. The sources do distinguish in a number of areas between the rights of Muslims and non-Muslims, men and women, and free persons and slaves. Premodern jurisprudence ranking males above females, Muslims above non-Muslims, and free persons above slaves became an ingrained feature of *shari'a* law.[2] Going beyond these distinctions, some of the early shapers of Islamic doctrine endorsed hierarchical features of local social structures, treating them as if they were mandated by Islamic law. The implications of these distinctions for today's societies are sharply debated. Although few would uphold the merits of slavery in current circumstances, in other areas contemporary Muslims sharply diverge regarding whether laws should respect the old juristic categories or reflect the idea that Islam was ultimately meant to afford equality to all human beings.

When it comes to deciding whether the principle of equality is compatible with Islam, one can distinguish between two different approaches on the part of those Muslims who wish to retain the premodern *shariʿa* rules affecting women and non-Muslims. One is to affirm that the principle of equality violates *shariʿa* law. Conservative Muslim clerics in the past have been outspoken in their condemnation of the principle of equality on the grounds that it makes equal those who under the *shariʿa* must be treated differently.[3] The other approach is to offer reasons why the principle of equality is not violated by the retention of the discriminatory rules of the premodern *shariʿa* according subordinate status to women and non-Muslims. Today one rarely encounters the former position; the second approach is the prevalent one.

In seeking to understand the position of Muslims who assert that the retention of discriminatory rules of the premodern *shariʿa* does not violate the principle of equality, one should bear in mind that "equality" may have a different connotation for many Muslims than it has for people in the contemporary West, who have grown up with the idea of the absolute equality of all human beings. Social conditioning plays a crucial role in how people think about the principle of equality, as is clear from the history of this principle in the United States. Although egalitarianism was a fundamental tenet of the political and legal order envisaged by the Declaration of Independence, almost no white males in the era of the Founding Fathers thought that the principle of equality extended to women and to black slaves, who were assumed to be inherently different and unequal. Thus, it was possible to affirm equality while at the same time supporting a regime of laws that discriminated based on sex and race. Not until the 1960s was the contradiction between the principle of equality and toleration of de jure discrimination tackled by civil rights legislation, which prohibited discrimination based on sex and race.

Because of the cultural conditioning that prevails in the Middle East, it is easy for conservative Muslims to assume that the distinctions made between different groups of persons in Islamic law are part of the natural order of things and to imagine that the retention of premodern Islamic rules does not in any way contravene the principle of equality. Thus, one finds Muslims who argue that Islam recognizes the principle of equality even while they uphold rules relegating women and non-Muslims to an inferior status.

From the perspective of Muslims who have been conditioned by their culture and traditions to think that such distinctions are natural and essential, Islam treats as equal all those who should be so treated. From this perspective, *shariʿa*-based discrimination is compatible with the principle of equality. However, those Muslims have a problem when they try to address international human rights standards, which clearly say that the principle of equality is not compatible with a regime of discrimination against women and non-Muslims.

Equality in Islamic Human Rights Schemes

In the case of the Islamic human rights schemes examined here, there is no real wish to abide by the principle of equality set out in international human rights law. Nevertheless, the authors appear reluctant to acknowledge their unwillingness to respect this principle. Perhaps conscious that by perpetuating a regime of discriminatory *shari'a* rules they are breaking with a widely respected tenet of modern political and legal thought, the authors attempt to disguise the extent to which they are repudiating the notion that all persons are entitled to equality.

They may attempt simply to steer clear of the issues. The Saudi Basic Law altogether avoids the topic of equality in rights, thereby obviating the need to stipulate the kinds of inequalities and discriminatory treatment that the Saudi law intends to perpetuate. In a misleading formulation, Abu'l A'la Mawdudi included "the equality of human beings" in his list of Islamic human rights.[4] In his discussion of this principle, he asserted that Islam outlaws discrimination among "men"—not among "men and women"—based on color, race, nationality, or place of birth.[5] In his comments on the principle of equality before the law in Islam, he stated that Islam also outlaws discrimination based on class.[6] (As will be seen, this formulation resembles the provision on equality in Article 3.a of the Universal Islamic Declaration of Human Rights [UIDHR].) Since in Muslim societies it is de jure discrimination based on sex and religion that constitutes the problem area, Mawdudi is writing around what should be central concerns.

In any social context, a critical measure of the human rights protections that are afforded by the law is the extent to which the laws aim at redressing ingrained patterns of discrimination. Where local laws have traditionally deprived certain classes of persons of their rights, it is essential that provisions on equality mandate an end to such discrimination. Therefore, it would have been hypocritical for the United States to have outlawed discrimination based, say, on caste while ignoring discrimination based on race, just as it would be meaningless in a Hindu environment to outlaw discrimination based on race while ignoring discrimination based on caste. In each case, the actual patterns of discrimination in the local culture would have been ignored. In a scheme like Mawdudi's—designed to be implemented in the Muslim world—it is disingenuous to talk about equality before the law without addressing the problems posed by discriminatory *shari'a* rules denying women and non-Muslims the rights and freedoms enjoyed by Muslim men. Mawdudi, because he failed to prohibit discrimination based on sex or religion, was effectively condoning the perpetuation of discrimination against these groups.

Article 19 of the Iranian Constitution uses a similar, evasive formula to deal with the principle of equality: "All people of Iran, whatever the ethnic group or tribe to which they belong, enjoy equal rights; and colour, race, language, and the like, do not bestow any privilege."[7] Significantly, Article 19 does not address the issue of whether equality can be denied on the grounds of sex or religion. The extensive discrimination practiced in postrevolutionary Iran against women and non-Muslims indicates that the omission of these categories was designed to accommodate patterns of discrimination that are endorsed by the government and conservative elements of society.

The gaps in the equality guarantee of Article 19 are significant, since they correlate with the practice of the government. However, the Iranian Constitution also has a provision that echoes one in the draft constitution. The draft constitution had provided in Article 22, the very first principle in the chapter on rights, that "all members of the people, both women and men, are equal before the law." In the section of the 1979 constitution setting forth the aims of the Islamic Republic, one finds in Article 3.14 that they include "securing the multifarious rights of all citizens, both women and men, and providing legal protection for all, as well as the equality of all before the law [*qanun*]." The fact that this provision was retained, even though it expressed a philosophy of equality that was radically at odds both with the actual policies of the regime and with other provisions in the constitution, is highly significant, because it shows how much normative force international human rights concepts retain in Iran despite the attempts by conservative clerics to discredit them.

Article 1(a) of the Cairo Declaration avoids stipulating that people are entitled to equal rights, stating instead that all human beings "are equal in terms of basic human dignity and basic obligations and responsibilities, without any discrimination on the grounds of race, color, language, sex, religious belief, political affiliation, social status, or other considerations." Given the evasiveness typically found in the wording of Islamic human rights schemes, one is alerted to the fact that the failure to stipulate equality in "rights" is not accidental and that the equality in "dignity" and "obligations" is not intended to signify equality in "rights." The declaration further provides in Article 19(a): "All individuals are equal before the law, without distinction between the ruler and the ruled." Viewed in isolation, this might seem to be an affirmation of equal rights, but in the context of a document that carefully avoids guaranteeing equal rights or equal protection of the law for women and non-Muslims, it should be read as meaning only that the law applies equally to rulers and ruled—that is, that rulers are not above the law. Similarly, Article 1(b) says that the persons most loved by God are those who are most useful to the rest of His subjects, and no one has superiority over another except on the basis of piety and good deeds. This last statement should, in context, be taken as an endorsement of the proposition that people are equal in God's eyes, which is not the same as affording a legal guarantee of equality. These weak provisions are not necessarily an advance over the Saudi Basic Law, which makes no provision whatsoever regarding equality in rights.

Sultanhussein Tabandeh expressed approval of Article 1 of the Universal Declaration of Human Rights (UDHR), which says that all human beings are born free and equal in dignity and rights, and declared that the UDHR reflects ideas in the Qur'an.[8] In discussing equality, however, he talked of prohibiting class-based or racially based discrimination only, omitting any mention of sex discrimination. He explicitly said that differences are recognized based on "religion, faith, or conviction," seemingly in the belief—unfounded—that the UDHR Article 1 provision on equality allows such religious discrimination.[9]

In his discussion of Article 2, the general provision of the UDHR prohibiting discrimination, Tabandeh also avoided addressing the issue of sex but did indicate his approval of Islamic rules according Muslims a higher status than non-Muslims and free persons a higher status than slaves.[10] He concluded that Islam could not accept certain parts of Article 2, "for it cannot deny the difference between Muslim and non-Muslim."[11] One gathers from Tabandeh's failure to mention the status of women in connection with these articles that the idea of female equality struck him as so farfetched that he did not need to bother explaining that it was unacceptable under the *shari'a*.

The Azhar draft constitution circumvents the issue of equality by avoiding any specific discussion of categories on the basis of which it is impermissible to discriminate. Article 28 does say that justice and equality are the basis of rule, but this vague provision is far from a stipulation that all persons enjoy equal protection of the law. One can speculate that the authors of the Azhar draft constitution may have been less comfortable than authors of some of the other Islamic human rights schemes with stipulating an equality that they deemed incompatible with Islamic law.

One sees in the contrasting treatment of equality in the Azhar draft constitution and the Iranian Constitution the impact of the very different circumstances in which the two documents were produced. The Iranian model is an actual constitution, unlike the Azhar draft, which was no more than a hypothetical agenda of rights formulations produced by Islamic conservatives, who did not have to deal with the arguments of Muslims who wanted to follow modern rights models. In Iran, the forces of Islamic conservatism had to engage in a dialogue with a real political opposition, since, at the time of the drafting, Iran's liberal opposition had not yet been quelled and held fast to the constitutionalist ideals that had influenced Iranian legal and political culture since the late nineteenth century. Iran's clerics also had to cope with a political reality in which spelling out their rejection of human rights concepts would have been unpopular and could have undermined the prospects for clerical domination of the government.

It is significant that in this real-world conflict among differing Muslim attitudes on human rights issues, conservative Muslims backed away from the more extreme positions they had traditionally advocated and agreed to accommodate—at least at the formal level—a number of fundamental human rights principles such as equality and equal protection.

In contrast, many other Islamic rights schemes lack an endorsement of equality or equal protection, highlighting the fact their authors did not have to respond either to popular pressures for such provisions or to the arguments of liberal jurists on behalf of established norms of constitutionalism. This is yet another reason for questioning whether the Islamic human rights schemes discussed here are at all representative of where Muslim opinion generally stands in practice on rights issues. They may merely reflect the ideas of conservative elements and repressive governments that are not answerable to public opinion.

Equal Protection in U.S. and International Law

The principle of equality before the law is closely related to the principle of equal protection of the law, which merits consideration at this juncture. The most influential formulation of the principle of equal protection of the law was set forth in the 1868 Fourteenth Amendment to the U.S. Constitution, which stipulates that "no State shall . . . deny to any person within its jurisdiction the equal protection of the laws."

The purpose of the U.S. equal protection clause in the aftermath of the Civil War was to end the legal regime of discrimination against blacks in the South.[12] Its original reach has been extended by judicial interpretation to provide protection against discrimination on a number of bases other than race. In general, one could say that classifications for the purpose of placing minorities at a disadvantage, and classifications based on the idea that one group is inherently inferior to another group or based on stereotypical views of the traditional victims of societal discrimination, violate the equal protection clause. That is, the principle of equal protection is understood to afford remedies in cases where one can identify laws that reinforce actual patterns of discrimination and inequality in U.S. society, which result in persons who are similarly situated being treated differently.

Although many features of U.S. equal protection jurisprudence necessarily reflect the peculiarities of U.S. history and the social environment, the basic concept has been emulated in other laws, and the idea of equal protection of the law is endorsed in international law. Article 7 of the UDHR stipulates: "All are equal before the law and are entitled without any discrimination to equal protection of the law. All are entitled to equal protection against any discrimination in violation of this Declaration and against any incitement to such discrimination."

One sees in Article 7 of the UDHR unequivocal endorsement of the idea that equal, nondiscriminatory treatment under the law is due all persons. According to Article 2 of the UDHR, it is impermissible to discriminate based on sex or religion, race, color, language, political or other opinion, national or social origin, property, or birth or other status. Any legal measures that discriminate among groups of people using these criteria violate the UDHR guarantee of equality and equal protection.[13]

Thus, both the U.S. constitutional principle and its UDHR counterpart envisage equal protection under a neutral law, a law that does not deny freedoms or rights to members of weaker or disfavored categories of society and that accords all people equal treatment.

Equal Protection in Islamic Human Rights Schemes

Although in Islamic law one can discern elements that in some ways anticipate modern notions of equality, one does not find any counterpart of the principle of equal protection under the law. For those trained in Islamic rather than in Western law, the meaning of equal protection may be obscure. In the past, when Muslims were first attempting to come to grips with the constitutional principles of equality, some tended to assume that the principle of equality was not violated as long as *shari'a* law, with its discriminatory features intact, was applied equally to persons within the separate categories that it established.[14] Where differences in religion were at issue, they took the position that equality before the law meant that all Muslims should be treated equally under the *shari'a* and that all non-Muslims should also be treated equally under the *shari'a*,[15] not that Muslims and non-Muslims should be treated alike or accorded the same rights under the law. This original confusion about the meaning of the modern principle of equal protection of the law appears to persist among Muslims who want to uphold traditional hierarchies. It will come as no surprise that the Azhar draft constitution, the Cairo Declaration, and the Saudi Basic Law offer no guarantee of equal protection of the law.

When equal protection of the law is included in the Islamic human rights schemes examined here, it does not have the same significance as it does in international law. As will be seen, the idea of equal protection is modified to accommodate forms of discrimination mandated by tradition and by premodern rules of Islamic law. In other words, the assumption is made that it is possible to have equal protection under a law that itself mandates unequal treatment.

In the English version of the UIDHR, Article 3.a provides that "all persons are equal before the Law and are entitled to equal opportunities and protection of the Law," which could leave the impression that the UIDHR has abolished the pattern of discrimination that *shari'a* law requires in the treatment of male Muslims versus women and non-Muslims. Although the uninitiated Western reader, having seen this formulation, might think that the authors had espoused the principle of equal protection of the law, this is not actually the case.

To understand the significance of the terminology, one needs to consult the Arabic version of Article 3.a of the UIDHR, which states that people are equal before the *shari'a,* and that no distinction is made in its application to them or in their protection under it. That is, people are not being guaranteed the equal protection of a neutral law but "equal protection" under a law that in its premodern formulations is inherently discriminatory and thereby in violation of international standards.[16] The misleading formulation of the English version of Article 3.a, which tends to disguise this difference, is only one of many aspects of the UIDHR that suggest that the authors are aware that their philosophy is incompatible with international norms and are trying to hide from international observers nonconforming aspects of their schemes.

Since one may presume that the authors of the UIDHR intend to uphold rules discriminating against women and religious minorities, the claim in the Arabic version of Article 3.a that all people are to enjoy equal protection before the *shari'a* seems self-contradictory. However, as will be shown in the discussion of the corresponding Arabic text, there are specifications in the Arabic version revealing that the authors do not believe that the principle of equal protection is violated where the discrimination is based on sex or religion. In other words, sex and religion are not included in the categories on the basis of which it is impermissible to discriminate. Thus, according to this approach, it becomes as legitimate to deny women and religious minorities the rights granted to Muslim males as it would be in Western legal systems to discriminate against noncitizens or convicted felons.

One finds the categories on the basis of which, according to the UIDHR, it is impermissible to discriminate in the Arabic version of Article 3.a. Following the statement that all persons enjoy equal protection of the *shari'a,* there are in the Arabic text of Article 3.a quotations from the Prophet and the caliph Abu Bakr, his first successor. These quotations support the notion that there should be no discrimination based on ethnic background, color, social standing, and political connections.[17] These are, in fact, categories on the basis of which *shari'a* rules do not ordinarily discriminate. It is noteworthy that the categories do not include sex or religion.

Some clarification of the real meaning of the UIDHR can be obtained by comparing provisions of various articles. Such internal comparisons reinforce the conclusion that the guarantee of equality and equal protection in Article 3.a does not intend to abolish discrimination based on sex and religion, since such discrimination is endorsed in other provisions. Some of these will be treated in Chapters 6 and 7, but a few will be presented here to illustrate how the rights that women and minorities enjoy under international law fail to receive protection in the UIDHR.

Conservative Muslims generally claim that the *shari'a* excludes women and non-Muslims from most, if not all, governmental positions. Article 11 provides for a right to participate in public life. The Arabic version provides that all members of the *umma,* or community of believers in Islam, who are possessed of the requisite *shari'a* qualifications are eligible to serve in public employment and public office. In the Arabic version it is specifically provided that race and class cannot be utilized as a basis for excluding people from such positions, but the possibility is left open that discriminatory *shari'a* rules may exclude women and non-Muslims from public office and employment as people lacking "requisite qualifications." Moreover, by its terms the article seems to exclude non-Muslims from its protections since they are not members of the *umma.*

Dealing with the specifics of equality seems to have presented great problems for the authors of the UIDHR, leading to the production of extremely convoluted and ambiguous formulations. Since it is very easy, if one actually endorses full equality, to provide for it using the international standards, the obscurity of the UIDHR provisions on equality suggests that the authors had difficulty in finding formulations that would offer token recognition of the principle while restricting equality to domains where the principle would not threaten the advantages enjoyed by Muslim males.

Turning to Article 3.c of the UIDHR, one finds that in the English version under the rubric "Right to Equality and Prohibition Against Impermissible Discrimination" there is the following guarantee: "No person shall be denied the opportunity to work or be discriminated against in any manner or exposed to greater physical risk by reason of religious belief, color, race, origin, sex or language."

This differs significantly from the wording of the corresponding Arabic provision. In the Arabic version under the rubric "Right of Equality," the corresponding section, in Article 3.b, says that all people are equal in terms of their human value *(al-qaima al-insaniya),* that they are distinguished in merit (in the afterlife by God) according to their works *(bi hasab 'amalihim),* that no one is to be exposed to greater danger or harm than others are, and that any thought, law, or rule *(wad')* that permits discrimination between people on the basis of *jins* (which can mean nation, race, or sex), *'irq* (race or descent), color, language, or religion is in direct violation of this general Islamic principle *(hadha 'l-mabda al-islami al-'amm).*

As a result of the difference between the English and Arabic texts and the ambiguity in the Arabic, one cannot tell whether the intent was to abolish discrimination based on sex with regard to the areas covered.[18] In light of the pattern of evasiveness that one finds in the provisions in the UIDHR, one has reason to assume that the wording here has been deliberately made opaque. Moreover, the range of discriminatory laws and practices affected by the Arabic Article 3 is so narrow as to afford no valuable guarantees against discrimination for any categories of persons. The English version in Article 3.b does seem to bar discrimination in work opportunities, but there is no corresponding provision in the Arabic version of Article 3. The Arabic version does not say that no one should be discriminated against "in any manner" based on the categories mentioned. Instead, it appears merely to endorse the notion that people should not be discriminated against in the sense of being exposed to greater danger or harm by reason of those categories. It is not clear what kind of discrimination this greater exposure to danger or harm would involve, but regardless of the construction placed on these terms, it seems certain that it would cover a narrower area than is indicated in the English version.

Although the Arabic version of Article 3.b does not correspond to any tenet of international human rights law, it could herald a concern for advancing rights protections if it addressed an actual pattern of rights deprivations in Muslim countries. However, the principle that groups of people should not be exposed to greater danger or harm does not seem to address the actual problems of discrimination faced by women and non-Muslims in Muslim countries. Members of these groups complain that they are discriminated against in education, employment, and political participation. To the extent that Islamic law is applied in the rules of evidence and in criminal law, members of these groups also object to being relegated to inferior status. Feminists condemn patterns of sex discrimination in personal status law and restrictions on women's freedoms, while non-Muslims protest the favored status accorded to Islam and complain of denials of religious freedoms.

Therefore, in context, the protections offered in Article 3.b seem quite trivial. There is every reason to assume that discriminatory rules relegating women and non-Muslims to a subordinate status could coexist with this provision. In fact, other provisions of the UIDHR indicate that such discriminatory rules are being retained. Furthermore, the lack of protection against discrimination afforded in the Arabic version of Article 3 is not mitigated by the initial stipulation that all persons have the same human value. In context, this seems to be an abstract moral proposition, not a principle designed to establish full equality before the law.

The great disparity between the English and the Arabic versions of Article 3 of the UIDHR has been demonstrated. It is noteworthy that the English, not the Arabic, version of Article 3 was invoked in a recent court case in Pakistan.[19] In the case, the petitioner charged that the appointment of women as judges in Pakistan was un-Islamic. Although the petitioner was unable to adduce any support from the Qur'an or *sunna* for his argument, he did manage to cite prestigious medieval jurists who had ruled that women could not be judges. The attorney general of Pakistan in turn found a medieval jurist who held the contrary view and also argued that the other jurists had drawn an overly broad conclusion from a statement by the Prophet on women's capacity to rule. The court found that the petitioner had been mistaken in his interpretations of many of the requirements of Islamic law as they would affect the ability of women to serve as judges. Although the decision did not turn on the UIDHR, the court did refer to Article 3 of the English version to support its decision that Islamic law did not prohibit women from serving as judges. It characterized the article as follows: "It deals with the equality before Law, entitlement to equal opportunities and protection of the Law [and] also provides firstly that all persons shall be entitled to equal wage for equal work and secondly that no person shall be denied the opportunity to work or be discriminated against in any manner or exposed to greater physical risk by reason of religious belief, color, race, origin, sex, or language."[20] Obviously, had the court examined the Arabic version of the same article, it would have had much greater difficulty finding support for the proposition that under Islamic law women should not be discriminated against in employment or excluded from serving as judges. Women aspirants to the bench were fortunate that in Pakistan competence in the Arabic language was not more widespread.[21]

It is not only in the provisions of Islamic human rights that deal expressly with equality or discrimination that one finds Islamic rules being applied to restrict the rights of women and non-Muslims. Careful scrutiny may be needed to identify discriminatory biases in measures dealing with other rights issues. Frequently, attempts are made to disguise these discriminatory features. A number of such instances of hidden biases in seemingly neutral provisions will be discussed in the next two chapters, but one example will be given here, where the objective is to deny to non-Muslims rights that are accorded to Muslims.

One might get the impression from a reading of the English version of Article 14 of the UIDHR that it endorses a right to freedom of association. In fact, on closer reading, the provision mandates inequality between Muslims and non-Muslims in terms of their rights of association and expression. The "Right of Free Association" in the heading of Article 14 of the English version of the UIDHR seems to be qualified by the requirement in Article 14.a that such associations enjoin the good and prohibit the evil. The UIDHR provision states: "Every person is entitled to participate individually and collectively in the religious, social, cultural and political life of his community and to establish institutions and agencies meant to enjoin what is right (ma'roof) and to prevent what is wrong (munkar)." No protection is afforded for participation in institutions or agencies with other purposes.

This provision relates to the Qur'anic command in 3:104 to Muslims to enjoin the good and prohibit the evil. Since the right to freedom of association as understood today was unknown in premodern Islamic law, there are no established guidelines for interpreting the Qur'anic command in 3:104 as a principle affecting freedom of association. It therefore is unclear what the limits set in Article 14.a would mean for that right.[22]

When one looks at the heading of the Arabic version of the same provision, it is evident that one is not even dealing with what would be considered a right to freedom of association in the sense current in international law. Instead, according to the Arabic heading of Article 14, the provision deals with *haqq al-da'wa wa'l-balagh*, or the right to propagate Islam and to disseminate the Islamic message. Among the Qur'anic passages cited in the Arabic version of Article 14 is part of 12:108: "Say, this is my way. I call on Allah with sure knowledge, I and whosoever follows me."

From this, one understands that the only freedom of association that is being guaranteed is one that protects activities connected with spreading Islam. It is possible to interpret the provision of this restricted freedom as an indication that there is no intent to recognize a broader freedom of association. It is highly unlikely that the right to spread religions other than Islam or to disseminate works tinged with secularism or atheism could be accommodated within the scope of this wording. The Arabic Article 14 therefore actually seems to result in a curb on the associational freedoms of non-Muslims and also on freedom of expression more generally.[23]

The drafters of the Iranian Constitution, who, as noted in Chapter 4, included an equal protection clause in Article 20, were apparently aware that it was, at least from the standpoints of constitutional theory and international law, a contradiction in terms to guarantee equal protection under the *shari'a*. Thus, the first sentence in the article provides for equal protection under the *qanun*, or secular law. This makes the Iranian equal protection clause look more like the international standard set forth in Article 7 of the UDHR than Article 3.a of the UIDHR. The intent is not, however, to guarantee equality to all persons under the law; in the Iranian Constitution, discrimination against women and non-Muslims is legitimated by other provisions. As we have seen, the second sentence of Article 20 provides that all human rights are determined by Islamic criteria, and Article 4 provides that Islamic principles in general prevail over constitutional principles. These provisions indicate that discriminatory *shari'a* principles would prevail over the secular equal protection principle.

The inclusion of an equal protection clause in Article 20 suggests the powerful influence that Western and international ideas of equal protection have had. Today, an equal protection clause seems to have become part of the necessary apparatus of a nation's constitution, so it is included even where the philosophical premises on which the concept of equal protection rests are rejected—as they are in the case of the Iranian Constitution. In any event, the incongruous inclusion of an equal protection clause in the Iranian Constitution is perfectly emblematic of that document's awkward blend of Islamic principles and dissimilar and imperfectly integrated elements of international human rights.

The question remains: How do the authors of the Iranian Constitution rationalize the conflicting provisions they have included in the text? It is interesting to consider the treatment of equality in an article by a Shi'i cleric and strong supporter of Ayatollah Khomeini, Ayatollah Yahya Nuri, who played a prominent and active role in the postrevolutionary regime.[24] Nuri attempted to adjust the idea of equality so that it could fit within a framework of premodern *shari'a* rules mandating inequality. He argued that the principle of equality is the basis of Islam and that Islam shuns the violation of human rights and grants freedom to all under the law.[25] However, in listing impermissible bases for discrimination, he enumerated only the categories of race, color, social class, "weakness," and poverty.[26] This pattern of omitting the critical categories, sex and religion, is by now familiar.

Ayatollah Nuri elaborated on his philosophy of equality. He said that Islam supports the idea that all men (here the omission of women is probably not accidental) should have equal political and social rights, but with the qualification that "equality must be established by the law and it must not transgress the law."[27] For Nuri, the law, by which he means the *shari'a*, serves as a necessary corrective to the principle of equality, which, if not adequately curbed, would have undesirable effects on society, whence his formula "equality must be established by the law" but "must not transgress the law." By holding that equality should be confined within legal limits so that excessive equality can be avoided, Nuri is effectively saying that some inequalities should be imposed by law. Ultimately, he is appropriating the ideal of equality while at the same time calling for upholding laws that favor some at the expense of others.

Nuri's formula, which is designed to enforce legal inequality at the same time that it proclaims support for the ideal of equality, is in the final analysis a cousin of the conceit of the elite pigs in George Orwell's *Animal Farm*, according to which all animals were equal but some were more equal than others.[28]

A comparison of Nuri's formula and the treatment of equality in the Islamic human rights schemes shows that they share a common assumption—that the right to equality is acceptable as long as people who should not be made equal are kept in their proper place by the retention of the rules of Islamic law. In contrast, in international law, as embodied in UDHR Articles 1 and 3, the rights to equality and equal protection of the law are not subject to any conditions. The UDHR assumes that there can be no legitimate societal or governmental interest in mandating inequality.

Summary

On the basis of these examinations, one can say that Mawdudi, Tabandeh, the Azhar draft constitution, the Cairo Declaration, and the Saudi Basic Law, which never fully and unequivocally endorse the notions that all persons are equal and that no discrimination based on religion and sex is permissible, are less internally inconsistent than the Iranian Constitution, which is a remarkable admixture of international human rights principles concerning equality and assertions of the supremacy of Islamic law that directly contravene them. It is more difficult to characterize the treatment of equality in the UIDHR because of the numerous ambiguities and inconsistencies in the provisions regarding equality and equal protection, as discussed above. However, in general the UIDHR treatment of equality resembles that in the models of Mawdudi, Tabandeh, and the Azhar draft constitution more closely than the treatment of equality in the Iranian Constitution.

Taken together, these schemes reveal the profound ambivalence that conservative Muslims feel about the principle of equality, a principle that they are in general reluctant to condemn openly but that they seek to circumvent by a variety of subterfuges. In these circumstances, the principles of equality and equal protection of the law as mandated in international human rights law are unlikely to be replicated in human rights schemes whose authors maintain the superiority of Islamic criteria.

CHAPTER 6

Restrictions on the Rights and Freedoms of Women

In this chapter I shall examine the significance of Islamic human rights schemes for women's rights. I shall first consider the problem of determining what constitutes "Islamic law" on this topic. Specific principles found in Islamic human rights schemes will be analyzed in connection with aspects of actual state practice in the area of women's rights. The role of sex stereotyping as a factor in assigning certain roles to women will be assessed. I shall briefly review the stances of Muslim countries regarding the Women's Convention and women's rights issues raised in international human rights conferences.

Islamic Law and Women's Rights

The basic features of premodern Islamic law affecting women's rights must first be outlined. To avoid endless and repetitive qualifications, I shall resort to generalizations, referring to "Islamic law" and "Islamic principles" without detailing all the diverging positions of the various schools of law and different sects. Although this oversimplification is necessary to avoid converting this background discussion into a treatise on the Islamic law of personal status, it should be borne in mind that such generalizations about where "Islam" stands on questions of women's status can be misleading, since even within the law schools of Sunni Islam one often encounters diverging rules.

Where women's rights are involved, Muslims may perceive a cleavage between the earliest sources and the later juristic tradition. Increasingly, feminists and reformers are asserting that the Qur'an and the example of the Prophet provide material that is supportive of expanded rights for women, whereas opponents of feminism turn to the juristic tradition and the associated cultural norms, which reflect the values of patriarchal societies.

The Qur'an, as divine Revelation, is obviously a central source of guidance, and it devotes considerable attention to women. Qur'anic innovations tend in the direction of enhancing women's rights and elevating their status and dignity. In an environment where women were so devalued that female infanticide was a common and tolerated practice, the Qur'an introduced reforms that prohibited female infanticide, permitted women to inherit, restricted the practice of polygamy, curbed abuses of divorce by husbands, and gave women the ownership of the dower, which had previously been paid to the bride's father. As the thrust of the Qur'anic reforms in women's status is an ameliorative one, it seems reasonable to conclude, as Fazlur Rahman, an eminent liberal scholar of Islam did, that "the principal aim of the Qur'an was the removal of certain abuses to which women were subjected."[1]

Not only did the Qur'an dismantle existing institutions that contributed to women's degraded and vulnerable status, but Islam conferred rights on women in the seventh century that women in the West were unable to obtain until quite recently. Muslim women, for example, enjoyed full legal personality, could own and manage property, and, according to some interpretations of the Qur'an, enjoyed the right to divorce on very liberal grounds. The historical accounts regarding the status of women in the first decades of the Islamic community under the Prophet Muhammad suggest that women were originally accorded considerable freedom, that within the family the rights given them by Islam enabled them to defend their interests, and that they participated in public and religious affairs on a footing of approximate equality with men.[2]

It is natural that contemporary Muslim feminists, when they look at the history of their religion, are very skeptical when assured that Islam, which initially aimed to remove the disabilities women had suffered in pre-Islamic Arabia, provides the rationale for keeping women in a subjugated, inferior status. They have tended to place the blame for what they see as distortions of the original, authentic Islam on male interpreters of the Islamic sources who had vested interests in the preservation of patriarchal privilege. Thus, Fazlur Rahman argued that, as a result of social conditions and the interpenetration of many diverse cultural traditions, the inferior status of women was written into Islamic law.[3] Feminists have been inclined to dispute the authority of the later juristic tradition, which seems full of male biases and influences from local cultures that are at odds with Qur'anic ideals.[4]

The notion that Muslims can and should disregard the juristic tradition is controversial. The *shari'a* has generally been viewed as being set forth in the works of jurists. Depending on their allegiances to various sects and schools of law, Muslims at a given time or place would refer to one or another of the many recognized juristic treatises for legal guidance. In many milieus, it was unthinkable to challenge established juristic doctrines.

The premodern jurists treated women as needing male tutelage and control, imposing many disabilities on women, putting them in a distinctly subordinate role vis-à-vis men within the family, and largely relegating them to secluded domesticity. Jurists condoned child marriages, which in practice meant that women were married off at early ages and against their wills by male marriage guardians. Women were required to be monogamous, whereas men could have up to four wives at a time. Wives owed obedience to their husbands, who were entitled to keep them at home and to beat them and withhold maintenance for disobedience. Husbands could terminate marriages at their discretion simply by uttering a divorce formula, whereas wives according to many jurists needed to overcome difficult hurdles to obtain a divorce over their husbands' objections. Men enjoyed great power as the guardians of minors, and after a divorce, men got custody of children once they passed the stage of infancy. In the scheme of succession, women got one-half the share of males who inherited in a similar capacity.[5]

As has been noted, jurists were rarely unanimous on points of family law and inheritance affecting women—areas where the rules in the Qur'an and *sunna,* although subject to diverging interpretations among the various schools and sects, were very extensive. One finds many tensions and ambiguities in the juristic tradition. Women were commanded to dress modestly, but what modesty entailed was disputed. In domains such as access to education, employment, and participation in public life, relevant textual authority was conflicting or wanting. The lack of explicit texts in the Islamic sources left many questions as to how women were meant to function in the society at large very difficult for the jurists to answer conclusively. Furthermore, there was an unresolved question of how to reconcile the rights that women were granted by the *shari'a,* such as managing their own property and conducting business, with other *shari'a* rules that seemed to be in direct conflict with them, such as the rules allowing the husband to control his wife's activities and to keep her at home, isolated from all but close family members.

Since the late nineteenth century, members of the elites in Muslim societies have been gradually won over to the idea that the premodern *shari'a* rules need to be reformed. Except for Saudi Arabia, Middle Eastern countries have introduced reforms to improve women's status and remove many, if not all, of the disabilities formerly imposed under the *shari'a.*[6] Until the forces of Islamization became so powerful that they were able to reverse the trend in favor of granting women greater rights, it seemed that changes in the legal status of women were moving in the direction of their achieving greater equality.

Liberal political forces have generally welcomed the expanded opportunities that political, economic, and social changes have meant for women, but Islamic clerics and established Islamic institutions have by and large manifested strong opposition to allowing the role of women to evolve apace with these changes. As feminist ideas circulated through urban milieus and among the newly literate female population, Muslim conservatives rallied to denounce the idea of expanded freedoms for women.[7] The example of the Afghan Taleban, discussed below, shows how in the case of extreme clashes between evolved urban societies and archconservative village mores, the hostile reaction to changes can provoke interpretations of Islam that call for women to be demeaned to the status of chattel. Indeed, as modernization has unsettled old patterns, conservatives have often tried to expand Islamic rationales for depriving women of rights. Islamic rationales have been concocted for forbidding women to drive, banning women from participating in sports, and excluding them from working in television, radio, and entertainment programs. New contraceptive techniques and expanded medical care have increased the ability of women to control their fertility. Ignoring the established views of Islamic jurists, who by and large accepted contraceptive measures, conservatives have argued that Islam forbids abortion and limits or precludes the use of contraceptives. With the adoption of modern political institutions, new questions about women's political role have been raised. Conservatives have argued that "Islam" bars women's participation in politics and precludes them from voting.

As undertaking salaried employment outside the home has become common and even necessary for many urban women, conservatives have asserted that "Islam" mandates that women should not work outside the home, that they should not be allowed in jobs where they will have contact with men, and that they should only take jobs dealing with women and children. With the growth of public education, questions have arisen about the degree to which women should have access to schooling and opportunities for advanced study. Muslim conservatives argue that Islam calls for sexual segregation in education and that women should only be allowed to study subjects suitable for females—which tend to be ones that prepare women for a life oriented toward the home and family.

Arrayed against the foes of women's emancipation are Muslims—generally among the better-educated classes of society—who have reappraised and discarded many traditional interpretations of the Islamic sources and concluded that Islam supports reforms in the premodern *shari'a* rules, reforms designed to ensure the equality of the sexes. Abdullahi An-Na'im, formerly a law professor in the Sudan and now working in exile in the United States, and Fatima Mernissi, a Moroccan sociology professor who was one of the founding members of the Moroccan Organization for Human Rights, are prominent examples of contemporary Muslims who have reexamined the sources and concluded that Islam calls for equal rights for men and women.[8] Just as feminist perspectives have challenged the gender biases in Christian and Jewish theology, so Muslim feminists are reappraising the theological justifications that have been offered for restricting women's rights.[9] The kinds of restrictions that conservative Muslims wish to impose on women's rights tend to be dismissed by Muslim feminists as representing nothing more than male biases and cultural traditions disguised as religious precepts.

Conservative Muslims routinely attack Muslims who advocate equality for women as being servile imitators of the West who are disloyal to the Islamic tradition, as in Iran, where women who object to the local version of Islamic morality are lambasted as "foreign dolls." Feminists are condemned as agents of Western cultural imperialism who aim to destroy sound customs and morality and to deviate from *shari'a* principles.[10] Abu'l A'la Mawdudi sneered at "Oriental Occidentals," his pejorative epithet for Muslim women who espouse Western-style philosophy, moral concepts, and social principles.[11] Mawdudi complained that in the works of Muslims who support feminist interpretations of the Islamic sources, "the limited and conditional freedom that women had been allowed by Islam in matters other than home science is being used as argument to encourage the Muslim women to abandon home life and its responsibilities like the European women and make their lives miserable by running after political, economic, social and other activities shoulder to shoulder with men."[12]

One also encounters Muslims who may not believe that full equality of the sexes is compatible with Islamic doctrine but who are nonetheless unsympathetic to the arguments of conservatives that Islam requires that women be kept enshrouded, subordinated, and secluded. A substantial portion of the Muslim community seems to espouse views on women's status that constitute a middle-ground position.[13]

Because of these competing trends in Islamic thought, one cannot predict from the fact that someone is a believing Muslim what that person's position on issues of women's status will be. Given the intense controversies that have developed regarding the status of women in Islam, Muslims can no longer rely on settled doctrine in this area but must decide which of the great variety of competing views on how Islam treats women they find most persuasive.

The authors of the Islamic human rights schemes that are being examined here aim to deprive women of the extensive rights to which they are entitled under international law. However, just as the authors were loath to concede that *shari'a* norms conflicted with the principle of equality, so, with the exception of Sultanhussein Tabandeh, they go out of their way to avoid confessing that they want women to be subjugated. Since the details of their rights schemes and policies—or, in Mawdudi's case, the principles set forth in his writings—amply demonstrate that they believe in denying women equality and keeping women in restricted roles, it is noteworthy that they seek to avoid formally acknowledging that the de jure status of women in their schemes is a decidedly inferior one. It seems that they have been profoundly impressed by international norms that teach that men and women are entitled to equal rights, and that they fear that any frank admission that women cannot be equal with men in Islam will lead to their schemes being branded "backward," "reactionary," or unacceptable under international law. They are therefore responding to the challenge posed by the prestige of international law in their formulations of principles even as they advocate substantive rules that are in conflict with international human rights.

Tabandeh's Ideas

Sultanhussein Tabandeh is exceptional in his forthright assertion that Islam opposes the idea of male-female equality. His candor on this point may be a by-product of his general lack of political sophistication, which is much in evidence in his commentary. He himself conceded: "I have never taken part in politics, and know nothing of any political aspects or implications which the Declaration [the Universal Declaration of Human Rights] may have. It is only from the religious angle, and in particular the relation to the sacred theology of Islam and of Shi'a beliefs, that I shall discuss the matter."[14] Tabandeh not only considered that the Islamic sources were authoritative, but he even proposed that, where there were discrepancies, it was the UDHR that should be rewritten to make it conform to Islam.[15] That is, he had much more real confidence in the definitive and binding character of Islamic law than did the other authors, who often seem genuinely confused and uncertain in their own minds about whether Islamic law can still be deemed viable if its rules fly in the face of international law.

Thus, Tabandeh was unusually candid in his reaction to Article 16 of the UDHR, which provides for equal rights for men and women in matters of marriage and divorce and guarantees the right to marry without any limitations due to race, nationality, and religion. He flatly stated that the declaration contained several points that are contrary to Islam,[16] roundly castigating the representatives of Muslim countries who were involved in the drafting of the UDHR for not rejecting this article and explaining at the United Nations what Islamic teachings had to say about the status of women.[17]

The Islamic rules that in his view are violated by Article 16 include the *shari'a* ban on Muslim women marrying non-Muslims[18] and the right to initiate a divorce being reserved to men.[19] Tabandeh also professed his opposition to the notion of male-female equality embodied in Article 16 if it meant "that a natural equality exists between men and women, fitting them to undertake identical tasks and to make equal decisions."[20] He said that a wife must obey her husband, consult his wishes, not go out of the house without his permission, take due care of the property, look after the household equipment, invite a guest only with the husband's agreement, uphold the family's good name, and maintain her husband's good standing whether he is present or absent.[21] In addition, Tabandeh stated that Islam forbids women from "interference in politics."[22] He also made much of women's obligation not to stir up male lust, charging that "liberty granted to women, contrary to all reason and religion, results in libertinism, licence, lust, lechery, and libidinousness."[23] He supported the Islamic curbs on women's freedom that conservative interpreters of the *shari'a* call for as part of a woman's duty not to provoke male lust, asserting:

> Islam has taken measures to prohibit practices which would lead to stimulating of sensual passion or to deviation from chastity. Women are therefore ordered not to do what would titillate men's feelings of lust. She must therefore cover her body, and not show her adornments of beauty or of jewelry or make-up to the outside world or to strangers. She must not frequent, more than absolutely essential, public gatherings attended by men. She must spend much time at home.[24]

Themes in Tabandeh's exposition of the status of women in Islam are characteristic of the ideas that are set forth by Muslim conservatives generally. It is assumed that all women will marry, so the primary determinant of an adult woman's life will be her relationship with her husband. In this relationship, she is required to submit to her husband's authority and follow his wishes. It is expected that her life will be passed at home fulfilling domestic duties. There is no concern for protecting women's rights to develop as individual persons with distinct identities and abilities, to become educated in ways that fit their specific talents and interests or that enable them to become productive members of society, or to ensure that they play a part in the social, economic, or political institutions that shape their destinies. Women are seen not as actors but as passive, dependent beings—all of whom are basically fungible, not diverging in personality and capacity as males do. Furthermore, women are assigned the burden of preserving morality: It is their responsibility to stay secluded and enshrouded so that they do not provoke sexual excitement in men. Sexual importunities or advances on the part of men are attributed to the flouting of norms of modesty by women, not to any lack of morality or to any blameworthy, lascivious attitudes among the male population. As will be indicated in the following discussion, although other authors are less frank than Tabandeh, when one scratches the surface, one finds that they have similar philosophies.

Mawdudi's Ideas

Abu'l A'la Mawdudi, in his human rights pamphlet, avoided the subject of women's rights. Unlike Tabandeh, Mawdudi was a canny politician who seems to have appreciated the damage that it would do to the credibility of his human rights scheme if he admitted that it aimed at denying fundamental rights to one-half of the population. However, Mawdudi's views on women are on record in his other writings, and they are similar to Tabandeh's, with the exception that Mawdudi believed that women should be able to sue for divorce on liberal grounds.[25]

In his book defending purdah, the custom of keeping women veiled and secluded, Mawdudi listed as doctrines of Western society the principles of male-female equality, economic independence of women, and "free intermingling of the sexes";[26] he then went to considerable lengths to document his abhorrence of these ideas and to argue that they lead to the undermining of the family, lower birthrates, immorality, promiscuity, perversion, and social decay.[27] Because of such an environment, people in the West "perpetually remain in a feverish condition on account of nude pictures, cheap literature, exciting songs, emotionally erotic dances, romantic films, highly disturbing scenes of obscenity and ever-present chances of encountering members of the opposite sex."[28] He accused Muslims who advocate the kind of rights for women that he associates with the West of abandoning the concepts of "the sense of honour, chastity, moral purity, matrimonial loyalty, undefiled lineage, and the like virtues."[29]

Perhaps realizing that it would seem strange if he failed to provide any rights for women in his human rights pamphlet, Mawdudi did list as one of his "basic human rights" respect for the chastity of women.[30] However, as has been amply demonstrated in practice in many Middle Eastern countries and, particularly, in the treatment of women in Afghanistan under the Taleban, the obsession with preserving women's chastity has led to a policy of nullifying women's rights and freedoms. Mawdudi himself has indicated that he associates preserving chastity with confining women to the home. Thus, the only "right" Mawdudi stipulated for women, respect for their chastity, does not really qualify as a human right but is a principle that is, in context, being used to keep women enshrouded, cloistered, and helpless.

Furthermore, Mawdudi's stance raises doubts about whether he has any grasp of what civil and political rights involve. Persons who would violate a woman's right to chastity will usually be criminal offenders, who by virtue of their criminal conduct indicate their unwillingness to be bound by the law. Protecting individuals from criminals is a task that is normally left to the police forces and criminal justice systems of individual states. International human rights law is no more designed to protect chastity against violation than it is to protect people from robbery, murder, or arson. International human rights standards are addressed to presumptively law-abiding officials and governmental institutions. Thus, Mawdudi's chastity right is not a human right as understood in international law. (International law may become concerned with related issues in the event of mass rapes when these are perpetrated as instruments of state policy, as when they are used as a tool of ethnic cleansing.)[31]

Mawdudi tried to implicate Western governments in patterns of crimes against women's chastity by linking the issue to military policies and practices:

> This concept of the sanctity of chastity and the protection of women can be found nowhere else except in Islam. The armies of the Western powers need the daughters of their own nations to satisfy their carnal appetites even in their own countries, and if they happen to occupy another country, the fate of its womenfolk can be better imagined than described.
>
> But the history of the Muslims, apart from individual lapses, has been free from this crime against womanhood. It has never happened that after the conquest of a foreign country the Muslim army has gone about raping the women of the conquered people, or, in their own country, the government has arranged to provide prostitutes for them.[32]

Mawdudi's resentment of the West seems to have impelled him to make the patently false charge that no legal systems other than the *shari'a* protect a woman from sexual molestation and assault or rape.[33] Moreover, contrary to his boasts, there is no evidence that Muslim armies have historically acquitted themselves any better in their treatment of vulnerable women than their counterparts in other societies. The extensive rapes during the recent internecine strife in Afghanistan and Algeria and after the 1990 Iraqi conquest of Kuwait indicated that abuse of women is not the sole proclivity of non-Muslim armies. One is prompted to inquire why this curious, contrary-to-fact assertion was included in Mawdudi's human rights pamphlet.

Mawdudi's comments came after a notorious mass rape that was carried out by the Pakistani army in the course of the 1971 civil war fought in East Pakistan, which culminated in the independence of Bangladesh.[34] In this context, Mawdudi's insistence that a Muslim army had never raped women served at least two functions. It was designed to comfort members of his audience who were still smarting from the embarrassment of the international condemnation following the Bengali mass rapes by denying that rape by Muslim armies was even possible.[35] It was also designed to put the West on the defensive by accusing it of systematic sexual exploitation and mistreatment of women in wartime. This correlates with Mawdudi's general approach to Islamic law, which is infused with a polemical spirit and serves as a vehicle for anti-Western propaganda.

Given Mawdudi's intense cultural nationalism and disinclination to engage in self-criticism, he could not be expected to appreciate how the patriarchal cast of an Islamization program and the attendant rhetoric about protecting women's chastity could coexist with and even encourage a tolerance of rape. This has proved to be the case in Pakistan, where rapes have been recently committed with impunity and may even be employed systematically as a device to keep women in their place and to reinforce male dominance.[36]

The UIDHR

Aiming to present Islamic human rights in a diplomatic fashion, the Universal Islamic Declaration of Human Rights (UIDHR) treats women's status in a deliberately obscure fashion. The UIDHR does not admit that women are to be accorded second-class status. Nonetheless, from a careful reading of the UIDHR one can glean that, under the guise of applying Islamic principles, it denies women a number of rights and freedoms. However, many of the provisions assigning women to a subordinate role do so only indirectly and are written in such a convoluted style that their significance may not be obvious to readers—and especially not to readers of the English version of the document.

For example, in Article 19.a of the English version, a provision begins with the following tenet: "Every person is entitled to marry, to found a family, and to bring up children in conformity with his religion, tradition and culture." This should be compared carefully with the wording of its international counterpart in UDHR Article 16.1: "Men and women of full age, without any limitation due to race, nationality or religion, have the right to marry and to found a family."

In international law the freedom to marry is unqualified. In contrast, UIDHR Article 19.a qualifies the entitlement to marry: The qualification "in conformity with his religion" means that rules of the *shari'a* will impose restrictions.[37] For example, Muslim women will be barred from marrying non-Muslims. Furthermore, a Muslim man will only be allowed to marry a woman who is either a Muslim or a member of the "people of the book." In addition, other Islamic rules could apply, to prohibit marriages, say, between persons related by suckling or between Muslims and apostates.[38] Therefore, the impact of this UIDHR provision is directly contrary to the principle in the UDHR that men and women should be allowed without any religious restrictions to choose their own spouses. The UIDHR provision is not designed to protect the right of the individual to choose a spouse freely but rather to deny that right according to Islamic criteria.

Article 19.a of the English version of the UIDHR continues: "Every spouse is entitled to such rights and privileges and carries such obligations as are stipulated by the Law." This language should be contrasted with the international rule in UDHR Article 16.1: "They are entitled to equal rights as to marriage, during marriage and at its dissolution." In the international standards of the UDHR, there is unequivocal endorsement of equality of husband and wife. There is no talk of equal rights in the English version in the UIDHR but only rights "stipulated by the Law." In the UIDHR, "the Law" means the *shari'a;* thus all the discriminatory rules of the premodern *shari'a* rules can be upheld. Qur'anic verses are referred to in the English version of Article 19.a in the fine print of the references section in the back of the document, where Islamic sources are noted.[39] The actual texts to which references are being made are not, however, reproduced in the references section.

In the Arabic version of UIDHR Article 19.a, the implications for rights in marriage and divorce are much clearer, since the Islamic sources are incorporated into the text. The citation of one of the Qur'anic verses implies that the inequality of the sexes is an underlying assumption of the UIDHR. The verse, 2:228, says that "[women] have rights similar to those [of men] over them in kindness, and men are a degree above them." This is one of the texts that is traditionally interpreted by conservatives to confirm that male superiority is mandated by Islam.[40] Given the conservative thrust of the UIDHR, this traditional interpretation is most likely incorporated.

It is also interesting to contrast the impressions created by the English and Arabic versions of Article 19.h. The English provision runs: "Within the family, men and women are to share in their obligations and responsibilities according to their sex, their natural endowments, talents and inclinations, bearing in mind their common responsibilities toward their progeny and their relatives." This English version suggests that men and women share family obligations and responsibilities, although it qualifies this sharing in problematic ways. Depending on what one might read into these qualifications, the English-language provision might or might not be taken to mean that a fairly equal division of duties in the home between husband and wife was intended, particularly since factors other than sex are listed as determinants of the spouses' obligations and responsibilities.

The Arabic version of Article 19.h, presumably the authoritative one, deals with quite a different subject. It says that the responsibility for the family is a partnership *(sharika)* among its members, each contributing according to his capacity and the nature of his character, and that this responsibility goes beyond the circle of parents and children and extends to close relatives and distant kinsmen *(al-aqarib wa dhawi'l-arham)*. In contrast to the English version of the article, the Arabic version establishes a right to collect support from members of one's extended family—a right not recognized in international law. The article potentially places binding support obligations on persons only distantly related to each other in accordance with the system of mutual obligations among members of the extended family that is reinforced by premodern *shari'a* rules.[41]

The great disparity between the English and Arabic versions suggests that the English version was redrafted to make it more attractive to and meaningful for a Western audience, who would presumably recoil from the burden of supporting distant relatives. This idea would have little appeal in an environment where nuclear families are the norm and where the financial burden of maintaining distant relatives would typically be much more onerous than in traditional societies.

The UIDHR contemplates retaining the premodern *shari'a* rules that impose disabilities on women. The one major exception is the provision in Article 19.i providing that no one may be married against his or her will. Rules developed by some jurists, especially in the Maliki school of law, allowed a girl's marriage guardian to marry her off at any age and without her consent.[42] Girls in traditional Muslim society were frequently forced into marriages as soon as they reached puberty. Parents continue to compel their daughters to marry young in many parts of the Middle East today, causing much heartbreak for young women made to wed men they dislike—and who are often much older than they are—and to give up their hopes of pursuing studies and employment.[43]

A controversial case involving a woman's right to choose her husband came to a head in Pakistan in 1996 and proved the continuing relevance of the tradition that the marriage guardian is entitled to force his ward to marry the man of his choosing. Saima Waheed, an educated adult women, married the man she loved over the objections of her father, who wanted to force her to marry an older and wealthier man. He tried to have his daughter's marriage dissolved on the grounds that she could not validly enter into a marriage without his permission. After winning a court judgment affirming the validity of their marriage, the couple was subjected to threats and forced into hiding to escape retribution from Saima Waheed's relations and other infuriated upholders of tradition.[44] Her attorney, Asma Jahangir, one of Pakistan's bravest and most accomplished human rights activists, was subjected to such dire threats that she felt obliged to employ three bodyguards.

Many Muslims consider the premodern rules of *jabr* or *ijbar*, "forced marriage," outdated and incompatible with the ideal of marriage as a union freely consented to by both parties, and legal reforms in most Middle Eastern countries have officially eliminated the marriage guardian's traditional right to compel his ward to marry.[45] Other Muslims confuse the ingrained patriarchal practice of fathers selecting husbands for their daughters regardless of their daughters' wishes with *shari'a* rules. Thus, conservatives who supported Saima Waheed's father spoke as if the prerogatives accorded the father in Pakistani custom were mandated by Islamic law. In so doing they showed how upholding tradition and the status quo may be incorrectly attributed to Islamic requirements. In reality, the Hanafi school of law prevalent in Pakistan allowed a guardian to force his minor ward to marry but upheld the right of an adult woman to contract herself in marriage to a Muslim man of her choosing. Because the practice of forced marriage has not ceased, the UIDHR is performing a service by going on the record as supporting the idea that as a matter of Islamic principle no one should be compelled to enter a marriage. This stands out as an isolated instance in the literature under discussion, in which a real human rights problem in the Middle East is confronted, the premodern jurisprudence is rejected, and an enlightened interpretation of Islamic requirements is offered.

The most extensive UIDHR provision dealing with women is Article 20. The rubric for Article 20 in the English version of the UIDHR is "Rights of Married Women." It is significant that no provisions in the document are made for the rights of unmarried women—just as there is no provision on the rights of married men or unmarried men. Given the nature of the document, one can hypothesize several reasons for this: All Muslim men are expected to marry, so the status of a single male is not significant. Married men will presumably all enjoy the husband's rights and privileges, which are counterparts of the wife's duty to obey and serve the husband. Given the apologetic nature of this exercise, it is understandable that the authors would not have wanted to include a separate article detailing the rights of the Muslim husband. To do so would make it all too obvious that they were endorsing a traditional, patriarchal system in which the law supports a regime of male privilege in matters of marriage and divorce. For example, if the authors catalogued as rights of the husband his entitlements to beat his disobedient wife, to have four wives at a time, and to have sexual intercourse regardless of his wife's wishes unless she has religiously acceptable grounds for refusing him, this would give their whole scheme the retrograde appearance that they were seeking to avoid.

The existence of autonomous adult women who are not answerable to male authority is not envisaged in this scheme, so there is no need to specify the rights of unmarried women. In Muslim countries, all women are expected to marry. It is natural for the authors of the UIDHR to assume that the contours of an adult woman's life are primarily shaped by her domestic obligations to her husband as his wife and as the mother of his children. By speaking exclusively of the rights of married women, the authors of the UIDHR reveal that they do not envisage a system where women escape male tutelage. Instead, they share the perspective that is pervasive in traditional Muslim societies that a female child should be under the control of her father or other close male relative until she marries, at which time she is to submit to the control of her husband.

It is important to note the significant disparity here. In international human rights schemes, the focus is on the rights of individuals, irrespective of their marital status. Because spouses enjoy equal rights in international law, although there are specific rights provisions dealing with marriage, marital status cannot be a prime determinant of rights in the way it appears to be in the UIDHR.

What are the "Rights of Married Women" granted by the English version of the UIDHR? Article 20 provides that every married woman is entitled to:

A. live in the house in which her husband lives;
B. receive the means necessary for maintaining a standard of living which is not inferior to that of her spouse, and, in the event of divorce, receive during the statutory period of waiting (Iddah) means of maintenance commensurate with her husband's resources, for herself as well as for the children she nurses or keeps, irrespective of her own financial status, earnings, or property that she may hold in her own right;
C. seek and obtain dissolution of marriage (Khul'a) in accordance with the terms of the Law. This right is in addition to her right to seek divorce through the courts;
D. inherit from her husband, her parents, her children and other relatives according to the Law;
E. strict confidentiality from her spouse, or ex-spouse if divorced, with regard to any information that he may have obtained about her, the disclosure of which could prove detrimental to her interests. A similar responsibility rests upon her in respect of her spouse or ex-spouse.

A review of these provisions dealing with support and inheritance rights can illustrate how this scheme reinforces the discriminatory treatment of women. For example, in the English version, Article 20.b seems to be concerned with ensuring a wife's maintenance by her husband, but it actually limits her ability to claim support. Although the premodern jurists disagreed about exactly how much maintenance a husband owed his wife during marriage and in the 'idda, or waiting period, following divorce (either three months or, if the divorcée turned out to be pregnant, until the birth of the child), they agreed that this was a unilateral obligation on the part of the husband—as was to be expected in a system where it was assumed that the women would be dependent. However, at the end of the 'idda, the husband's obligation to support the wife ceased. The woman was then expected to be supported by her relations or by a subsequent husband.

This cutoff of support obligations can leave a woman destitute. The economic predicament of divorced women who are not wealthy or gainfully employed has worsened in modern times as urbanization and economic changes have undermined the extended family and diminished a divorced woman's ability to secure support from relatives. The recent tendency in family law reform in the Middle East has been to extend the husband's support obligations beyond what they were in the premodern shari'a. It is therefore noteworthy that the UIDHR fails to address the financial hardships of the indigent divorced woman while limiting the husband's financial obligations to the period of the 'idda. In context, this constitutes a rejection of the reformist position and a reaffirmation of the premodern rules sharply limiting the husband's support obligation to a divorced wife, which in contemporary circumstances can expose such women to acute economic hardship.

The English version of Article 20.b makes no mention of the Qur'anic verse 4:34, which is cited in the Arabic version of the same article. The cited verse connects male control over women to the maintenance that men pay for women: "Men are in charge of women, because Allah has made the one of them to excel the other, and because they [the men] spend of their property [for the support of women]." This verse is invoked by Muslim conservatives to justify according men superior rights.[46] It is significant that this very verse is quoted in the text of the Arabic version of Article 20.b, a subsection of an article purportedly concerned with the rights of married women. Its quotation in this context reinforces the idea that male superiority comes from the fact that men support women economically. Women's financial dependence on men is in turn the consequence of other *shari'a* rules that keep women housebound and excluded from remunerative activity. The inclusion of this Qur'anic verse in the Arabic text conveys a different impression than the English version does.

Similarly, Article 20.d seems innocuous in its English version, saying that a married woman has a right to inherit from her husband and other relatives in accordance with the law, this law being the *shari'a*. *Shari'a* inheritance law discriminates against women generally, allowing them to take only half the share that males do, and against widows in particular. In the Arabic version of this article, the impact of the *shari'a* on a woman's ability to inherit is more obvious. The Qur'an 4:12, quoted in the text, assigns the widow (a maximum of) one-quarter of her husband's estate if there are no children and (a maximum of) one-eighth of the estate if there are children. These Qur'anic shares constitute the legal maximum that the widow may take because, according to prevailing opinion, Islamic law does not allow the spouse relict (widow or widower) to inherit more than the Qur'anic share.[47] Moreover, the *shari'a* allows the Muslim husband to have up to four wives simultaneously, and if the husband dies and leaves more than one widow, the widows have to divide the one-quarter or one-eighth share that otherwise would go to a sole wife, in which case their shares will be very much reduced. Meanwhile, a widowed husband takes one-half of the estate in the absence of children and one-fourth if there are children, a portion that he does not have to share with any other heir. Thus, in incorporating the Qur'anic standards for inheritance by the spouse relict, Article 20.d reaffirms discriminatory *shari'a* inheritance rules and restricts a wife's right to inherit from her husband in a way that is very much to her disadvantage. This article does not afford protection for any human right as understood in international law, nor does it make an attempt to adjust the inheritance scheme to take into account the erosion of the extended family network that the original Qur'anic scheme assumed would ensure a widow's livelihood.

Regarding divorce, the reader of the English version of Article 20.c, cited above, might interpret the language to mean that a woman who wanted to terminate her marriage could claim a divorce as of right. The article provides that the wife "is entitled to seek *and obtain* dissolution of marriage" (emphasis added), an entitlement that is said to be "in addition to her right to seek divorce through the courts." This suggests that women are being guaranteed a right to divorce, which is not actually the case. When one consults the authoritative Arabic version of Article 20.c, one sees that no such right is being offered. The Arabic version says that a woman may *ask* her husband to agree to dissolve their union via a consensual termination of marriage, known as a *khul'*, or may *ask* a judge for a dissolution within the scope of *shari'a* rules *(fi nitaq ahkam al-shari'a)*. When one considers the implications of this wording, one appreciates that it is not much of a "right" for a wife to be allowed to *ask* her husband to agree to terminate a marriage or to *ask* a court for a *shari'a* dissolution. According to the *shari'a,* the husband is under no obligation whatsoever to grant her request and, except in the doctrines of the Maliki school of law, a woman must meet difficult requirements before she can obtain a divorce from a judge over her husband's objections.

The provisions in the Arabic version of the UIDHR are meant to reassure a largely Muslim audience that the *shari'a* regime of male privilege was being maintained, whereas the English version, the audience for which would be largely non-Muslim, was meant to disguise deviations from international norms.

The remaining "rights" that are provided to married women in Article 20 are simply frivolous or meaningless. For example, in Article 20.a, a woman is given the right to live in the house in which her husband lives. This would appear to be a solution to a nonexistent problem under present circumstances in the Middle East, particularly in the urban areas that have grown so quickly in the past few decades. Few men today can afford to maintain separate residences for their wives, even if they might wish to live separately from them. In countries like Egypt, where the population pressure is enormous and the stock of urban housing is woefully inadequate, it would be virtually impossible for the average husband to find and afford two residences so that he could house his wife separately. Indeed, so serious is the shortage of housing in some urban areas that even couples who are divorced may have to continue to live together in the same dwelling, because neither ex-spouse can find affordable alternative housing. Moreover, since the UIDHR does not abolish polygamy, this "right" might be interpreted to mean that cowives could not demand that the husband provide separate residences, as they could under the premodern *shari'a* rules, but would have to live together in their common husband's home. The beneficiary of this "right" would be the husband, who would be spared the expense of maintaining his cowives in separate residences.

Article 20.e purports to give a woman a right to have any potentially damaging information that her husband may have about her kept confidential, but it accords the same right to the husband regarding any confidential information that his wife may have about him. Thus, listing this right with the rights of married women is misleading. Here, there is no significant difference between the Arabic and the English versions, but in neither case does the principle embodied in the provision rise to the stature of a human right. A puzzling aspect of this article is that no Islamic legal rule prevents spouses from disclosing detrimental information about each other; on the contrary, the husband may need to do so to annul a marriage and the wife may need to do so to obtain an annulment or a divorce under *shari'a* rules. Depending on circumstances, the ability to disclose evidence about her husband's defects, failings, and misconduct may be the only means a Muslim woman has at her disposal to terminate a marriage.[48] Therefore, such a rule could conceivably inhibit a woman's ability to terminate a marriage over her husband's objections by barring her testimony about relevant evidence. Since this provision offers no significant rights for married women, its inclusion may amount to an effort to pad the very limited list of rights afforded women in the UIDHR scheme.

Islamization in Iran and the Iranian Constitution

The 1979 Iranian Constitution does not expressly relegate women to second-class status. There are even provisions in the constitution that, taken in isolation, might indicate that it was proposing equal rights for men and women. A section of the Preamble titled "Women and the Constitution" portrays the revolution as being sympathetic to women's rights, saying that after the overthrow of the shah, people will regain their original identities and human rights *(hoquq-e ensani)* and that, in consequence, women "should benefit from a particularly large augmentation of their rights."[49] Article 3.14 includes in a listing of the goals of the Islamic Republic "securing the multifarious rights of all citizens, both women and men, and providing . . . the equality of all before the law *[qanun]*." Article 21.1 calls for the creation of "a favorable environment for the growth of women's personality and the restoration her rights, both material and intellectual."

However, one sees provisions of a very different sort as well, ones that are much more in keeping with the spirit of the Islamic human rights that are under discussion here. It has already been noted that the Iranian Constitution provides in Article 20 that citizens' rights are qualified by Islamic standards and that women's rights are so qualified in Article 21. The negative implications of such qualifications will by now be familiar.

In the section of the Preamble on women and the constitution, one also sees that women's function is primarily to bear children committed to the regime's ideology. The Preamble says, in part:

> The family is the fundamental unit of society and the main centre for the growth and edification of human beings. Compatibility with respect to belief and ideal, which provides the primary basis for man's development and growth, is the main consideration in the establishment of a family. It is the duty of the Islamic government to provide the necessary facilities for the attainment of this goal. This view of the family unit delivers woman from being regarded as an object or as an instrument in the service of promoting consumerism and exploitation. Not only does woman recover thereby her momentous and precious function of motherhood, rearing of ideologically committed human beings *[ensanha-ye maktabi]*, she also assumes a pioneering social role and becomes the fellow struggler of man in all vital areas of life. Given the weighty responsibilities that woman thus assumes, she is accorded in Islam great value and nobility.

In the context of Iranian history, the emphasis on the family and women's role in raising children signaled that the aim was to return Iranian women to a domestic role after decades in which they had made progress in the areas of education, employment and the professions, and government service. Among Islamic conservatives, emphasizing the family has become a code for programs designed to keep women in domestic roles.

This family theme is repeated in Article 10, along with a claim that the framework for family structure should be taken from Islamic rights and morality: "Since the family is the fundamental unit of Islamic society, all laws, regulations, and pertinent programmes must tend to facilitate the formation of a family, and to safeguard its sanctity and the stability of family relations on the basis of the law and the ethics of Islam *[hoquq va akhlaq-e eslami]*."

One of the first measures that Khomeini took after coming to power was to nullify in February 1979 the Iranian Family Protection Act of 1967 as amended in 1975. The Family Protection Act was one of the two most progressive reforms of Islamic personal status law (the other being the Tunisian Code of Personal Status of 1956) enacted in the Middle East in the latter half of the twentieth century. The act included rules requiring that all divorce actions be brought before a court (thereby eliminating the husband's right of extrajudicial divorce by uttering a divorce formula), significantly broadening the grounds on which women could seek divorce, assigning custody based on the best interests of the child (instead of automatically giving custody to the father after age two for boys and age seven for girls), and requiring a married man to get a court's permission before taking a second wife, which would only be granted if he convinced the court of his ability to provide justly for both wives.[50]

Claiming that these reforms violated *shari'a* law, Khomeini and other conservatives condemned the Family Protection Act. In its initial years, the regime encouraged early marriages for girls, lowering the minimum age for marriage from eighteen to thirteen.[51] Eager to have women concentrate their energies on motherhood, the regime adopted a vigorous pro-natalist policy. The regime also promoted the Twelver Shi'i institution of temporary marriage, in which a man may contract for a woman's sexual services for a limited period of time.[52] This institution has been widely condemned by Iranian feminists as degrading to women and is regarded by most Sunni Muslims as a form of prostitution.

One might wonder how the Article 10 idea of exalting women's role in the family fits with Article 28, which provides in part: "Everyone has the right to choose any occupation he wishes, if it is not contrary to Islam [*mokhalef-e eslam . . . nist*] and the public interest, and does not infringe the rights of others." To understand Articles 10 and 28, one has the record of many years of praxis on the part of Iran's government that provide a gloss on these provisions. The accumulated evidence indicates that postrevolutionary Iran at first tried hard to push women back into the role of caretaker of the home and children. However, the regime was sufficiently pragmatic to revise its policies when they engendered untoward consequences. Unable to cope with the severe strains occasioned by the soaring population growth that the exaltation of motherhood and accompanying pro-natalist policy necessarily engendered, the regime has sharply reversed its course, relaxing restrictions on women's participation in the workforce and energetically promoting birth control to reduce population growth to a manageable rate.[53]

Under Iran's official version of Islamic morality, many restrictions were placed on women. Women's ability to participate in sports activities was drastically curtailed by rules mandating that women not engage in athletic activities where men could observe them and that when in public women must wear cumbersome, baggy, concealing clothing—even while swimming or skiing. Generally, women have been forced to wear all-enveloping chadors or similar covering in dark, dull colors and have been exposed to harsh criminal penalties for minor contraventions of the dress rules. Morality police engaged in systematic intimidation and harassment designed to discourage women from appearing in public with unrelated males.[54] Women's educational opportunities were restricted by a variety of measures; women were fired and excluded from a wide spectrum of prestigious jobs, and they were practically eliminated from politics and government. Women were barred from serving as attorneys in court and as judges. That is, they were quite deliberately excluded from having a say in the legal order that was seeking to return them to a cloistered existence within the family. Women were displaced from employment in the media and the entertainment industry.

An incident occurred on January 21, 1986, that graphically epitomized the official Iranian mind-set on women. In the course of a trip to Zimbabwe, President Ali Khamene'i, later to become Khomeini's successor, refused to attend a state banquet in his honor, in part because wine was to be served, but also because women were to be seated at the head table. The Iranian delegation demanded that all women, including a woman cabinet member, be relegated to the table that was farthest away from the head table. The Zimbabwe leadership refused, saying that women were entitled to equal standing with men. The Zimbabweans understood that the Iranian demand that women be confined to the remotest table did not just indicate sexual segregation at the dinner but was also symbolic of the inferior status to which the Iranians assigned women. In rejecting the Iranian demand, the Zimbabwean foreign minister noted that the roles played by women in Zimbabwe's struggle for majority rule and for development "entitle them to an equal status and standing in every respect with their male counterparts." The parallels between Khamene'i's attitude and the attitudes of white racists in the United States in the era when racial segregation was imposed are striking. Measures like the physical segregation of an "inferior" group by a more powerful group reveal how the "inferior" group is stigmatized.[55]

Iran's rulers have belatedly recognized that their reactionary polices affecting women have seriously tarnished their revolutionary credentials and undermined their popularity. Thus, Iran has begun to show acute embarrassment over being exposed as a violator of international law on women's rights, and the Iranian leadership has proffered strained arguments to justify its policies on women's rights as consonant with international law.[56] It has chosen to exploit the public relations implications of symbolic gestures. In 1996 Iran decided to offer a whole new image to the world after years of barring Iranian women from participating in the Olympics and sending all-male teams, which had refused to march into Olympic stadiums behind women from the host countries carrying the placards with Iran's name. Although its women athletes could only compete in events where they could wear their cumbersome and concealing Islamic dress, at the Atlanta Olympics Iranian women were included on the team, and a woman athlete dressed in a smart white coverall carried the flag and led the team into the stadium. This, Iran announced, was in order "to neutralise poisonous propaganda on the status of women in Iran."[57] That is, the hallowed rules of Islamic dress could be compromised in situations where following such rules could tarnish the progressive image that the clerical elite was struggling to project to the outside world.

Although the clerical elite has remained adamant about upholding the requirements of Islamic dress, even strengthening the penalties for noncompliance in 1996 by adding imprisonment and fines as penalties, the official stance on women's rights has been liberalized, with the result of adopting some positive reforms and rescinding many restrictions on women—such as the bar to their serving in the legal profession.[58] Certain women like former President Ali Akbar Hashemi Rafsanjani's daughter Faezeh Hashemi have been allowed to assume a prominent public role and to advocate women's rights.[59] After the 1997 election of President Mohammed Khatami, Iran even witnessed the appointment of a woman vice president. However, Iran's growing acceptance of an expanded role for women had limits; in 1997 all of the would-be women candidates for president were disqualified from running by the Council of Guardians.[60] Apparently, the prospect of having a woman heading the Islamic Republic was more than the council members could stomach. Moreover, the regime long prevaricated on whether it should rescind the ban on women in the judiciary, waiting until December 1997 to allow a few women to serve as judges. In 1997 Khamene'i was still admonishing Iranian women not to embrace Western feminist ideas, insisting that these ideas simply brought sexual promiscuity and that Iranian women had to follow "Islamic models" of sexual equality.[61] Moreover, on the occasion of the intense national jubilation over Iran's soccer team qualifying in 1997 for the World Cup finals, the regime refused to relax its rule barring women from attending male sports events to permit women fans to enter the stadium for the ceremony welcoming home the national soccer team. That thousands of women defied this ban and stormed into the stadium to join the celebration reveals how the impact of clerical appeals to Islamic morality has diminished.

Once having shifted gears, in its efforts to disassociate its official Islam from what was becoming disparagingly called "gender apartheid" in international human rights parlance, Iran eagerly exploited the contrast between its relatively lenient policies on women and the extraordinarily retrograde policies of the Taleban in neighboring Afghanistan. In 1996 Ayatollah Jannati publicly denounced the Taleban's fossilized policies, complaining: "What could be worse than committing violence, narrow-mindedness and limiting women's rights [thereby] defaming Islam?"[62] For a regime that had long appealed to Islam as the rationale for depriving women of rights and freedoms, this signaled a remarkable turnabout.

The sharp differences between Iran and Afghanistan, both of which officially followed Islamic policies on women's rights, proved that there was no monolithic Islam that determined countries' laws affecting women. Moreover, the changes in policies on women's rights in Iran in the relatively short period since the revolution have shown that even within one country that is supposedly committed to following Islamic law, readings of Islamic law may shift dramatically in response to local conditions and changing political trends.

The Sudan Under Islamization

Women's rights were not the focus of the Islamization program undertaken in the Sudan by Ja'far Nimeiri in the period 1983–1985. However, in the course of the second Islamization campaign, undertaken by the military regime of General Omar al-Bashir in 1989, the imposition of Islamic law became associated with much the same kinds of oppression that one saw in Iran after the Islamic Revolution. According to Bashir, the ideal Sudanese woman was one who took care of her husband and children, did her household duties, attended to her reputation, and was a devout Muslim.[63] Women were dismissed from public service and discriminated against in hiring and promotion; women in the legal profession were particularly targeted for removal. Women, regardless of age, were prohibited from traveling unless chaperoned by a male relative, a prohibition that was not lifted until 1996. Women who were not supporters of the Islamization program of the powerful National Islamic Front were subjected to harassment. In 1996 a law was enacted imposing many curbs on women's freedoms under the rubric of protecting Islamic morality. Measures were introduced such as mandatory segregation of the sexes in public places, the requirement that women be chaperoned by male relations in marketplaces at night, and the requirement that women's sports be conducted in private. Vague new crimes against morality were manufactured; women could be prosecuted for offenses against public order such as suspicion of intent to commit prostitution.[64]

The Azhar Draft Constitution

The Azhar draft constitution has some features that are very similar to those found in the Iranian Constitution, although the former is a much briefer and sketchier document. Article 7 in the section on rules governing "Islamic Society" provides that the family is the basis of society and that the family's foundations are religion and morality *(al-din wa 'l-akhlaq)*, and Article 8 says that safeguarding the family is a state duty. As has been noted, "protecting the family" is a code phrase used by conservative Muslims to denote an order where women are kept confined in the domestic sphere and subordinated to men.

In the Azhar draft, Article 8 provides that the state should encourage early marriage and provide "the means according to which the wife would obey her husband and look after her children and consider keeping the family the first of her tasks." This shows how in these schemes the state winds up as the enforcer of supposedly traditional values at a time when the tradition itself has crumbled and ceased to have its former normative force. It reflects the Azhar sheikhs' abhorrence of the situation that has developed in contemporary Egypt, where many women are educated and work in full-time jobs. In Egypt, as in other countries that have undergone similar changes, women have been less inclined than they formerly were to view their domestic roles as the center of their lives. Women's earning power has weakened the control that their husbands formerly enjoyed as the sole providers and has facilitated wives' challenging their husbands' authority. The Azhar draft therefore envisages a situation where socio-economic transformations have weakened the husband's power over the wife and changed marital relations in fundamental ways. To reestablish the old order of things, the state must be enjoined to intervene to make the wife obey her husband and accord primacy to her duties as mother and housewife.

In addition to the general guarantee of the right to work in Article 37 of the Azhar constitution, there is a separate provision in Article 38 that says that women have the right to work within the limits of the precepts of the *shari'a (hudud ahkam al-shari'a al-islamiya)*. It is significant in this regard that there are no Islamic qualifications imposed on men's right to work—and no idea, therefore, that a man's working might infringe *shari'a* principles. There is no further explanation of what the Islamic limits on a woman's ability to work might be, but extrapolating from the general attitudes of Muslim conservatives, one can presume that women will need their husbands' permission to work, that they will be allowed to work in only a limited range of jobs deemed suitable for women, and that they will be barred from work that would bring them into inappropriate proximity with men.

The most distinctive provision in the Azhar draft constitution is Article 14, which in the English version provides: "Bedizement [bedizenment, or gaudy dress] is forbidden and observing others' feelings is a duty. The government is to pass the laws and decisions to preserve the feelings of the public against profligacy according to the rules of the Islamic Sharia." Like portions of the English translation of the UIDHR, this English translation of Article 14 seems disingenuous. The reader of the article may not realize that this prohibition of bedizenment is a call for governments to take measures to force women to go about veiled and to discourage them from leaving their homes or associating with men from outside the family circle. The use of the term "profligacy" is misleading in this context, since it gives the impression that the concern is for the curbing of wastefulness and dissipation generally, when in reality it is only "shameless" conduct by women that is targeted.

In the Arabic version of Article 14, the word corresponding to what should be "bedizenment" in the English version is *tabarruj*. The reference is to the command in the Qur'an 33:33, which in an English translation that favors archaisms reads: "[B]edizen not yourselves with the bedizenment of the Time of Ignorance."[65] The verse is widely interpreted to mean that women must avoid immodest or provocative clothing and ornaments, and by Islamic conservatives to mean that heavy veiling and no makeup are de rigueur for women whenever they are exposed to the sight of men who are not members of their own family circles.[66] Prohibitions like the ban on "bedizenment" are rarely interpreted as having any bearing on how men dress, however, and Muslim men who abandon traditional Middle Eastern dress and adopt conventional Western styles of clothing are not considered to be committing any offense against public decency. (The policies of the Taleban, discussed below, are a major exception in this regard.) Thus, this provision sets the stage for government-imposed, uniform standards of dress for women but leaves men free to dress like Europeans. Their enshrinement of the ban on female "bedizenment" in the early fundamental provisions of the Azhar draft constitution reveals the authors' mentality, their social priorities, and their attitudes toward women's rights.

In the Arabic version of Article 14, the ban on bedizenment is followed by statements that preserving female honor is a duty *(al-tasawun wajib)*. This could be interpreted as justifying the retention of Arab concepts of honor, which have been used traditionally to justify keeping women segregated and secluded and for imposing harsh penalties on women (not men) for violating sexual taboos.[67] The Azhar draft also provides that the state must issue laws to prevent offenses to the public sense of decency according to the principles of the *shari'a (ahkam al-shari'a al-islamiya)*. This could mean measures beyond just requiring that women be veiled in public; it could be interpreted to entail legislation that allows the familiar kinds of prosecution and harassment of women for going about without male chaperones or for dress that is deemed "immodest."

The Cairo Declaration and the Saudi Basic Law

As has been noted, the Cairo Declaration is carefully drafted so as to avoid providing for equality in rights regardless of gender—as one would expect in a document endorsed by countries like Iran and Saudi Arabia, where sex-based discrimination is state policy. In an evasive formulation, Article 6 provides that women are equal to men in "human dignity"—but not equal in "rights." However, the term "rights" is used later in the same article, when it is stipulated that a woman "has rights to enjoy as well as duties to perform." The duties are left unspecified and only three rights are enumerated as such: a woman's right to legal personality, to own and manage her property, and "to retain her name and lineage." The first two were among the important improvements Islam made in women's rights over a millennium ago, but they are of less significance in the late twentieth century, when such minimal rights are taken for granted. The third "right" does not advance women's position in Middle Eastern societies, where women have traditionally kept their family names after marriage. Article 6 also imposes on the husband the duty to pay maintenance and to care for the family, thereby perpetuating the traditional spousal relationship, in which the husband is treated as both master and provider and the husband's rights over his wife flow from his duty to support her.

Furthermore, it seems that the Cairo Declaration envisages using Islamic criteria to restrict both women's freedom of movement and their ability to select employment. Article 12 provides that everyone shall have the right, within the framework of the *shari'a [fi utur al-shari'a]*, to freedom of movement. This seemingly neutral provision would accommodate restrictions on women's mobility, preventing women from leaving the home except with their husbands' permission and from traveling except when accompanied by a male relative. Although Article 13 provides that men and women are entitled to fair wages for work without discrimination—a positive step—it does not prohibit restricting the fields in which women are permitted to work. Instead, it provides that everyone "shall be free to choose the work that suits him best and which serves his interests and those of society," and that a person "may not be assigned work beyond his capacity." These conditions would permit excluding women from work on the grounds that it was unsuitable for them, that the demands were beyond their capacity, or that the interests of society dictated such exclusion. This is in violation of UDHR Article 23.1, which guarantees that everyone has the right to work and to free choice of employment, and Article 6 of the International Covenant on Economic, Social, and Cultural Rights (ICESCR), which guarantees the right of "everyone to gain his living by work which he freely chooses or accepts." Article 23 of the Cairo Declaration stipulates that the *shari'a* determines the right to assume public office, which could be exploited by conservatives opposed to women's participation in government.

The Cairo Declaration affords no guarantee for the right to marry the partner of one's choice, providing in Article 5 only that the right to marry should not have "restrictions stemming from race, color, or nationality," thereby leaving intact the old *shari'a* rules restricting the ability of Muslims to marry outside their faith, rules that are especially restrictive where women are involved. Not only can Muslim women not marry non-Muslims, but they may lose their Muslim husbands if and when, in the increasingly intolerant climate of their societies, their husbands run afoul of some would-be enforcers of orthodoxy who declare their husbands to be heretics or apostates. One is far, indeed, from the standards of the UDHR, which in Article 16.1 guarantees that both men and women have the right to marry without any limitations due to race, nationality, or religion.

The Saudi Basic Law has no provision directly addressing women's rights. However, in Article 10 it provides that the state is to "aspire to strengthen family ties" and to maintain "Arab and Islamic values." There are also stipulations in Article 9 that the family shall be inculcated with the Islamic faith and with obedience to God, the Prophet, and those possessing authority, and also with respect for the law. Taken together, these suggest an intention to employ appeals to Saudi family values and premodern Islamic law in order to maintain the traditional patriarchal family structure and to keep women subordinated and cloistered within its confines, denied any opportunity to participate in public life or government. In other words, the Basic Law accommodates the Saudi system of gender apartheid. Not surprisingly, whereas most countries were so appalled at the Taleban's rights abuses, especially their treatment of women, that they refused to recognize the new Afghan regime, Saudi Arabia was one of only three nations willing to accord recognition to the Taleban government.[68]

Women's Rights in Afghanistan

In the turbulent, strife-torn years just before the Taleban takeover, various factions competed for supremacy in Afghanistan, some of which vaunted their commitment to reinstating Islamic law.[69] During this period women suffered from abductions, displacements, abuse, torture, rapes, and slaughter.[70] All this was but a prelude to the even harsher crackdowns and more extensive abuses perpetrated under the Taleban, who succeeded in extending their rule over most of the country in 1996. They set loose fierce and undisciplined enforcers of their retrograde version of Islamic morality to terrorize the population into submission. Ironically, their Islamic dress rules had some elements that were more equitable than rules found in countries like Iran, since men were also affected, being required to don traditional Afghan attire and to leave their beards untrimmed. Women had to be completely swathed in the enveloping *burqa* any time they left their homes—but they were meant to stay within their homes, their mobility being sharply curbed.[71] As elsewhere under Islamization campaigns, much arbitrariness ensued in the application of Islamic rules: Even women wearing *burqas* were sometimes tormented and savagely beaten for trivial offenses, such as wearing white socks, which were somehow transformed into emblems of licentiousness.[72] The Taleban's policies blocked women from all education and virtually all employment outside the home, drastically reducing their access to the public sphere and to health care.[73]

The Taleban's draconian version of Islam was no more acceptable to the affected population than were the versions forcibly imposed by the Iranian and Sudanese regimes. Opponents of the Taleban who had fled to Tashkent issued a stinging denunciation of Taleban human rights violations and condemned what they labeled the Taleban's most inhuman and un-Islamic fanaticism. They called on the United Nations and powerful international organizations to use political and economic pressure to force the Taleban to end their rights violations.[74] Shiʻi Muslims of the Hazara ethnic group, both religiously and ethnically distinct from the assertively Pashtun and fervently Sunni Taleban, were particularly alienated, and they promised to field a battalion of women soldiers to fight the Taleban. A Hazara woman teacher condemned the Taleban as being "against all civilisation, Afghan culture, and women in particular."[75] The outrage that the Taleban provoked among their fellow Afghans on account of their policies shows why it is unreasonable to treat governmental positions regarding religion and culture as if they were necessarily representative of the views of a society as a whole or as if within the borders of one nation, all persons necessarily adhere to a unitary set of attitudes and values.

Apparently somewhat chastened by the international chorus of condemnation, the Taleban cleric Alhaj Mawlavi Qalamuddin, the head of the General Department for the Preservation of Virtue and Prevention of Vice, which was charged with enforcing Islamic morality, complained that the outside world had unleashed false propaganda against the Taleban by saying that they were violating women's rights, insisting: "But the reverse is true. . . . By strictly observing the Shariah law, we have given great honor and dignity to our women."[76] Similarly, the acting foreign minister, Sher Mohammed Abbas Stanakzai, insisted that the Taleban regime respected women's "human rights" as well as their nature.[77]

That is, even in the Taleban regime, whose leaders were most notoriously at odds with human rights, a pro–human rights stance was already being adopted by officials in their efforts to persuade the world that their imposition of Islamic law did not violate international law. There was a time when Muslims who found human rights incompatible with their interpretation of Islamic law were prepared unequivocally to denounce human rights as an alien institution. The prestige of human rights has since grown to the point that the claims of human rights are now given hypocritical acknowledgment by the most retrograde Islamic regimes, even where any intent to respect such rights is entirely wanting.

Summary of Islamic Approaches

In these various approaches to women's rights there is an absence of any willingness to recognize women as fully equal human beings who deserve the same rights and freedoms as men. Instead, discrimination against women is treated as something entirely natural—in much the same way that people in the West think it is natural that mentally defective persons and young children must be denied certain rights and freedoms. However, the authors of Islamic rights schemes are generally reluctant to spell out their belief in inherent female inferiority. In this regard, the invocations of *shari'a* law are very useful, since the *shari'a* qualifications that are placed on rights tend to look harmless to a casual observer but signal the authors' actual intentions to an informed audience. The vagueness in the Islamic criteria limiting women's rights also affords great leeway to governments in choosing what kind of discriminatory measures they will impose.

International human rights documents aim to afford protection for human rights, not to provide rationales for restricting or denying rights. In contrast, as the examination of these Islamic human rights schemes shows, in the area of women's rights, the latter serve the function of justifying the taking away of rights. Islamic human rights schemes would seem to permit many direct forms of sex discrimination. Of course, insofar as the application of Islamic criteria means that Muslim women are confined in the home and excluded from situations where they will have contact with men, they will also be indirectly denied many other freedoms as well.

Islamic Versus Women's International Human Rights

The Convention on the Elimination of all Forms of Discrimination Against Women (CEDAW), also known as the Women's Convention, entered into force in 1981. Measured by the standards of this convention, the treatment of women in Islamic human rights schemes seems particularly deficient. Article 1 defines discrimination as including "any distinction, exclusion or restriction made on the basis of sex which has the effect or purpose of impairing or nullifying the recognition, enjoyment, or exercise by women, irrespective of their marital status, on a basis of equality of men and women, of human rights and fundamental freedoms in the political, economic, social, cultural, civil, or any other field." Article 2.f of the convention calls on states to take all measures necessary to eliminate all laws, regulations, customs, and practices discriminating against women. CEDAW lists many specific kinds of sex discrimination that are to be eliminated. For example, Article 16 requires eliminating all discrimination between men and women in the family and ensuring that men and women have the same rights and responsibilities during marriage and at its dissolution.

Many Muslim states have ratified CEDAW without reservation—as if they found its principles unexceptionable—but there is no indication that the authors of the Islamic human rights schemes reviewed here share any of the goals of CEDAW. Their aim seems instead to enlist the state as the primary enforcer of discriminatory principles taken from the premodern *shari'a* and to shore up the restrictions on women's rights and freedoms that were traditionally imposed in Middle Eastern societies.

It is not surprising, then, that one bloc of Muslim countries has refused to ratify CEDAW, including Afghanistan, Bahrain, Iran, Saudi Arabia, the Sudan, and the United Arab Emirates. However, a larger number of Muslim countries have ratified CEDAW with significant reservations that have qualified their adherence to the convention's provisions. Many non-Muslim countries have also entered reservations in ratifying CEDAW, but often these reservations have affected relatively peripheral matters. What stands out in the case of Muslim countries is that so many of their reservations amount to rejections of the most central CEDAW provisions, such as Articles 2 and 16, and that many of them specifically invoke Islamic law as the reason why they are making these reservations.[78] Like the Islamic human rights schemes examined here, these ratifications effectively pay lip service to international law while using Islamic reservations to qualify their adherence to such law.

In entering their Islamic reservations, Muslim states treat Islamic law as if it were a supranational religious law that binds them, whereas in reality, where Islamic law survives, it does so in the form of very dissimilar national laws enacted by local governments and changed by them at will. Moreover, Muslim countries do not all make Islamic reservations to the same provisions of CEDAW, again indicating that they have dissimilar opinions regarding which CEDAW articles conflict with Islamic law. Furthermore, many reservations have been entered by Muslim countries to CEDAW provisions on the basis of discriminatory domestic laws that are in no way connected to Islamic law, indicating that the real reason for their nonacceptance of CEDAW may be their overall policies of upholding regimes of sex discrimination.[79] That is, despite the Islamic reservations entered by some Muslim countries to CEDAW, it is questionable whether Islam per se has prompted their reservations.

The Influence of Sex Stereotyping

CEDAW recognizes that sex stereotyping constitutes an obstacle to realizing full equality for women and calls on governments to attack the attitudes and practices that stereotype women as inferior beings whose nature disqualifies them from enjoying freedoms on a par with men. Article 5.a binds the parties "to modify the social and cultural patterns of conduct of men and women, with a view to achieving the elimination of prejudices and customary and all other practices which are based on the idea of the inferiority or the superiority of either of the sexes or on stereotyped roles for men and women."

One sees no concern for transcending or eliminating sex stereotyping in the Islamic human rights schemes reviewed here; on the contrary, such stereotyping is a central feature of the schemes, if sometimes only an implied one. All of them show evidence of being shaped by the idea that men and women have fundamentally different natures and roles and should, accordingly, have distinct rights and obligations. By examining the substantive provisions in the schemes, one can see whether assumptions about inherent, sex-linked differences are implicit in the schemes and thereby draw some inferences about the authors' attitudes. Whether express or implicit, the stereotypes that correlate with the treatment of women in the Islamic human rights schemes under discussion here are all similar.

Given Sultanhussein Tabandeh's general level of candor, it is not surprising that he expressed his sexual stereotypes quite freely and unselfconsciously in the course of explaining why Islam cannot accept the human rights accorded women in the UDHR. Women, according to Tabandeh, are touchy and hasty, volatile and imprudent. They are generally more gullible and credulous than men. Their sexual desire makes them easy prey for the blandishments of salacious individuals.[80] He invoked these female characteristics to justify the restrictions that he argued Islam imposes on women's right to obtain a divorce, but, obviously, these same female shortcomings would justify male superiority in other areas as well. In Tabandeh's opinion, nature made men and women capable of performing different functions. Women were designed for "cooking, laundering, shopping, and washing up," as well as for taking care of children. Men, in contrast, were created for field work, warfare, and earning a living.[81] Women are deficient in the intelligence needed for "tackling big and important matters"; they are prone to making mistakes and lack long-term perspective. For this reason, he said, they must be excluded from politics.[82] Women cannot fight in war because they are "timorous-hearted," affected by physical weakness, and might get frightened and run away.[83]

Abu'l A'la Mawdudi took a similar line, although not in his publication on human rights. In his book on purdah he argued that nature has designed men and women for different roles, treating menstruation, pregnancy, and nursing as incapacitating disabilities.[84] Women, he asserted, are created to bear and rear children. They are tender, unusually sensitive, soft, submissive, impressionable, and timid. They lack firmness, authority, "coldtemperedness," strong willpower, and the ability to render unbiased, objective judgment.[85] Men have coarseness, vehemence, and aggressiveness, which make them suited to assume roles as generals, statesmen, and administrators. The education of men should, therefore, aim at training them so that they can support and protect the family, whereas a woman should be educated to bring up children, look after domestic affairs, and make home life "sweet, pleasant, and peaceful."[86]

Similar observations are made by Ayatollah Javad Bahonar, a cleric who briefly served as Iran's prime minister before being assassinated. Bahonar was one of Khomeini's closest aides, and his thinking may be taken as representative of many of the leading clerics in Khomeini's regime who fashioned or supported the regime's policies vis-à-vis women. In an article on Islam and women's rights in an English-language journal distributed in the West by the

Iranian regime, Bahonar said that men are bigger and stronger and have larger brains, with more of the brain section "dealing with thought and deliberation."[87] A relatively larger percentage of the smaller female brain is "related to emotions," and women have more in the way of the affection and deep tender sentiments that suit them for child care and nursing. Women's sentiments and emotions make them ill equipped to cope with earning a livelihood, which calls for farsightedness, perseverance, strength, tolerance, coolness, planning ability, hard-heartedness, connivance, and the like—characteristics that women lack. Therefore, it is men who are equipped by nature to deal with "the tumult of life," and who can fight on the battlefield or manage the affairs of government and society.[88] A note at the end of the article offers some statistics on female physical inferiority, including the comment that "a man's brain weighs 100 grams more than a woman's." Bahonar summed up his evidence by saying that the "differences in physical structure are reflected in the mental capacities of the two sexes."[89]

Bahonar included in his recital of women's natural deficiencies and infirmities the assertion that "Islam considers men and women equal as far as the basic human rights are concerned."[90] However, one could predict that any human rights scheme that he might devise would be bound to relegate women to the subordinate status mandated by his sex stereotypes of female weakness and physical and mental inferiority. Indeed, although Bahonar proposed many ways that men and women share similar religious and moral obligations—for example, both have to pray, be faithful and obedient believers, command the good and prohibit the evil, keep their looks cast down, and accept punishment for crimes—the only rights that he actually lists that the two sexes share on an equal basis are the rights to own and use property and to inherit.[91]

We do not have such direct descriptions of the sex stereotypes that were on the minds of the authors of the Azhar draft constitution and the UIDHR, but in those documents we can see implicitly many similar prejudices regarding women. Like the other Islamic human rights schemes, rather than serving the CEDAW goals of dismantling discrimination and eliminating stereotypical ideas of the different roles of men and women, they provide Islamic rationales for maintaining discrimination.

Because the Islamic legal tradition developed in traditional, patriarchal milieus and because the authoritative works on the legal status of women in Islam have been exclusively written by men, it is not surprising that male stereotypes of women were incorporated by that tradition and that they have been retained as part of Islamic rights schemes. However, there is very little in the original Islamic sources that supports these stereotypes, and there is, moreover, nothing distinctively Islamic about the self-interested and biased appraisals of women's characteristics that they offer. Even an example like the Saudi ban on women driving, which is currently associated with conservative Islamic precepts, has historical counterparts in the efforts once made by men in the United States to exploit sex stereotyping to justify preventing women from driving.[92]

In fact, the sex stereotyping that one sees in the Islamic tradition resembles very closely that developed in other contexts, such as in a variety of Christian faiths. For example, it is evident in the Catholic Church, only one of the many denominations where sex stereotyping was used to support the insistence of the exponents of Church doctrine—all males—to the effect that women had to be kept subjugated due to their "natural" inferiority to men. It is not a coincidence that Catholic theologians, having stereotyped women in much the same way that Muslim jurists had, developed a similar set of rules discriminating against women and restricting their freedom and opportunities. To be reminded that sex stereotyping has common features that can be projected into very dissimilar religious traditions, one should briefly consider aspects of the Christian tradition. Among the characteristics that the Church Fathers attributed to women were fickleness, shallowness, garrulousness, weakness, slowness of understanding, and instability of mind.[93] Saint Augustine asserted that in comparison with men, women were small of intellect.[94] Two priests, in a book designed to persuade Catholic women that, due to their sex, their "entire psychology is founded upon the primordial tendency to love," asserted that a woman's brain "is generally lighter and simpler than man's."[95]

Pope Pius XII in 1945, in a public speech to women, described "the sensibility and delicacy of feeling peculiar to woman, which might tempt her to be swayed by emotions and thus blur the clearness and breadth of her view and be detrimental to the calm consideration of future consequences."[96] He asserted that as a result of their characteristics, women were suited for tasks in life that called for "tact, delicate feelings, and maternal instinct, rather than administrative rigidity."[97] A Jesuit theologian who offered an outline of a divine plan for women asserted in the course of his discussion on the nature of a woman: "She has not lost the dispositions of impressionability and mobility which Eve had manifested in the initial drama of humanity. She remains fragile, more subject to an unreflected impulse, and more accessible to seduction."[98]

As a major feminist critic of Catholic doctrine has pointed out, the sex-role stereotypes upheld and disseminated by men in the Church hierarchy became closely intertwined with the Catholic teachings calling for the subordination of women, because "the very emancipation which would prove that women were not 'naturally' defective was denied them in the name of that defectiveness which was claimed to be natural and divinely ordained."[99]

The same nexus between culture-bound presuppositions about inherent female characteristics and religious doctrine exists in the Islamic tradition. As in the case of sex stereotypes that have been ascribed to religious authority in the West, the question remains whether the sex stereotypes associated with Islamic doctrine really have support in the Islamic sources or are only being read into them by biased interpreters.

Stances of Muslim Countries
at International Rights Conferences

Given the basic similarity between Vatican views and conservative Muslims' positions regarding women's rights, it was no surprise when the Vatican and some conservative Catholic countries made common cause with the Islamic bloc that emerged in two important conferences involving women's rights. In resisting proposals for expanding women's international human rights at the 1994 International Conference on Population and Development in Cairo and the 1995 Fourth World Conference on Women in Beijing, Muslim conservatives found that they had Catholic allies.

The Cairo conference was meant to address issues such as overpopulation and human development; conference participants envisaged advancing women's equality and empowerment and supporting women's right to control their sexuality and fertility. Opponents of the conference argued that such an agenda would destabilize the family and promote immorality. Several Muslim countries, including Saudi Arabia and the Sudan, boycotted the Cairo conference. Egypt, Iran, and Pakistan collaborated in insisting that they had to place Islamic law first and in criticizing the idea that the individual possessed rights in sexual matters.[100] Muslim countries were instrumental in securing a pledge that the implementation of the conference document should be consistent with "full respect for the various religious and ethical values and cultural backgrounds."[101] Iran's head delegate announced his pleasure over Iran's success in obtaining the concession to religious values and in establishing the basis for cooperation with the Vatican "in the defence of religious and spiritual values."[102] Muslim countries at this conference were associated with a policy of upholding cultural particularism at the expense of universal human rights and subordinating women's rights to local cultures and religious values, but this policy was far from being uniquely associated with the defense of Islam.

So sinister did the idea of a conference devoted to women's international human rights appear to Muslim conservatives that some states refused to allow official delegations to attend the 1995 Beijing conference. For example, the government of then President Borhanoddin Rabbani of Afghanistan barred the Afghan delegation from attending, saying that the issues being discussed at the conference were against basic Islamic principles.[103] Saudi Arabia boycotted the conference on the grounds that it was un-Islamic.[104]

Although the Vatican and some Catholic countries worked against the feminist agenda in Beijing, the most salient challenges to controversial feminist initiatives in the Platform for Action came from Muslim countries.[105] Some of the specific reservations to the platform were explained on the grounds that provisions actually or potentially violated Islamic law; other reservations indicated that Muslim countries were agreeing to provisions only to the extent that they did not violate Islamic law. Among the principles that Muslim countries were disposed to object to were the calls for states to take action to ensure respect for women's human rights and provisions relating to reproductive health, autonomy in decisions relating to reproduction, and women's right to control their own sexuality. They also rejected the ideas that abortion should be safe in countries where it was not illegal and that states should enact legislation guaranteeing equal rights of inheritance.[106]

Iran's head delegate announced that Iran would not implement any conference proposals that conflicted with its Islamic view of the role of women.[107] She also emphasized women's role as the pillar of the family and complained that the conference was not sufficiently emphasizing the role of the mother.[108] In effect, she indicated that Iran's official Islamic ideology was to override any conflicting human rights for women, and women's roles within the family and as mothers were to be prioritized, a practice that has typically correlated with official policies restricting women's role.

The official Sudanese women's delegation at Beijing objected to the call for eliminating violence against women, which consisted of physical, sexual, and psychological violence in the family and female genital mutilation, and also to a call for governments to "condemn violence against women and refrain from invoking any custom, tradition or religious consideration" to avoid their obligations under CEDAW.[109] Since the Bashir regime has not defended female genital mutilation, a common practice in the Sudan, it seems likely that these objections rested on a desire to defend rules of the premodern *shari'a*, which does not recognize marital rape and allows husbands to beat their wives. This stance would correlate with other policies on women's rights adopted under Bashir, which have tended to treat women as wards subject to male tutelage and control, much as women were viewed by the premodern jurists.

Thus, both in Cairo and Beijing, the conduct and statements by some Muslim countries indicated that they were insisting on upholding the primacy of religion and culture at the expense of women's human rights. They were also indicating in various ways that they were unprepared to accept the notion that women should be autonomous individuals meriting equality in liberty. One sees in these examples how the treatment of women's rights in the Islamic human rights schemes reviewed here correlates with the positions formally endorsed by Muslim countries in international forums; according to these positions, Islam precludes Muslim women from enjoying the rights to which they are entitled under international law.

CHAPTER 7

Islamic Human Rights Schemes and Non-Muslims

The Treatment of Religious Minorities in Muslim Countries

The issue of the rights of non-Muslim minorities in the Middle East has a peculiar historical background that casts a shadow over any discussion by a Western observer. Critical assessments of the use of Islam as a rationale for discriminatory treatment of non-Muslims are likely to be interpreted as being prompted by Western neocolonialist politics or Orientalist biases. The historical background is summarized here in an attempt to show that important distinctions should be made between the past, when imperialist campaigns were aimed at undermining the sovereignty of Muslim countries by exploiting the issue of their treatment of non-Muslim minorities, and the present, when calling for respect for international human rights law has—or should have—different connotations.

For centuries, the status of non-Muslims in the Middle East was determined by *shari'a* law. At the time of the growth of European commercial connections with the Ottoman Empire, European powers were able to wrest concessions from the Ottomans for their own citizens, who were given extraterritorial status. In response to European pressures, the Ottoman sultans promulgated special edicts in 1839 and 1856 that formally granted equality to non-Muslim Ottoman citizens.[1] In the nineteenth century, European powers with political ambitions in the Middle East appointed themselves the protectors of the various local Christian minorities, and Europeans began to monitor aggressively the treatment of non-Muslims, using allegations of mistreatment of non-Muslims as a pretext for interfering in Middle Eastern politics.

The treatment of non-Muslims thus became a bone of contention between Middle Eastern governments and European countries with imperialist ambitions. Where Europeans dominated Middle Eastern societies, they inevitably favored non-Muslim minorities, the most important instance being Great Britain's use of its mandate over Palestine to foster the development of a Jewish homeland.[2] In addition to according privileged treatment to the non-Muslim segment of the population, Europeans invoked the need to protect non-Muslims from oppression by the Muslim majorities as a rationale for their rule.[3] Since European powers were notably lacking in sympathy for the aspirations for freedom on the part of Muslim Middle Easterners, European expressions of solicitude for non-Muslims naturally became associated with hypocrisy and selfish political ambitions. Christian missionary activities in the Middle East, which flourished when the region was under European domination, suggested that there was a Christian plot to undermine Islam. In this context, European expressions of concern for the rights of non-Muslims could not be severed from the political agendas of the European powers.

Eventually, Middle Eastern countries became independent of European domination. In most cases this happened in the wake of World War II. Many members of non-Muslim minority communities then emigrated from the newly independent states. The old Christian communities of Egypt, Syria, and the Levant largely stayed behind, but overall the proportion of non-Muslims in the Middle East dwindled, leaving relatively few people who today are affected by *shari'a* rules governing the treatment of non-Muslims.

Events since World War II, in particular the strong Western support for Israel, have tended to exacerbate Muslim resentment and suspicion of Western policies concerning non-Muslim minorities. Muslims were aggrieved that the former colonialist powers par excellence, Britain and France, ignored the right of self-determination of the native Palestinian population in order to accommodate the remnants of a Jewish community long persecuted by European Christians. This disregard for the right of Palestinian self-determination and the strong U.S. support for Israel has reinforced the impression that there is a link between neocolonialist designs and Western powers' support for religious minorities in the Middle East. The latter are seen as pawns in U.S. strategies that aim to oppress and exploit the largely Muslim population of the region, goals that entail dismantling Islamic law.[4]

Muslims tend to view any discussion of the status of non-Muslims in the contemporary Middle East in relation to this particular historical background. Muslim resentment has been exacerbated by the callous indifference shown by the United States and western Europe to the atrocities and genocide in Bosnia, which decimated and martyred Bosnia's Muslim population. Given this background, any critical evaluations of *shari'a* standards for the treatment of religious minorities are bound to provoke negative reactions.

Suspicions of U.S. designs will only be aggravated by measures like the Freedom from Religious Persecution Act, considered by the U.S. Congress in 1997–1998. Under the bill, significant abuses against religious minorities would trigger automatic U.S. sanctions against offending countries.[5] Although concerns for minorities like Baha'is and Buddhists were belatedly included—apparently with the aim of avoiding charges of sectarian bias— the original focus was clearly meant to be on anti-Christian persecution, which is not surprising, given that Christian groups were the prime advocates of the initiative.[6] Although some countries like China are included in the list of putative offenders, there has been sufficient initial targeting of Middle Eastern countries to provoke anger and wariness in the region. This bill has been spearheaded by a coalition of politicians and lobbyists apparently seeking to curry favor with and build bridges to certain domestic constituencies, notably the religious Right.

Not surprisingly, this bill has been criticized by human rights nongovernmental organizations, who see in its privileging of religious freedom a threat to the overall integrity of the human rights system. Persons genuinely concerned for the well-being of beleaguered Christian minorities grasp that associating calls for improvement in their status with aggressive U.S. intervention on their behalf can only aggravate suspicions that local Christians are pawns in a neoimperialist plot—which is hardly likely to ameliorate their present difficulties. If the United States, which already stands accused of having a neoimperialist strategy and using gross double standards in its approach to Middle Eastern human rights issues, espouses the cause of Christian minorities in the same fashion that Britain, France and Russia once did, this will only heighten Muslims' inclination to believe that Western professions of concern about human rights violations affecting religious minorities are a cynical cover for a superpower agenda that is nefarious for the sovereignty of Middle Eastern countries. In the long run, such measures can only tarnish the prestige of human rights and diminish the effectiveness of groups working to advance the cause of human rights in the region.

Leaving aside ill-judged governmental initiatives like the proposed Freedom from Religious Persecution Act, the implications of criticizing the rights accorded non-Muslims in Islamic human rights schemes are in general different from the implications of Western criticisms of the treatment of non-Muslims in the nineteenth century. Independent Muslim countries have themselves imported constitutional models from the West and have adopted twentieth-century concepts of citizenship designed for application in the modern nation-state. According to these models, discrimination based on religion should be prohibited. Proponents of Islamization who demand the adoption of Islamic forms of government and the imposition of laws discriminating against non-Muslims have to combat other political factions inside their own societies that favor respecting modern norms of citizenship and constitutional equality guarantees.

Furthermore, the significance of *shari'a* rules for religious minorities is changing. Islamization has particularly serious implications for the rights of non-Muslims, but it also has implications for dissidents and nonconformists who consider themselves Muslims but whose ideas offend the version of Islam endorsed by governments and allied religious establishments. Such persons can wind up being reclassified as non-Muslims or heretics. That is, the rules for the treatment of religious minorities are relevant not just for persons who are avowedly non-Muslim but also for persons within the Muslim community who run afoul of the version of Islam endorsed by the local arbiters of orthodoxy. In the light of these altered conditions, it is time to stop automatically associating critiques of the treatment of religious minorities under *shari'a* rules with neocolonialist mentalities and objectives.

International Standards Prohibiting Religious Discrimination

Just as it is not permissible under international human rights norms to deny people equal protection of the law or to discriminate against them on the basis of sex, so it is not permissible to do so on the basis of religion. This principle is enshrined in the Universal Declaration of Human Rights (UDHR) in Article 2, and in the International Covenant on Civil and Political Rights (ICCPR) in Articles 2 and 26. More recently, the Declaration on the Elimination of All Forms of Intolerance and of Discrimination Based on Religion or Belief, proclaimed by the UN General Assembly on November 25, 1981, reaffirmed this principle in Article 2, elaborating on it in Article 2.2 to define impermissible discrimination as "any distinction, exclusion, restriction or preference based on religion or belief and having as its purpose or as its effect nullification or impairment of the recognition, enjoyment or exercise of human rights or fundamental freedoms on an equal basis."

Article 4.1 requires all states to take effective measures to prevent and eliminate discrimination on the grounds of religion. Article 4.2 calls on governments to take affirmative steps to dismantle patterns of discrimination and eliminate religious prejudice: "All States shall make all efforts to enact or rescind legislation where necessary to prohibit any such discrimination, and to take all appropriate measures to combat intolerance on the grounds of religion or belief in this matter."

Shari'a Law and the Rights of Non-Muslims

The premodern *shari'a* rules affecting the status of non-Muslims were formulated by Islamic jurists at an early stage of the history of the Islamic community and reflect the circumstances of that era. The nascent community was weak and beleaguered, faced with the difficult task of absorbing non-Muslim communities in newly won territories while having to meet the military threat of powerful non-Muslim foes.[7] The jihad, or Islamic holy war, was undertaken both to expand the territory subject to Muslim control and to spread the Islamic religion.[8] However, contrary to Western images of Muslim conquerors presenting the conquered peoples with a choice of conversion to Islam or the sword, conquered Christians and Jews were allowed to persist in their beliefs. In Islam, Christians and Jews are regarded as the recipients of earlier divine revelations, which were deemed to have culminated in God's final Revelation to the Prophet Muhammad. Christians and Jews are known as *ahl al-kitab,* or people of the book, an indication of Islamic respect for their scriptures.

Although the premodern doctrines of jihad remain part of the Islamic cultural legacy and jihad may be proclaimed in a variety of military and political contexts by contemporary leaders, conducting holy war is obviously incompatible with the modern scheme of relations between nation-states. Muslim governments know that under international law they cannot invoke religious doctrines to justify military campaigns to conquer the non-Muslim world. In practice, many of the premodern doctrines regarding jihad and treatment of non-Muslims have been discarded, having been recognized as anachronisms in present circumstances, in which the Muslim community has burgeoned to over 1 billion adherents and its existence is no longer threatened.[9] A few aspects of the *shari'a* that do remain relevant for the status of non-Muslims will be summarized here.

In the early Islamic conquests, numerous Christian and Jewish communities refused to embrace Islam as the culmination and perfection of their own faiths. A major concern of the leaders of the new Islamic community became how to treat the Christians and Jews who continued in their old beliefs.[10] Jews and Christians ruled by Muslims had the political status of *dhimmis,* being accorded toleration in return for submitting to Muslim rule and accepting a number of conditions governing their conduct.[11] *Dhimmis* had to pay a special capitation tax known as the *jizya* and were excluded from serving in the military, since, as non-Muslims, they could not be expected to fight in holy wars on behalf of Islam. Depending on the jurists' opinions, *dhimmis* could be either excluded from serving in government altogether or excluded only from high government positions. Although they were generally subject to *shari'a* law, *dhimmis* were allowed to follow their own rules of personal status, except in cases where persons of different faiths interacted, especially when one party was a Muslim.[12]

In theory, other faiths were not tolerated. In premodern *shari'a* doctrine, non-Muslims who were not Christian or Jewish were categorized as polytheists or unbelievers. When conquered by Muslims, they theoretically either had to embrace Islam or accept death.[13] In practice, as Islam expanded eastward, the premodern doctrines had to be adjusted and Muslims had to learn to coexist with Hindus and other polytheists.[14]

Despite incidents of mistreatment of non-Muslims, it is fair to say that the Muslim world, when judged by the standards of the day and the European record, generally showed far greater tolerance and humanity in its treatment of religious minorities.[15] In particular, the treatment of the Jewish minority in Muslim societies stands out as fair and enlightened when compared with the dismal record of Christian European persecution of Jews over the centuries.[16]

With the rise of secular nationalism in the Muslim world in the nineteenth century, it seemed that the significance of distinctions between Muslim and non-Muslim was destined to diminish.[17] Although the *shariʿa* prohibitions affecting intermarriage persisted and most Muslim countries retained the legal requirement that the chief of state be Muslim, in many respects non-Muslims gained the status of citizenship on a par with Muslims.

Today, as the influence of secular nationalism has waned and the influence of Islam as a political ideology is mounting, issues of the status of non-Muslims that seemed closed have recently been reopened.[18] Proponents of Islamization are calling for reinstating rules on *dhimmi* status in contemporary Middle Eastern societies. For example, a leader of the Egyptian Muslim Brotherhood in April 1997 announced that Egypt's Coptic Christians should be excluded from the army and posts related to national defense and that they should also pay the *jizya*, a symbol of subjugation to Muslim rule. Although Copts have a long history of patriotic commitment to Egyptian independence, the Muslim Brotherhood leader claimed they could become enemy agents if an Egyptian Islamic state were attacked.[19] So fierce were the attacks by other Egyptians on the author of these remarks that he felt obliged to back down and deny ever having made them.

The kind of robust, vigorous advocacy of feminist ideas that one commonly encounters within the Islamic tradition today is not matched when one moves to the topic of equal rights for non-Muslims. Still, one finds Muslims representing a variety of currents of Islamic thought who have taken the position that Islam can accommodate equal treatment for non-Muslims. For example, the Lebanese scholar Subhi Mahmassani argued in his work on Islam and human rights that there can be no discrimination based on religion in an Islamic system.[20] His approach basically seems to assume that there must be harmony between Islam and international law, which entails tacitly suppressing or discarding any features of the *shariʿa* that would be incongruous in the scheme of international human rights. Mahmassani places great emphasis on aspects of the original sources and examples from early Islamic history that demonstrate the tolerant and egalitarian strains that have from the beginning constituted important components of the Islamic tradition.[21]

The conviction that there must be a natural affinity between Islam and the tenets of international human rights law has led other Muslims as well to embrace the principle that full equality for all citizens is compatible with Islam.[22] Sometimes arguments justifying this conclusion seem to be relegated to an afterthought. For example, the Egyptian political theorist Tariq al-Bishri, concerned with the status of Egypt's Copts and insisting that they should enjoy equality, has called on specialists to reconcile this equality with Islamic law but has expressed confidence that in a tradition as flexible and egalitarian as the Islamic one this should present no great problem.[23] However, he has also examined the implications of the political changes in the Muslim world that are relevant for evaluating whether the premodern *shari'a* rules remain applicable. Al-Bishri noted that the nature of the modern state is so different from the kind of government envisaged by medieval Islamic theorists that the *shari'a* restrictions on non-Muslims holding high political office no longer logically apply.[24] The interpretations of Islamic law that have been offered by Abdullahi An-Na'im show much more concern than al-Bishri's for establishing the methodological basis for the belief that Islam allows absolute equality of Muslim and non-Muslim.[25] An-Na'im's system is based on the teaching of the late Mahmud Muhammad Taha, who said that the applicability of legal rules in various Qur'anic verses must be rethought. By distinguishing verses that were meant to govern the early Islamic community from those that were meant to have enduring validity, Taha was able to derive Islamic human rights principles that abolish the status of *dhimmis* and mandate an end to all discrimination on a religious basis.[26]

Against such persons are arrayed Muslim conservatives like Sultanhussein Tabandeh and Abu'l A'la Mawdudi, who want either to preserve or revive discriminatory *shari'a* rules affecting non-Muslims. Even where the Islamic human rights schemes reviewed here do not expressly advocate assigning non-Muslims to an inferior position, they have been deliberately drafted so as to accommodate the continued application of discriminatory rules from the premodern *shari'a*. Whereas Islamic human rights schemes envisage that non-Muslims will continue to be governed by the *shari'a*, international human rights law assumes that a neutral, nondiscriminatory law will be applied to all citizens of a country, not accepting that a person's rights can be denied by reason of discriminatory religious laws.[27] However, with the exception of Tabandeh, the authors of these human rights schemes formulate their provisions regarding non-Muslims in such a manner that their intention to discriminate against non-Muslims will not be too obvious. That is, as with their evasive treatments of the status of women, they are reluctant to state forthrightly that they refuse to endorse the principle of equality as understood in international law.

Tabandeh's Ideas

Sultanhussein Tabandeh demonstrated a rare candor in his willingness to concede that, according to his conception, the *shari'a* precludes equality between Muslims and non-Muslims. In commenting on the UDHR Article 1 guarantee of equality, Tabandeh insisted that the principle of equality does not apply when it comes to differences of religion, faith, or conviction. This is because "nobility, excellence and virtue consist in true worship of the One God and obedience to the commandments of Heaven." According to Tabandeh, the *ahl al-kitab* deserve respect because of their belief, but "since their faith has not reached the highest level of spirituality, but obeys commands which we believe to have been abrogated, and puts other laws in place of these revealed through Islam by the means of the Prophet and most righteous Judge, therefore [the *shari'a*] makes certain difference between them and Muslims, treating them as not on the same level."28

For those non-Muslims who are not *ahl al-kitab,* he has only contempt. Humanists, he said, are "the gangrenous members of the body politic,"29 and those who have not accepted the one God are "outside the pale of humanity."30 Given his attitudes, Tabandeh naturally cannot concede that persons in the latter categories are deserving of any human rights protections. The view that non-Muslims who are not among the *ahl al-kitab* are not entitled to the status of legal persons is common among Muslim conservatives. This idea corresponds to features of the premodern *shari'a,* but it leads to a sharp conflict with international human rights, which do not recognize that a person may be denied legal personality because of religion or belief. The ICCPR says in Article 16 that everyone has a right to recognition everywhere as a person before the law.

Tabandeh's conviction that the polytheist must be treated as a nonperson also comes up in comments regarding the issue of intermarriage. He insisted on preserving the premodern *shari'a* rules that absolutely prohibit marriage with polytheists.31 He is equally adamant about preserving the premodern *shari'a* rule that prevents a Muslim woman from marrying a Christian or Jew, while allowing a Muslim man to marry a woman from those faiths.32 According to Tabandeh, a marriage between a Muslim woman and a non-Muslim man is invalid and any child born of such a marriage is illegitimate; moreover, if the woman knew before her marriage that the man she was marrying was a non-Muslim, she must be punished.33

It is at this point in Tabandeh's argument that one sees how the inferior status of women and the inferior status of non-Muslims are linked—a linkage that is made by many Muslim conservatives. Tabandeh argued:

The scripture says: "Men are guardians of women and guarantors of their rights" [Qur'an 4:34]. The wife must obey her husband. But, if she weds a non-Muslim husband it means that she as a Muslim is subordinating herself: and Islam never allows a Muslim to come under the authority of a non-Muslim in any circumstance at all, as is made perfectly plain in "God will never make a way for infidels (to exercise lordship) over believers" [Qur'an 4:41]:

and therefore He never granted permission that Muslims should by marriage voluntarily subordinate themselves to non-Muslims. . . . In Islam every distinction is abolished except the distinction of religion and faith; whence it follows that Islam and its peoples must be above infidels, and never permit non-Muslims to acquire lordship over them.[34]

Here one consequence of the anti-individualistic approach taken by Muslim conservatives is apparent: The rights of the individual man and woman who wish to marry despite religious differences are totally absent from Tabandeh's concerns. Instead of the concern that one finds in international human rights law for the freedom of the individuals involved, the concern is for the prestige of the Muslim community, the honor of which is sullied if one of its members is subordinated to a member of the inferior group, the non-Muslims. The assumption is that, just as Muslims are placed above non-Muslims, so men are placed above women, meaning that wives are necessarily subordinated to their husbands. Therefore, the Muslim man who marries a female *dhimmi* does not infringe the hierarchy of status, since by virtue of her sex the non-Muslim wife will be subordinate to her husband, who as a Muslim and a male ranks above her on two counts. In contrast, the Muslim woman who marries a *dhimmi* violates the rules of status, since as a wife she has lower status than the man to whom she is married even though by virtue of her adherence to the Islamic religion she should rank above him. These *shariʿa* rules regarding marriage have the effect of allowing Muslim men to exercise the powers that they enjoy as husbands both over their own women and *dhimmi* women, while allowing *dhimmi* men to exercise their marital prerogatives solely over women who are likewise relegated to *dhimmi* status.

On the questions of political rights and freedom of expression, Tabandeh is opposed to according to non-Muslims rights that are guaranteed by international human rights standards. Non-Muslims, he said, must be entirely excluded from the judiciary, the legislature, and the cabinet.[35] Furthermore, no "propaganda" for any non-Muslim religion may be allowed.[36]

The UIDHR

The disposition of the authors of the Universal Islamic Declaration of Human Rights (UIDHR) to evade hard questions regarding the compatibility of *shariʿa* rules with international human rights law has already been established. Where the status of non-Muslims is concerned, the authors of the UIDHR are much less forthright than Tabandeh in spelling out the specifics of the discriminatory rules that they mean to apply.

The UIDHR addresses the situation of non-Muslims in Article 10. This article does not guarantee equal treatment for religious minorities or state that discrimination based on religion is impermissible. It provides in Article 10.a that the religious rights of non-Muslim minorities are governed by the principle that there is no compulsion in religion, which is based on the Qur'an 2:256. The traditional interpretation of this verse is that *dhimmis* should not be forced to convert to Islam. In contrast, it has not traditionally been interpreted to mean that the prohibition against compulsion in religion precludes *dhimmis* or other non-Muslims from being subjected to discrimination based on their religion.

What the UIDHR seems to contemplate is the use of the *millet* system that flourished under the Ottoman Empire, in which the various non-Muslim communities were governed under their own religious laws in internal matters and lawsuits involving members of the same faith while they were subject to the *shari'a* in mixed cases and in all other matters. In most Muslim countries today, remnants of this system persist, since personal-status matters remain for the most part governed by the religious law of the parties involved.

In the English version of Article 10.b, "religious minorities" are given the right to be governed either by Islamic law or by their own laws on personal-status or civil matters. Not limited in terms to Christians and Jews, Article 10.b appears to go beyond the premodern *shari'a* rules, which gave only *dhimmis* the right to be judged under their own law. The article seems to allow all non-Muslims to follow their own laws in personal or civil matters. However, the Arabic version of the same provision resurrects the old distinction between Christians and Jews on the one hand and other non-Muslims on the other, suggesting that only members of the *ahl al-kitab* enjoy this right. In a peculiar formulation, the Arabic version of Article 10.b provides that non-Muslims may appeal to Muslims for judgment, but that if they do not do so, they must follow their own laws, provided that they (seemingly, the non-Muslims) believe that the latter are of divine origin. This would seem to mean that where non-Muslims did not elect to be governed by the *shari'a,* their subjective convictions that the laws of their own communities were divinely inspired would mean that their laws would be controlling. However, the references in the same provision to the Qur'an 5:47, dealing with people of the Gospel, and 5:42, dealing with the followers of the Torah, give reason to believe that this right of religious minorities to be bound by their own religious rules actually pertains only to Christian and Jewish minorities. That is, as in the premodern *shari'a,* no provision is made allowing non-Muslims who are not Christians or Jews to follow their own religious law in civil and personal-status matters among members of their own communities. This leaves open the question as to what status is contemplated for such non-Muslims, who under the *shari'a* were considered nonpersons.

In another article, the UIDHR echoes an idea put forth by Mawdudi in his human rights pamphlet saying that Muslims must show respect for the feelings of non-Muslims. Mawdudi stated that Islam does not allow Muslims to use abusive language that may injure the religious feelings of non-Muslims.[37] The UIDHR says in Article 12.e that no one shall hold in contempt or ridicule the religious beliefs of others. Both of these principles seem to be ethico-moral injunctions rather than enforceable legal rights. Again, as frequently happens, Islamic human rights schemes are not directed against laws or governmental action, which are the most pervasive causes of infringements of liberty, but against private individuals, whose actions are less likely to have as great an impact on non-Muslims as discriminatory laws and governmental policies.

Article 12.e of the UIDHR elaborates on this idea, saying that "people" should not incite hostility toward non-Muslims. This is a laudable ethico-moral precept, and the Islamic Council is performing a valuable public service by taking a stance condemning such incitement, which, in the volatile Middle Eastern setting, can be a prelude to violence. However, for this principle to have teeth—and legal force—further definition of what constitutes such impermissible incitement to violence would be required. As the UIDHR now stands, it lays down no guidelines for enforcing this principle. All speech is allowed within the limits of the *shari'a*, according to Article 12.a, a standard that is far too vague to determine what kinds of speech would constitute unacceptable incitement to public hostility toward non-Muslims.[38]

The Iranian Constitution

The article of the Iranian Constitution dealing with religious minorities seems to contemplate a model similar to the *millet* system, where there are two categories of persons, Muslims and the *ahl al-kitab*, which Iran deems should include Zoroastrians. With emphasis added, Article 13 provides: "Zoroastrian, Jewish, and Christian Iranians are the *only* recognized religious minorities, who, within the limits of the law *[dar hodud-e qanun]*, are free to perform their religious rites and ceremonies, and to act according to their own canon in matters of personal affairs and religious education."[39]

That is, aside from acts of religious observance and personal status matters, the *ahl al-kitab* are to be governed by Iranian laws. As has already been discussed, Iranian laws are subordinate to Islamic law, which, under Article 4 of the constitution, is treated as the norm to which all laws must conform. This means that the *ahl al-kitab* will be subject to discriminatory laws. The nonrecognition of religious minorities other than the *ahl al-kitab* in this *shari'a*-based system means that these other minorities can claim no constitutional protections. The problems of non-Muslims who are not accorded the status of recognized minorities will be discussed after a review of the implications of constitutional provisions for the rights of recognized minorities.

The disabilities imposed on non-Muslims under the postrevolutionary regime have been severe, in many instances going beyond those that would be required under the premodern *shariʿa*. Since in the postrevolutionary Iranian environment Islam is interpreted to be an ideology—much as communism was in the East Bloc countries—the fact that non-Muslims are persons who by definition do not subscribe to the official Islamic ideology of Iran has provided additional grounds for discriminating against them. Iran has imposed tests of ideological purity on applicants for public employment that effectively exclude non-Muslims.[40] Of course, Muslims who oppose the peculiar ideologized version of Islam that is sponsored by the regime have also been excluded.

Mawdudi, who believed that Islam must be the official ideology of Muslim countries, had a similar attitude. Although he did not discuss this in his human rights pamphlet, elsewhere he indicated that he considered discrimination against persons who did not share a state's official Islamic ideology perfectly reasonable.[41] However, as a committed Sunni, Mawdudi would hardly have been pleased by the consequences of Iran's ideologization of Shiʿism, which has led to a pattern of discrimination and even persecution directed against Sunni Muslims. Members of Iran's ethnic minorities are largely Sunnis, which means that these Sunnis may suffer discrimination and abuse on combined ethnic and religious grounds. Since the revolution, Iran has been castigated for mistreating its Sunni minorities, and several prominent Sunni figures have been executed or have died in suspicious circumstances.[42] This pattern turns out to be a mirror image of trends in neighboring Pakistan in the wake of the Islamization program of Muhammad Zia ul-Haq, which had a strong pro-Sunni bias. Pakistan's large Shiʿi minority has become increasingly beleaguered and subjected to threats and assaults, and lethal sectarian violence has frequently broken out. A militant Sunni group has campaigned for laws that would stigmatize Shiʿis and has called for declaring Pakistan a Sunni state, just as Iran has been declared a Shiʿi state.[43] When a state imposes an ideologized version of Islam, Muslims who dissent from this version may be effectively relegated to a subcategory where they are exposed to discrimination similar to that meted out to non-Muslims and where they are subjected to mistreatment that may at times be even be more severe, because the regime may feel directly threatened by their challenges to the official orthodoxy.

An example of the consequences of ideologization of Islam can be seen in the Iranian Constitution. There is an ideological test for those who wish to serve in the Iranian military. A close reading of Article 144 reveals that non-Muslims will be excluded from the military, just as *dhimmis* were in premodern Islamic civilization. The article provides: "The Army of the Islamic Republic of Iran must be an Islamic Army, i.e., committed to Islamic ideology and the people, and must recruit into its service individuals who have faith in the objectives of the Islamic Revolution and are devoted to the cause of realizing its goals." Obviously, Iran's non-Muslim minorities will have no place in an Islamic army set up under these criteria.[44]

Article 14 of the Iranian Constitution provides in part: "The government of the Islamic Republic of Iran and all Muslims are duty-bound to treat non-Muslims in conformity with ethical norms and the principles of Islamic justice and equity, and to respect their human rights [*hoquq-e ensani*]. This principle applies to all who refrain from engaging in conspiracy or activity against Islam and the Islamic Republic of Iran." Here, following "Islamic justice" entails qualifying non-Muslims' rights via the application of *shari'a* law. Far from granting non-Muslims protections for the rights to which they are entitled under international law, the constitution reinforces the principle that all rights are subject to *shari'a* qualifications.

In addition, Article 14 provides that the human rights that non-Muslims enjoy, which one may assume will be very limited to begin with, are to be forfeited if the non-Muslims become involved in activity against the Islamic Republic, a vague standard affording a broad range of potential justifications for curbing their rights. It is interesting that this article provides special grounds for depriving non-Muslims of human rights, even though there is already a general provision in Article 26 that enables the government to curb the activities of groups, including "minority religious associations," if they are "contrary to the principles of Islam or the Islamic Republic." Article 14 seems to contemplate even more extensive deprivations of human rights than those involved in the curbs placed on the freedom of association by Article 26. Taken together, they betoken a suspicion on the part of the drafters of the constitution that non-Muslims are likely to be disposed to oppose Iran's Islamic Republic. Of course, given the Islamic bias in the system, such opposition would only be natural.

Although Iran denies Jews, Christians, and Zoroastrians many rights, the latter are distinctly better off than other non-Muslims who do not qualify as *ahl al-kitab*. The exclusion from the Article 13 status of "recognized minorities" was particularly ominous for Iran's Baha'is.

The Baha'i religion, sometimes called Babism, originated in Iran in the nineteenth century. It is named after one Baha'ullah, who in 1863 announced that he was a messenger from God and espoused liberal and ecumenical teachings. It teaches veneration for the founders of all the major world religions and insists on the brotherhood and equality of all persons, stressing that men and women are meant to be equal. Baha'ism denies that clerics are needed as intermediaries in understanding religion, calling instead for universal education so that individuals can pursue the path of enlightenment. It also supports the idea of a world government and world peace.[45] Baha'i doctrines appealed to many of Iran's Muslims and led them to convert from Islam to the new faith.

In Iran, the position of the Baha'i community has always been precarious, and its members have suffered from periodic waves of persecution. From the beginning, Baha'ism has been perceived as a threat by Iran's clerics, and many of them have been violently hostile toward the religion. Shi'i clerics have, since the nineteenth century, supported attempts to eliminate Baha'ism from Iran through massacre, torture, intimidation, and discrimination.[46] This clerical animus had several grounds. Baha'ism challenged the doctrine of the finality of God's Revelation to the Prophet Muhammad. It aimed at winning converts from Islam in violation of the *shari'a* prohibition of any conversion away from Islam to another faith. Its egalitarian doctrines challenged the hierarchy of privilege mandated by the *shari'a,* according to which men were superior to women and Muslims superior to non-Muslims. Its members showed no inclination to defer to the views of Iran's clerics.

Given this long history of animosity toward the Baha'i community, which by the time of the Iranian Revolution may have numbered 200,000–300,000, it was natural that when Shi'i clerics achieved political dominance in the postrevolutionary regime, they would seek to eliminate Baha'ism once and for all. The government, sometimes acting directly and at other times indirectly through allied groups, has carried out a campaign of terror against Baha'is. They were fired from jobs, their property was confiscated, their homes were subject to invasion at any time by persons bent on harassment and plunder in the guise of investigating crimes, and they were murdered with impunity. Hundreds of Baha'is were arrested, imprisoned, and subjected to brutal torture, and Baha'i leaders were executed on a variety of trumped-up charges. In addition, their shrines and houses of worship were destroyed and desecrated, and all of their associations were forcibly disbanded. The widespread persecution of the Baha'is has been extensively documented by neutral observers and international human rights organizations.[47]

Embarrassed by the bad publicity that its discriminatory and cruel treatment of religious minorities has received, Iran has recently gone to some pains to improve its image. In efforts to establish that it is benignly disposed toward non-Muslims, the regime has elected to pose as the friend and protector of Armenian Christians, apparently hoping that this will win it credit with influential Armenians in the West.[48]

Mawdudi and Pakistan's Ahmadi Minority

Abu'l A'la Mawdudi's treatment of equality has already been indicated earlier in this chapter, but his vague, ambiguous position merits further examination in connection with his views on the rights of non-Muslims. Just as Mawdudi avoided detailing his views on women's rights in his human rights pamphlet, so he steered clear of any specifics on how the *shari'a* affects non-Muslims. He merely mentioned *dhimmis* in passing, saying that their lives and properties are as "sacred" as those of Muslims.[49]

However, his views on this subject are on record in other publications. Mawdudi advocated discrimination against non-Muslims. According to him, Muslims are to be accorded superiority over non-Muslims. He favored reinstating the *jizya* tax traditionally imposed on *dhimmis*,[50] excluding them from military service,[51] and eliminating them from high positions in government.[52] He asserted that Islam "does not permit them to meddle with the affairs of the State."[53] Because Mawdudi believed that Islamic law should control personal-status matters as long as one party is a Muslim,[54] he believed that the *shari'a* prohibitions regarding intermarriage should be retained. Thus, although Mawdudi did not follow Tabandeh in acknowledging in the course of his discussion of human rights in Islam that he supported a regime of discrimination against non-Muslims, his views are similar to Tabandeh's.

Mawdudi's Jama'at-i-Islami party was among the instigators of the Pakistani campaigns against the country's Ahmadi minority, who were later to be badly affected by Zia's Islamization program. The Ahmadi example demonstrates that in an era in which governments are adopting official versions of Islamic requirements as the law of the land, it is not just those who formally adhere to religions other than Islam who need to be concerned about their status in society; Muslims who adhere to minority sects or schools of thought may be demoted by governmental policy to the category of "non-Muslims." The treatment of the Ahmadi Muslim minority in Pakistan, which may number about 1 million, provides a good illustration of how this can happen.

The Ahmadi sect was founded by Mirza Ghulam Ahmad (d. 1908) in India. Ahmadis, their opponents charge, treat their founder as a prophet, thereby violating the Islamic doctrine of the finality of the Prophethood of Muhammad. Although Ahmadis fervently believe that they are Muslims, they are considered heretics by many other Muslims. For a variety of reasons, Mawdudi's followers in the Jama'at-i-Islami and the Ahmadis became bitter foes, and the Jama'at was implicated in the serious disturbances that resulted from their anti-Ahmadi agitation in the Punjab in 1953.[55] Mawdudi wrote an anti-Ahmadi tract and was even incarcerated after being convicted of playing a leading role in anti-Ahmadi agitation.

In a concession to anti-Ahmadi sentiment, Prime Minister Zulfikar Ali Bhutto amended the constitution in 1974 to declare the Ahmadis non-Muslims. President Zia, who was closely allied with the Jama'at, went further and in 1984 issued a decree, the "Anti-Islamic Activities of the Quadiani Group, Lahori Group and Ahmadis (Prohibition and Punishment) Ordinance XX of 1984," forbidding Ahmadis to "pose" as Muslims or to call their religion Islam, to use Islamic terminology, to use the Islamic call to prayer, to call their houses of worship mosques, and to preach or propagate their version of the faith—all prohibitions under sanction of criminal law.[56] Extensive criminal prosecutions of Ahmadis ensued.

There have been various challenges to Ordinance XX, the most important of which was decided in *Zaheeruddin v. State* when the Supreme Court rejected the Ahmadis' claim that the ordinance violated the constitutional guarantee of freedom of religion.[57] This case showed how using the legal system to endorse the persecution of a religious minority can lead to consequences that have ominous implications for rights and freedoms generally. A 1991 bill, the Enforcement of Shari'ah Act, had already proclaimed that the Qur'an and *sunna* were the supreme law of Pakistan and that law should be interpreted in the light of the *shari'a,* but the Court had initially resisted applying this principle to fundamental rights.[58] In *Zaheeruddin* the Supreme Court decided that the constitution itself was subject to "the Injunctions of Islam" and that fundamental rights should likewise be subordinated to Islamic criteria.[59] However, the Court never troubled to define what "the Injunctions of Islam" meant for rights protections, leaving this vague term open to being construed broadly enough to nullify rights altogether. That is, via this judicial precedent, the Court adopted the same position that one sees in Iran's constitution in Articles 4 and 20. Breaking with precedents that had upheld the supremacy of the constitution and safeguarded fundamental rights, the Court proceeded to rule that under Islamic law, Ordinance XX did not violate the constitutional guarantee of freedom of religion.

In the course of the decision, the Court treated Islam as if it were a trademarked commodity and as if the Ahmadis were guilty of an offense akin to trademark infringement in claiming to be Muslims when the government said that they were not. Although it did not expressly assert that Pakistan's government held the trademark, the opinion implied that Islam was the property of the government of Pakistan. If Islam belongs to the government and if the government has the discretion to set the Islamic criteria that determine rights, what protection remains for any Pakistani deprived of human rights under the rubric of applying the official version of Islamic law? It seems that it is not only Ahmadis who have reason to be concerned about the negative repercussions that this decision portends for human rights in Pakistan.

The Cairo Declaration, the Saudi Basic Law, and the Azhar Draft Constitution

Against the background of the prior Islamic rights schemes, one would expect that the Cairo Declaration, which duplicates so many of the flaws of its precursors, would also fail to ensure equality for non-Muslims. As I have already noted, there is no provision for equality in rights in the Cairo Declaration, even though the guarantee of equality in "basic human dignity" and "basic obligations and responsibilities" in Article 1(a) does prohibit discrimination in these respects on the grounds of religious belief. The Cairo Declaration will not protect religious minorities any more than it protected women from being denied rights established in international law, particularly in a system like the one that it envisages, in which all rights and freedoms are subject to the *shari'a*. There is a vague provision in Article 18(a) to the effect that everyone shall have the right to live in security for himself and his religion, his dependents, his honor, and his property. This provides no real protection for religious minorities against discrimination, as can be seen in Article 23(b), which imposes *shari'a* restrictions on the right to serve in public office, in effect allowing the use of religious criteria to exclude non-Muslims.

The Saudi Basic Law offers no protections whatsoever for the rights of non-Muslims. Virtually all Saudi citizens are Muslim, and Article 34 provides that the defense of the Islamic faith is a duty imposed on every citizen. There is no notion that other faiths should be protected. However, Muslims are not insulated from mistreatment. According to Saudi officialdom, Islam is Wahhabism, and members of the large Shi'i minority in Saudi Arabia are exposed to persecution, often being treated like heretics.[60] Non-Muslims, who are largely expatriates and exposed to discriminatory treatment on this score, continue to be bereft of legal protections against persecution and harassment. Because of the absence of any requirement for arrest warrants and the secrecy in which Saudi criminal proceedings are conducted, it is hard to ascertain which jailings and prosecutions of expatriates are based on discriminatory treatment because of alienage as opposed to religious affiliation. In the Saudi system, violations of human rights based on a person's religion can blend with and overlap with violations motivated by other factors. Thus, focusing on the failure to protect the religious freedom of non-Muslims to the exclusion of the much broader pattern of human rights abuses in the country would be to isolate a problem that is in reality inseparable from the context from which it emerged, which is a legal order where discrimination against minorities, repression of nonconformity, and violations of the civil and political rights of dissidents are pervasive.

In November 1997 Amnesty International published a catalogue of these and related ills and a denunciation of the Saudi criminal justice system as blatantly unfair from start to finish.[61] This and other negative publicity in the Western media, which had been making much of the detention and secret prosecutions of two British nurses for murder, prompted a riposte from the Saudi interior minister. He tried to shift the discussion away from the arbitrary and discriminatory features of Saudi justice by insinuating that Western criticisms of what he called "the Islamic judiciary" were motivated by animus toward Islam and *shari'a* law.[62] In reality the focus of Amnesty International was not on the practices required by Islamic law but problems such as the institutionalized practice of torture and the preponderance of persons from developing countries among defendants who were given the death penalty. As in other instances, accusations that criticisms of human rights abuses were prompted by anti-Islamic animus seemed to be leveled very cynically.

The Azhar draft constitution avoids dealing with the status of non-Muslims. In the context of a document that seems to support the general applicability of premodern *shari'a* rules, the failure to address the issue suggests that the intent was to retain discriminatory rules governing the status of non-Muslims.

Summary

The Islamic human rights schemes discussed here do not respect the requirements of international law regarding protections for the rights of religious minorities. In fact, to the extent that they deal with the question of the rights of religious minorities, they seem to endorse premodern *shari'a* rules that call for non-Muslims to be relegated to an inferior status if they qualify as members of the *ahl al-kitab* and for them to be treated as nonpersons if they do not qualify for such inclusion.

Not only does the record of the treatment of religious minorities in countries undergoing Islamization show that policies are being implemented that relegate religious minorities to second-class status, but the record also establishes that Middle Eastern regimes are in some instances ready to engage in actual campaigns of religious persecution directed at non-Muslims. Moreover, as indicated, regimes that are prepared to discriminate against their non-Muslim citizens tend to be equally ready to mistreat their Muslim minorities and Muslims who refuse to defer to their version of orthodoxy.

CHAPTER 8

Freedom of Religion in Islamic Human Rights Schemes

International Human Rights Law and the *Shari'a* Rule on Apostasy

In the West, people do not tend to think of the freedom to change religion as the central concern of provisions guaranteeing religious freedom. There, the right to freedom of religion is most often conceived of as a guarantee against religious persecution and protection from discriminatory treatment. Although religious discrimination was common in the West until recently, the concept of apostasy as a criminal offense has long vanished. In Muslim milieus the perspective is different, and the question of whether there should be freedom to convert remains relevant. Muslim attitudes are still influenced by the *shari'a* rule prohibiting conversion from Islam, and the transformation of Islam into state ideologies has encouraged the equation of abandoning Islam with treason.

Under the interpretations of the premodern jurists, apostates were to be given an opportunity to repent and return to Islam, but if they refused, they were to be executed if they were male and imprisoned until they changed their minds if they were female. Premodern *shari'a* rules also provided that apostasy constituted civil death, meaning, among other things, that the apostate's marriage would be dissolved and the apostate would become incapable of inheriting. Naturally, the *shari'a* imposed no penalties on converts to Islam from other faiths. Given this background, when one evaluates Islamic versions of human rights, it is particularly important to see whether the schemes contemplate the retention of the *shari'a* ban on apostasy.

International human rights law allows no constraints on a person's religious beliefs: Freedom of religion is an unqualified freedom. One of the most influential statements of this freedom is in Article 18 of the Universal Declaration of Human Rights (UDHR). Article 18 states: "Everyone has the right to freedom of thought, conscience and religion; this right includes freedom to change his religion or belief, and freedom, either alone or in community with others and in public or private, to manifest his religion or belief in teaching, practice, worship and observance." Freedom of religion is unqualified in International Covenant on Civil and Political Rights (ICCPR) Article 18.1. Although the wording is basically similar to UDHR Article 18, this ICCPR provision does not specifically mention the freedom to change religion.

It is historically significant that the phrase guaranteeing the right to change religion was added to the UDHR at the behest of the delegate from Lebanon (a Christian). Lebanon in the 1940s and 1950s was an oasis of toleration, where large Christian, Muslim, and Druze communities coexisted in a pluralistic society. The Lebanese Christian community objected to *shari'a* rules like the ban on conversions from Islam. Not surprisingly, when the Lebanese representative proposed that this language be added, he faced strong objections from the delegates of some Muslim countries.[1] The Saudi Arabian representative was particularly outspoken in condemning this provision on the grounds that Islam did not permit Muslims to change their religion. A voice favoring the Lebanese delegate's suggestion was Pakistan's representative, an Ahmadi, who spoke forcefully in defense of the proposition that freedom of religion as presented in this article was fully consonant with Islam. In the end, no Muslim countries other than Saudi Arabia refused to vote for the UDHR.[2]

Objections similar to those that had been raised by Saudi Arabia were later raised by Iran in discussions of the 1981 Declaration on the Elimination of All Forms of Intolerance, expressing the government's position that Muslims were not allowed to convert from their religion and were to be executed if they did so.[3] The Convention on the Rights of the Child (CRC), the most widely ratified of all the human rights conventions, guarantees a child's freedom of religion in Article 14. Although many Muslim countries ratified the CRC without reservation, Iraq, Jordan, Kuwait, Morocco, and Syria specifically reserved to Article 14. Perhaps these countries were more willing to indicate their nonacceptance of freedom of religion in a context where paternal control over children was at issue. After all, in Arab countries it is assumed that children must adhere to the religion of their father, family solidarity and paternal authority being treated as sacrosanct. Iran, Pakistan, and Saudi Arabia entered sweeping reservations when ratifying the CRC, indicating that they would not be bound by provisions contravening Islamic law, potentially encompassing Article 14.[4] These public statements by Muslim governments indicated ongoing differences regarding their willingness to accept the principle of freedom of religion.

Since Islam is the world's fastest growing religion and attempts to convert from Islam are uncommon, one might object that the issue of whether

Muslims are free to convert to other religions in the Middle East would be an academic rather than a practical one. In these circumstances, one would expect that the number of persons whose freedom of religion might be affected by the imposition of the *shari'a* ban on apostasy would be minimal. However, the ban on conversion from Islam has broader ramifications and potentially limits the rights of a much larger segment of the populations of Muslim countries than one might initially think.

As interpreted, the ban can apply to people who are born into a non-Muslim religion but whose parents, grandparents, or even remoter ancestors converted from Islam. The notion that Baha'is are renegades from Islam has been one basis for their persecution in Iran since the revolution. The targeted individuals had not changed their religion, but Iranians believe that most Baha'is are descendants of Muslim converts. As Iran's example shows, such persons may be punished and persecuted as apostates by virtue of their ancestors' defections from Islam.

The ban can also affect Muslims who adhere to doctrines that are out of keeping with whatever standard of orthodoxy is currently being espoused by powerful Islamic institutions or governments pursuing Islamization. Although premodern Islamic culture was generally tolerant of diverging views on questions of Islamic theology and law, when contemporary Middle Eastern governments have pressed forward with Islamization campaigns, they have tended to demand adherence to a uniform version of Islam. As the official orthodoxy becomes identified with the regime's own ideology and legitimacy, modern governments have shown themselves inclined to label Muslims who do not accept the official version of Islam as heretics and apostates. The circumstances under which the Ahmadi minority in Pakistan was officially designated "non-Muslim" and was made a target of discrimination and persecution under the official Islamization program has already been discussed. Likewise, the Sudanese Republicans officially became "apostates" from Islam under Ja'far Nimeiri even though they never repudiated Islam and believed that they were following authentic Islamic teachings. Thus, the ban on apostasy has become a curb on the religious freedom of Muslims—not only on their freedom to convert from Islam but also on their freedom to follow their consciences in matters of faith. In the climate of intolerance that has been fostered by official Islamization campaigns, even if Muslim dissidents and minorities are not jailed or executed for beliefs that are officially deemed heretical, they may have to contend with discrimination, harassment, and assassination attempts along with governmental indifference to their plight.

Furthermore, the ban on conversion from Islam has implications for the freedom of Muslim women, preventing them from escaping being subject to *shari'a* law. The choice-of-law rules that are in force in most Muslim countries mean that religious affiliation decides which law is applicable to personal-status issues. Only in rare instances, like the reforms enacted in Turkey and Tunisia, have Muslim countries so modernized their personal-status rules that one national standard can apply to all citizens. Elsewhere, *shari'a* law still applies to personal-status questions where one or both of the parties is Muslim.[5]

In such systems, if there were no ban on conversion, a Muslim woman could change the personal-status law applicable to her simply by abandoning Islam or converting to another religion. Such conversions might not be inspired by theological considerations but would be undertaken for purely practical reasons, to avoid the strictures of an unfavorable law. In the Middle East, conversions from one religion to another—and sometimes switches from one Islamic sect or school of law to another—have long been used to change the applicable law in personal-status issues. These conversions are the equivalent of forum shopping in the United States, where litigants, by changing their domicile, can alter the law applicable to family law and inheritance issues—"shopping" for the law of a forum that is favorable by changing residence from one state to another.

Conversions—including conversions to Islam—potentially enable parties to accomplish objectives impossible to achieve under their original personal-status law. For example, in a Middle Eastern country a Roman Catholic woman married to a Catholic man would be barred from divorcing, but if she wanted a divorce, she could sever her marital tie by converting to Islam. Then her marriage would become void, for she would gain the benefit of the *shari'a* rule that a Muslim woman cannot be validly married to a non-Muslim. A non-Muslim man might convert to Islam to gain the benefit of a more favorable personal-status law, such as a lenient divorce rule. Penalizing conversion from Islam can be utilized to deter "conversions" undertaken out of expediency by preventing opportunists from converting back to their original faiths after they achieve a desired end made possible by their temporary status as Muslims.

One of the options, admittedly a drastic one, open to Muslim women who seek to sever their ties with their husbands but are unable to get divorced is that of apostasy. By virtue of becoming apostates, Muslims incur civil death, regardless of whether a criminal penalty is imposed, and the civil death of one party terminates a marriage. Thus, the Muslim woman who is willing to incur civil death can escape both from her marriage and from the applicability of *shari'a* law.

In the past, many informal social and cultural factors inhibited Muslim women from taking such a radical course, but these inhibitions are crumbling under the impact of drastic social changes. In intact traditional communities, the ostracism that apostasy from Islam entails would make women reluctant to resort to such an action, but such communities are being undermined by rapid urbanization and economic transformations that make it possible for women to become independent and self-supporting. Improved educational opportunities, exposure to different social models via the media, a more skeptical approach to traditions of women's subordination, and other factors may lead women to chafe under an onerous marital tie that might formerly have been accepted. The prospect of achieving freedom via apostasy comes to have more allure.

One reason why Islamic human rights schemes do not allow freedom to change religion is that their authors remain determined to uphold traditional personal status rules. Because Muslim women are emerging from their traditional roles and modern ideologies favoring equal rights for women are spreading, the authors of Islamic human rights schemes expect that Muslim women will be restive. In such circumstances, where *shari'a* rules are converted into a scheme for controlling and subjugating one-half of the population, it is essential that there be no means by which the subjugated half may evade the applicability of the *shari'a* via the manipulation of choice-of-law rules.

That Muslim women may be tempted to abandon Islam concerned Sultanhussein Tabandeh, who has identified a number of discreditable reasons for which Muslim men might convert, while positing a Muslim woman's desire "to exploit easier conditions for divorce obtaining under other religions" as the only reason for apostasy in a woman's case.[6] His sense that the temptation to escape a marriage by apostasy is a real threat and that a strong deterrent is necessary to prevent women from resorting to apostasy as a route to freedom led him to propose a penalty that has no counterpart in the premodern *shari'a:* life imprisonment at hard labor for the female apostate.[7]

In Kuwait, where a Muslim woman's ability to opt out of the *shari'a* system has likewise been perceived as a threat, a different legal solution was found. There, a law was enacted discarding the premodern *shari'a* rule that a Muslim woman's marriage would be automatically dissolved by her apostasy. The reason for this change was offered in an explanatory memorandum accompanying the text of the reform: "Complaints have shown that the Devil makes the route of apostasy attractive to the Muslim woman so that she can break a conjugal tie that does not please her. For this reason, it was decided that apostasy would not lead to the dissolution of the marriage in order to close this dangerous door."[8] One sees that in Kuwait fidelity to the *shari'a* takes second place to concerns for preserving the patriarchal order; the *shari'a* tradition of civil death for the apostate is abandoned due to worries that this traditional penalty has become insufficient to deter women from exploiting the apostasy rules to terminate their marriages. With the change in the law, Muslim women in Kuwait can no longer open "this dangerous door."

Given this background, one can see that in the Middle East the freedom to change religion constitutes a far more significant dimension of religious freedom than it does in the West. However, until recently, the progressive Westernization of Middle Eastern legal systems seemed to promise that the practical importance of *shari'a* concepts in this area would diminish. Because of the nineteenth- and twentieth-centuries reforms in the area of criminal law, the application of the *shari'a* death penalty for apostasy from Islam became a rarity. In this regard, the impact of Islamization on Middle Eastern law has made a great difference. What until recently seemed to be an anachronism has been revived in ways that have led to serious breaches of international human rights in the name of applying *shari'a* law.

Even where no rule mandating that apostates from Islam are to be executed has been incorporated in the criminal code, governments that have undertaken Islamization programs may nonetheless execute people for apostasy from Islam—as if the *shari'a* rules were binding even in the absence of corresponding provisions in the criminal code. It seems that even those governments that readily execute people as apostates from Islam are reluctant to proclaim publicly that they kill people for their religious beliefs or to enact laws that confirm that the death penalty applies to persons who convert from Islam. For example, trying to counter damaging publicity, Iran has proclaimed that apostasy is not a crime under its codified laws and in 1995 assured a UN rapporteur that "conversion was not a crime and no one had been punished for converting."[9] Thus, seeking to avoid more negative publicity, Iran does not admit to killing Baha'is as apostates; instead, they are executed for allegedly committing secular offenses, such as spying for Israel or treason, even though the fact that their "crimes" are pardoned if they recant and return to Islam reveals that they are in practice being prosecuted for apostasy.

In Egypt since the 1970s there have been insistent demands for a revival of the death penalty for apostasy from Islam.[10] These demands have met energetic opposition on the part of Egypt's large Coptic population and have also been opposed by liberal and secular forces. Although the Egyptian government in 1980 changed the constitution to make the *shari'a* the main source of legislation, it resisted attempts to have the death penalty for apostasy from Islam incorporated in its criminal law.

The notorious 1994–1996 case of the Egyptian university professor Nasr Hamid Abu Zaid, divorced against his will for his alleged apostasy, showed that Egypt's courts were prepared to penalize religious dissent in other ways.[11] Egypt's personal status laws do allow recourse to Islamic law in default of an applicable code provision, meaning that, where there are gaps, judges can treat the works of the jurists of the Hanafi school of law as authority. A third party, totally unrelated to Abu Zaid, was allowed to bring a personal status law claim asserting that, according to Hanafi jurisprudence, Abu Zaid's marriage to his Muslim wife had to be dissolved because his writings showed that he was an apostate. Ignoring the conventional view that a person who is a professing Muslim should be deemed a Muslim, the courts decided that Abu Zaid's religion had been placed in doubt. They reviewed Abu Zaid's writings, which called for revising conventional approaches to Qur'an interpretation, and agreed that his theories made him an apostate. On this basis, the courts declared his marriage to his Muslim wife dissolved. They referred to the constitutional protection for freedom of religion but treated it as if it had to be understood in relation to the Islamic legal tradition.[12] That is, although the constitution did not expressly place Islamic qualifications on religious freedom, the courts acted as if such qualifications were implicit and as if they supported ruling Abu Zaid an apostate.

Again one sees how human rights issues are interlinked. The upholders of the premodern *shari'a* insist that the wife must be subordinate to her husband, which makes it intolerable for her, if she is a Muslim, to be married to a non-Muslim, since Islam—the Muslim woman being a marker for Islam—should not be subordinated to another faith. They also refuse to accept the principle that both men and women should be allowed freely to choose their spouses, without any hindrances based on religion. One could say that the outcome of the Abu Zaid case could be as readily attributed to Egypt's failure to accord women equality as to Egypt's failure to uphold religious freedom.

Among other things, the Abu Zaid case proves that the quarrel of Sunni orthodoxy with Mu'tazilite ideas, which have been discussed in Chapter 3, is far from over, since many of his controversial positions are closely linked to the rationalist approach to Islam advocated by the Mu'tazilites.[13] Abu Zaid took stances at odds with the notion, popular among contemporary proponents of Islam as an ideology, that the Qur'an possesses a univocal meaning, emphasizing instead the diversity in interpretations.[14] Moreover, he disputed the tenet that Islam covers all domains, arguing that areas like human rights are based on developments outside the sphere of religion.[15] Although the actual implementation of the divorce ruling was ultimately stayed and Egypt subsequently changed its laws to prevent private parties from bringing such suits in the future, these belated responses did not protect Abu Zaid and his wife Ibtihal Yunis from the religious zealots who were ready to enforce their own version of Islamic justice, threatening to kill him for his supposed apostasy or to kill them both for living together in sin after they had been forcibly divorced. The couple was obliged to seek asylum in Europe. This outcome is a reminder that in the climate of intolerance prevailing in many Muslim countries, it is not necessary for the state to intervene to impose a death penalty for an "apostate" to be severely penalized.

The outcome of the case also shows why it is an oversimplification to ascribe such rulings violating human rights to Islamic law. After all, the concern of the death penalty for apostasy as devised by the premodern jurists was to punish Muslims who abandoned their faith and to deter defections from the early Islamic community. In Abu Zaid's case, a committed, professing Muslim who had been a member in good standing of the Muslim community and who wished to revitalize Islamic scholarship through his study of the Qur'an was cast out of the community against his wishes and on the flimsy basis of a decision by a secular court that happened to find his challenges to received opinions offensive. From punishment for a willful act of abandonment of the faith, "apostasy" had been converted into an arbitrary sanction that courts representing national governments, not the Islamic community, could mete out to Muslim believers who elected to take different paths to understanding scripture. In consequence of the "apostasy" ruling, two Muslims were forced to uproot themselves from their Muslim homeland and move for their own safety to live as exiles in non-Muslim territory. From a penalty designed to secure inclusion within the Islamic fold, apostasy had been transformed into a means of excluding believing Muslims from their place in the community.

Like the Iranian philosophy professor Abdolkarim Sorush, who has been persecuted for uttering similar views, Abu Zaid critically appraised the consequences of the monopoly over Qur'anic interpretation exercised by state theologians dependent on local rulers, claiming that such a scenario leads to repressing new interpretations and critical questions.[16] As if anticipating his own fate, he charged that this results in the ideological exploitation of the Qur'an to legitimize reality and in the branding of Muslims who fight against this situation as unbelievers, atheists, and heretics.[17] Both he and Sorush would likely concur that their problems were due less to the Islamic tradition than to politics.

Ironically, the same Egyptian courts that had ruled in a fashion that showed disregard for freedom of religion devoted considerable efforts to arguing that the forcible divorce of a couple on the grounds of the husband's allegedly heretical religious beliefs did not conflict with freedom of religion as set forth in the constitution.[18] Like the persons engaged in purveying the Islamic human rights schemes that are reviewed here, the judges refused to acknowledge that their recourse to Islamic criteria led to denying religious freedom.

As this book attempts to show, human rights violations that seem at first blush to be tied to the Islamic tradition often turn out upon closer inspection to be intertwined with local politics. Abu Zaid himself claims that the reason he was targeted for persecution as an apostate had nothing to do with his religious views but was retaliation for his criticisms of an Islamic investment scheme in which a powerful personage had an interest. Given the pressures for Islamization and the religious fervor whipped up by religious demagogues and given the government's disinclination to intervene to protect a controversial intellectual, the stage was set for the offended individual to obtain his revenge via the route of having Abu Zaid labeled an apostate.

However, even if the original impetus behind the lawsuit was revenge for embarrassment caused by criticism of a financial institution, Abu Zaid's liberal views and his arguments on behalf of a reformed understanding of the relationship of the believer to the Islamic sources were sure to anger conservatives and ideologues committed to Islamization. He was thus vulnerable to the same kinds of denunciations and assaults that have plagued other innovative Islamic thinkers and eminent literary figures and that have forced so many distinguished intellectuals into exile. As one author who has written about the Abu Zaid case laments, it is precisely the most creative, the brightest, and the most courageous spirits in the Muslim world who are slandered, attacked, persecuted, and killed by their own culture—this for trying to take up the challenge of preserving their culture and identity in a changing world.[19] One should bear this in mind when the impression is conveyed that Islam is a reactionary and oppressive religion: The Muslims who could transform Islam into a more open system and who offer an enlightened version of their faith are all too often threatened with becoming victims like Abu Zaid.

In any event, this grim case illustrates why freedom of religion issues are at least as important for Muslims as they are for the non-Muslim populations in predominantly Muslim countries. The notion that one can protect the religious freedom of a minority like Egypt's Copts in a system that allows members of Egypt's Muslim majority to be persecuted as Abu Zaid was must be an illusion.

Rethinking the *Shari'a* Rule on Apostasy

It is ironic that the apostasy penalty of the premodern *shari'a* has been revived after developments had suggested that many thoughtful Muslims were prepared to reform or discard the premodern Islamic jurisprudence on this topic and accept the concept of religious freedom. Contemporary Muslims who have repudiated the penalty argue that the premodern juristic interpretations were unwarranted by the texts of the Islamic sources and out of keeping with the principle that there is "no compulsion in religion" (based on the Qur'an 2:256).[20] The principle of tolerance of religious difference, which figures prominently in the Islamic value system and tradition, supports the notion that religious adherence should be left a matter of conscience. Liberal Muslims note that there is no verse in the Qur'an that stipulates any earthly penalty for apostasy and that the premodern jurists' rules on apostasy were extrapolated from incidents in the Prophet's life and from historical events after his death that actually lend themselves to a variety of interpretations. Having drawn distinctions between the Qur'anic concern for freedom of conscience and the concerns of public order that historically led jurists to devise a rule that the apostate should be punished by death, a Muslim scholar has concluded that the Qur'anic principle of religious liberty shares common foundations with the Western concept of religious liberty.[21]

Contemporary scholars have found many reasons for rethinking the jurists' rule that the apostate must be killed. For example, the Lebanese scholar Subhi Mahmassani asserted that the circumstances in which the penalty was meant to apply were intended to be narrow ones. He pointed out that the Prophet never killed anyone merely for apostasy. Instead, the death penalty was applied when the act of apostasy from Islam was linked to an act of political betrayal of the community. This being the case, Mahmassani argued that the death penalty was not meant to apply to a simple change of faith but to punish acts such as treason, joining forces with the enemy, and sedition.[22] Another Muslim understands the Qur'an to say that God wants submission to Islam "in full consciousness and freedom," indicating that religious liberty is fundamental to respect for God's plan for humanity. This plan includes the mysterious privilege of rejecting Islam's message of salvation. In turn, the privilege of rejecting Islam means the total impermissibility of recourse to compulsion or killing in matters of faith.[23]

Muslims who currently call for the execution of apostates are not compelled to do so by unambiguous Islamic authority supporting this penalty. There are ample grounds for deciding that the juristic rules on apostasy no longer apply. Muslims can select alternative interpretations of the Islamic rules on apostasy that are more in keeping with the tenor of the Qur'an and with modern ideas of religious freedom. Where they elect not to do so and insist that apostates are to be executed, one must wonder whether Islam or another concern provides their motivation.

Tabandeh's Ideas

Not surprisingly, Sultanhussein Tabandeh is the most candid of the authors in calling for the retention of premodern Islamic rules restricting religious freedom. As we have seen, in his view, *dhimmis* do enjoy the right to follow their own religions, but this is not so in the case of adherents of other religions. Because they are largely descended from Muslims who converted, members of the Baha'i faith are considered by Tabandeh to be defectors from Islam who must be forced to recant and return to the fold. In what appears to be a thinly veiled attack on the Baha'i faith, Tabandeh asserted that "followers of a religion of which the basis is contrary to Islam, like those who demand Islam's extirpation, have no official rights to freedom of religion in Islamic countries or under an Islamic government, nor can they claim respect through their religion, any more than in certain countries definite political parties which are contrary to the ideology of the regime can claim freedom since they are declared to be inimical to the welfare of the land and people."[24]

This view relates to Tabandeh's assumption that in Islam religion and politics are not separated, and thus the government cannot be divorced from the official religion.[25] Since his version of Islam is effectively ideologized and treated like a political philosophy, Tabandeh can compare restricting freedom of religion to the curbing of a political party with goals "inimical to the welfare of the land and people."

Tabandeh said that "propaganda" for any religion other than Islam must be prohibited.[26] His position on this is a consequence of his unyielding insistence that conversion from Islam should not be tolerated because there is no legitimate reason for abandoning the Islamic faith: "No man of sense, from the mere fact that he possesses intelligence, will ever turn down the better in favor of the inferior. Anyone who penetrates beneath the surface to the inner essence of Islam is bound to recognise its superiority over the other religions. A man, therefore, who deserts Islam, by that act betrays the fact that he must have played truant to its moral and spiritual truths earlier."[27]

The reasons a person might desert Islam, according to a speech by the Egyptian UN representative cited by Tabandeh, include duress, bribes, and a woman's desire "to exploit easier conditions for divorce obtaining under some other religions."[28] As other possible inducements to abandon Islam, Tabandeh listed false promises by another religion, spite on the part of a Muslim who has been injured by another Muslim, and being led astray by carnal lusts that Islam forbids.[29] The nature of these reasons means, according to him, that conversions from Islam should not be given encouragement, "let alone by an international law." A person born in Islam who deserts after coming of age must be killed since he is "diseased ... gangrenous, incurable, fit only for amputation."[30] A person who was not born Muslim but converted to Islam and then leaves it is given three days to reconsider his apostasy, after which, if he fails to return to the faith, he must be executed.[31] To illustrate the solicitude of Islam for women's welfare, Tabandeh pointed out that the female apostate is not killed but is condemned, instead, "only to life imprisonment with hard labor."[32] In contrast, Tabandeh noted that "a person who gives up some religion other than Islam to accept Islam's sound faith is received and respected."[33]

It is obvious that this kind of attitude is incompatible with the protection of religious freedom; for Tabandeh, there are only the categories of truth and error. Seemingly unaware that such an approach is incompatible with international norms, he assumes that it is feasible to project these categories into international law. He apparently imagines that once those who make international law are made to understand the reasons why Islam forbids conversion, international law will also decree that conversions from Islam should be banned.[34]

It is worth considering how Tabandeh's arguments for banning conversion from Islam compare with central premises underlying the Islamic human rights schemes and with those underlying international human rights law. Tabandeh and Muslims who share his values start from the premise that one must accord primacy to the interests of Islam and the Muslim community when deciding whether individual freedoms are permissible. If it turns out that the interests of the religion or the community dictate that the individual should be deprived of freedom, this is entirely acceptable.

In contrast, in international human rights law a central premise is that individuals are the best judges of their own interests, because individuals ultimately have greater insight into what they need to be happy than do any other persons or institutions. International human rights law is based on the assumption that exercising the freedom to choose, a fundamental right, is part of what is involved in being human and achieving dignity and self-respect.[35] It is therefore disposed to afford strong protection for the individual's freedom of choice in a matter like religious belief and has little concern for whether the interests of a religious institution or the community in which the individual lives are served by that choice.

The UIDHR

The Universal Islamic Declaration of Human Rights (UIDHR) purports to treat the "Right to Freedom of Belief, Thought and Speech" in Article 12.a, but, again, it uses formulations in the English and Arabic versions that convey very different impressions. In the English, Article 12.a states: "Every person has the right to express his thoughts and beliefs so long as he remains within the limits prescribed by the Law. No one, however, is entitled to disseminate falsehood or to circulate reports that may outrage public decency, or to indulge in slander, innuendo, or to cast defamatory aspersions on other persons."

At first glance this provision appears to impose neutral, secular restraints on freedom of expression, while sidestepping the issue of freedom of belief. The idea that slanderous, defamatory speech can be curbed by law seems unobjectionable. The standards for curbing freedom of expression in this article are left sufficiently broad to allow for government interpretations that might make serious inroads in the area of freedom of expression, but if one assumed that the qualifications would be interpreted narrowly, one might find this formulation in substantial conformity with international norms.

The Arabic version of Article 12.a conveys a very different message because it reveals that Islamic criteria limit freedom of expression. It states:

"Everyone may think, believe and express his ideas and beliefs without interference or opposition from anyone as long as he obeys the limits *[hudud]* set by the *shari'a*. It is not permitted to spread falsehood *[al-batil]* or disseminate that which involves encouraging abomination *[al-fahisha]* or forsaking the Islamic community *[takhdhil li'l-umma]*."[36] Thus, *shari'a* rules set limits not just on freedom of expression but also on the freedoms of thought and belief. As has already been pointed out, such use of the criteria of one religion to set limits on rights are unacceptable under international human rights law.

One can surmise what specific rules in the *shari'a* would likely be employed to curtail these freedoms. For example, one would expect that in a system based on the *shari'a*, at a minimum people would be prohibited from attempting to convert Muslims to other faiths and forbidden to speak disparagingly of the Prophet. However, since there exist no established standards for how extensive the *shari'a* limits on the kinds of freedoms involved here may be, the scope of the *shari'a* restraints that could be imposed under this provision is open-ended.

The significance of the second sentence is difficult to ascertain. The English version suggests that defamation and slander are categories of expression that are not protected, but the Arabic version appears to deny protection to quite different categories of expression. Falsehood, the encouragement of abomination, or the forsaking of the Islamic community could be banned, but since these vague, value-laden terms have no settled meanings as they apply to limiting human rights, one cannot predict how the authorities would interpret them. It is conceivable that any speech that might threaten to diminish loyalty to the local version of Islamic orthodoxy could be banned. The provision would also seem to allow broad censorship in order to protect morality. Here, as in other instances, the open-ended nature of the qualifications has the potential to emasculate the very freedoms that the UIDHR makes a pretense of granting.

"Right to Freedom of Religion" is the rubric for Article 13 of the UIDHR. This article states in the English version that everyone has the right to freedom of conscience and worship in accordance with his religious beliefs. The wording is different from the wording of comparable international human rights principles, but the difference is a relatively subtle one.[37]

The significance of the difference between Article 13 and the relevant international standards is more readily ascertained if one consults the Arabic version, which says that everyone has freedom of belief and freedom of worship according to the principle, "you have your religion, I have mine." This line is taken from the Qur'anic sura *"al-kafirun,"* 109:6. *Al-kafirun* can mean "unbelievers," "infidels," or "atheists"; in any case, it has strong negative connotations. The complete sura runs as follows, in Marmaduke Pickthall's flowery translation: "Say: O disbelievers *[al-kafirun]*! I worship not that which ye worship; Nor worship ye that which I worship. And I shall not worship that which ye worship. Nor will ye worship that which I worship. Unto you your religion, and unto me my religion."[38] The sura contemplates a division between Islam and "unbelief." It lays the groundwork for coexistence but does not attempt to establish any principle of freedom of religion comparable to that found in international human rights documents. If there is a right implied in this provision, it is the right to follow one's own religion, which in a *shari'a*-based system would be a freedom accorded only to Muslims and, within limits, to the *ahl al-kitab*. As a consequence of being obliged to follow their own religion, Muslims would be bound by *shari'a* rules, which would mean that they would not be allowed to convert from Islam and could be executed if they did so.

Pursuant to Article 13, conversions to Islam would probably be encouraged but none from Islam allowed. This result would be consistent with the Arabic version of Section 7 of the Preamble of the UIDHR. The English version of this section seems quite neutral and innocuous, calling for a society in which "all worldly power shall be considered as a sacred trust, to be exercised within the limits prescribed by the Law and in a manner approved by it, and with due regard for the priorities fixed by it." In sharp contrast, the same section in the Arabic version is an expression of a commitment to a society where all people will believe that Allah alone is the master of all creation. This is tantamount to a commitment to converting the world's population to Islam, a commitment that is not compatible with the attitudes that shaped the international human rights norms regarding freedom of religion.

To establish an effective guarantee for religious freedom that would meet international standards, Article 13 would have to indicate that the premodern *shari'a* rules in this area were being discarded. The UIDHR has carefully refrained from making any such indications.

The Azhar Draft Constitution

The Azhar draft of an Islamic constitution is less evasive than the UIDHR on the issue of protection for freedom of religion. It says in the English version of Article 29 that "within the limits of the Islamic Sharia, the Government provides for the natural basic rights of religious and intellectual beliefs." In this obscure formulation, there is no mention of any freedom of religion. Given this omission, the article could provide the same kind of "right" to follow one's own religion—without granting any right for Muslims to change religion—that was set forth in Article 13 of the UIDHR, which has already been discussed. In contrast, the same article of the Azhar draft constitution expressly mentions "freedoms" of labor and expression and personal "freedom." The omission of the mention of "freedom" *(hur-*

riya) of religion is unlikely to be accidental, particularly given the fact that "the natural basic rights" set forth in the article are being offered only "within the limits of the Islamic Sharia." Any doubts about whether the application of these limits is intended to restrict the freedom of religion in accordance with premodern *shariʻa* rules are removed by Article 71 of the draft constitution, which provides for the application of the death penalty for apostasy. Since the *shariʻa* sets the governing standards, this can only apply to apostasy from Islam. The relative candor of the Azhar draft with respect to the death penalty for apostasy from Islam is in striking contrast to the evasiveness one normally encounters on the part of Muslims who wish to retain the rule that apostates are to be executed.

The willingness of al-Azhar to call openly for the execution of persons who abandon Islam is probably the result of several factors. The al-Azhar University is the oldest institution of higher learning in Islam and the most prestigious center for training in Sunni Islam. Given the emphasis on the study of traditional Islamic sciences and premodern jurisprudence in the Azhar curriculum, Azhar clerics are unlikely to be conversant with modern liberal, democratic values or well versed in international human rights law.

Moreover, the relatively candor of the Azharites regarding their unwillingness to allow Muslims to leave Islam may have been a natural outcome of circumstances in Cairo. The question of whether to execute apostates was at the time of the drafting of the Azhar constitution a very hotly contested issue on the Cairo scene. Given the liveliness of the controversy about the death penalty for apostasy, it would have been difficult for a Cairene institution like al-Azhar to sidestep the issue of punishment for apostasy even if the Azharites had been motivated to do so.

Furthermore, the draft was not an actual constitution but only a proposal for what Azharites would ideally like to see incorporated in a constitution. Because their exercise was an academic one, the authors of the Azhar draft were not forced to accede to political compromises with disaffected Egyptian Copts. Nor did the drafters have to accommodate those politicians and jurists who were abreast of modern trends in constitutionalism.

Mawdudi and Pakistani Law

Abu'l Aʻla Mawdudi was not prepared to confess in the text of his human rights pamphlet that he supported killing those who convert from Islam. As was his habit when he realized that his views were so far out of keeping with international human rights standards that, by expressing them, he would undermine the credibility of his human rights scheme, he simply avoided the issue. There is, therefore, no discussion of the problem of freedom of religion in his human rights pamphlet. However, Mawdudi is on the record elsewhere as supporting the death penalty for conversion from Islam.[39]

Mawdudi did not live long enough to see the enactment in Pakistan of Ordinance XX, discussed in Chapter 7, which provided a legal warrant for persecuting Ahmadis, but this ordinance can be seen as the culmination of the anti-Ahmadi campaign that he and his followers had waged. However, as the discussion of the ruling on the constitutionality of Ordinance XX in the *Zaheeruddin* case has shown, in using Islamic criteria to qualify the constitutional guarantee of religious freedom, Pakistan's Supreme Court has set a precedent that could be detrimental for religious freedom generally.

Whereas in some Muslim countries punishment for apostasy looms as a major threat to religious freedom, in Pakistan, where blasphemy laws were enacted under Muhammad Zia ul-Haq and where blasphemy has been a capital offense since 1991, blasphemy prosecutions have seriously undermined that freedom. These blasphemy laws have been used to initiate politically motivated prosecutions, mostly against Ahmadis and Christians, but also occasionally against Muslims. In one of the most infamous cases, a distinguished Muslim writer and sociologist, Dr. Akhtar Harold Khan, was charged with blasphemy on the basis of an allegorical poem he had written about a simpleton who was devoured by a lion that he had raised. The poem referred to General Zia's overthrow and execution of Zulfikar Ali Bhutto, to whom he owed his high military position, but accusations were made that it was a slur on the fourth caliph Ali, the cousin of the Prophet, who was known as the lion of God. By the mid-1990s, hundreds of blasphemy cases were pending in Pakistan.

Asia Watch has found that in the wake of Islamization in Pakistan, "the Islamic laws of religious offense are defined with reference to certain sacred 'truths' that may not be contradicted, challenged, satirized or ridiculed—it is the affront to the ideas themselves that is seen as threatening to the very fabric of Islamic society."[40] According to Asia Watch, Pakistan's sweeping blasphemy laws, although ostensibly concerned with religious offenses, have become a powerful weapon for the silencing of ideological enemies. Asia Watch concludes that these blasphemy laws have fostered a climate of intolerance and bigotry, in which persons accused of blasphemy have been terrorized, beaten, and murdered. Its assessment: In Pakistan, intolerance is becoming holy, a distinguishing badge of devotion to Islam.[41]

In this climate, it is not only apostates and non-Muslim minorities who need to fear becoming the targets of prosecutions or extrajudicial killings for what are ostensibly religious offenses; Muslims of a variety of persuasions may find their freedom constrained and even their lives jeopardized as well. For example, as of 1997, Shi'i and Sunni factions were engaging in retaliatory killing sprees in the Punjab and Karachi. In an especially ominous development, a Muslim judge who had courageously acquitted two Christians of blasphemy charges in a high-profile case was assassinated in

October 1997, apparently by angry members of the Sunni extremist group that had originally brought the blasphemy charges.[42] The defense attorney in the same blasphemy case was also terrorized. The overall collapse of the rule of law was becoming as great a problem as the laws that allowed personal and political vendettas to be carried out in the name of defending Islam. As a human rights monitor aptly observed in a discussion of Pakistan's deteriorating legal environment: "When politics invades religion, legality becomes merely emblematic."[43]

The Iranian Constitution

The rights provisions of the 1979 Iranian Constitution also fail to address the issue of religious freedom as such. It is significant that a constitution that in many respects copies the French model should have eliminated any protection for religious freedom from its list of rights. However, Article 23 does forbid interrogating or attacking people because of their beliefs. This provision might be interpreted as meaning that religious persecution should be outlawed. Whatever the original intent or hopes of the drafters of this article may have been, the Iranian government has certainly not interpreted it as a guarantee of freedom of religion or as a protection for religious minorities.

The conduct of the Iranian government can serve as a gloss on the meaning of the protections afforded by Article 23. The extensive persecutions of Iran's Baha'is unequivocally establish that the Iranian government does not believe that Article 23 prevents interrogating or attacking members of disfavored religious minorities because of their religious beliefs. Baha'is have been put under enormous pressure to recant their beliefs and return to Islam. It is well established that Baha'is are persecuted on the basis of their religious beliefs, because the trumped-up charges of offenses against Iran's secular laws have been dropped when and if accused Baha'is have been willing to repent of their theological errors and proclaim their adherence to Islam.[44] The religious nature of the persecution can also be seen in the fact that Baha'is are treated as persons who have incurred civil death, the consequence of apostasy from Islam under *shari'a* law. Thus, for example, all Baha'i marriages have been declared invalid, sexual intercourse between the former spouses has been treated as fornication (punishable by death), and the children of the dissolved marriages have been declared illegitimate, thereby depriving their parents of any claim to them.[45]

Despite the extensive evidence that the persecution of the Baha'is is religiously motivated, in communications designed for international audiences, the Iranian government has gone to great lengths to justify executions of Baha'is on the grounds that the deceased had been guilty of political crimes. Executed Baha'is are routinely alleged to be guilty of spying for Israel or the CIA. Reclassifying Baha'is as "traitors," "spies," and "conspirators" enables Iran to pretend that its criminal justice system follows a more conventional model than it actually does. In international forums, the regime insists that Baha'is who are not guilty of antiregime activities are not molested and asserts that Iran does not persecute Baha'is for religious reasons.[46]

A comment published by the Iranian attorney general intended to debunk charges that Baha'is were being persecuted for religious reasons is revealing of the regime's attitude:

> Now, if a Baha'i himself performs his religious acts in accordance with his own beliefs, such a man will not be bothered by us, provided he does not invite others to Baha'ism, does not teach, does not form assemblies, does not give news to others, and has nothing to do with the administration [of the Baha'i community]. Not only do we not execute such people, we do not even imprison them, and they can work within society. If, however, they decide to work within their administration, this is a criminal act and is forbidden, the reason being that such administration is considered to be hostile and conspiratorial and such people are conspirators.[47]

Even if one accepted this disavowal at face value, one would see that the regime had acknowledged its anti-Baha'i policies and its refusal to grant Baha'is religious freedom on a par with adherents of other faiths. The attorney general effectively admitted in this statement that the religion and its institutions were officially associated with treasonous, conspiratorial activities, making it impossible for Baha'is to worship or associate with each other without risking criminal prosecution.

In trying to argue to an international audience that the prosecution of the Baha'i population is political rather than religious in character, the Iranian government has pretended that a distinction is made in Iran between political and religious crimes. However, this is a distinction that by the terms of Article 168 of the Iranian Constitution cannot, in fact, exist. The second sentence in Article 168 reads: "The definition of a political crime, the manner in which the jury will be selected, their qualifications and the limits of their authority shall be determined by law, based upon Islamic principles *[mavazin-e eslami]*."[48] One sees in this article that it is not the secular law that defines political crimes but law based on Islamic principles. As befits a government following a religious ideology, religious categories and rules determine the definitions of political crimes; thus, political crimes are, ultimately, also religious crimes.

The lack of candor on the part of the Iranian government in its official representations to the international community about the reasons for its persecutions of Baha'is correlates with the patterns of obfuscation and evasiveness that one sees in Islamic human rights schemes generally. Given the fact that in the Iranian Constitution Islamic principles are treated as the supreme law of the land, one might have expected that the legality of the executions of the Baha'is in Islamic terms would be Iran's only concern, that it would publicly admit its policy of killing apostates, and that the government would proudly cite *shari'a* rules in response to any foreign criticisms of its actions. The Iranian government might, therefore, be expected to take a position like that taken in the Azhar draft constitution, where there was forthright endorsement of the rule that apostates were to be killed. However, in reality, the Iranian government is painfully aware that appealing to *shari'a* rules allowing it to kill people for their religious beliefs will only create embarrassment. It realizes that the persecutions and executions of Baha'is violate international human rights standards and that it is by reference to these international standards that the quality of Iran's Islamic justice will largely be judged—by Muslims as well as by non-Muslims. Iran's dissimulations reveal that it implicitly recognizes the authoritative, universal character of the international human rights standards—even as it continues to violate them.

One notes the irony of Iran's theocratic government, ruled by an Islamic jurist, trying to its disguise its religious persecutions as secular political cases, whereas in the far more secular political order in Pakistan laws specifically target a religious minority for criminal prosecution and elevate blasphemy, a religious offense, to the status of a capital crime. Obviously, strategic calculations play a major role in shaping how different regimes decide whether to ascribe their treatments of minorities and their prosecutions of people for what amount to religious offenses to the need to enforce Islamic law. In these circumstances, outsiders need to appraise with skepticism all official rationales for such persecutions and punishments.

However, not all Iranian officials were attuned to the attitudes of the world community or were able to gauge how their initiatives would be judged under international law. Like Tabandeh, Ayatollah Khomeini was relatively uninfluenced by and uninterested in international law. The veil that more diplomatic and cosmopolitan members of the regime had sought to draw around policies antithetical to religious freedom was lifted in the Salman Rushdie case. Khomeini quite deliberately courted international notoriety in the Rushdie affair, seeking thereby to buttress his faltering image as the leader of militant Islam, an image that had been undermined by his having had to accept a UN plan to end the Iran-Iraq War, which he had earlier promised to pursue until victory was achieved and Saddam Hussain was overthrown.

Khomeini issued his death edict for Rushdie on February 14, 1989, claiming that Rushdie's book *The Satanic Verses* was an attack on Islam, the Qur'an, and the Prophet. Khomeini was undeterred by concerns about whether it was legitimate for an Iranian Shi'i cleric to issue a death edict for a person of Sunni background who was a British citizen, whether it was just to condemn Rushdie without affording him a trial or a chance to defend himself, and whether it was reasonable to kill a novelist on the basis of charges about what he had written when Iranian clerics had not scrutinized the contents of the novel. On February 19, Khomeini added to the death sentence the order that, even were Rushdie to repent of his offense, he would still have to be executed.[49]

Muslims' responses to Khomeini's death edict, which ranged from enthusiastic plaudits to outspoken condemnation, proved that they were deeply divided about whether Rushdie should be executed and whether Islamic law supported this edict.[50] Despite the risks, courageous Muslims raised their voices in protest over the death edict.[51] Not a single Muslim country opted to endorse Khomeini's call for killing Rushdie, even though on March 16, 1989, the Organization of the Islamic Conference did label the book blasphemous and Rushdie an apostate.

Iran's clerical leadership seemed in its subsequent propaganda to lack confidence in the legitimacy of killing Rushdie solely on grounds that his novel proved that he had abandoned the Islamic faith. As the regime attempted to justify Khomeini's call for Rushdie's execution, efforts were made to portray Rushdie, in actuality a leftist supporter of Third World causes, as an antirevolutionary agent of the forces of capitalism and Zionism, an agent of both the CIA and its Israeli counterpart, the Mossad, and a participant in a British imperialist plot to destroy Islam. Just as in the case of the prosecutions of the Baha'is, there was a strained attempt to portray the criminal charges as being based on secular offenses, not on religious beliefs.

After Khomeini's death in 1989, many officials seem to have wished that they could safely rescind the Rushdie death edict, and Iranian factions have subsequently quarreled over whether Iran remained religiously bound to carry out Khomeini's order.[52] In an apparent effort to disassociate Iran from the practice of killing people for their religious beliefs, Iranian officials have argued that it is essential to differentiate between the responsibilities of the Iranian government and a religious ruling[53]—a claim that is particularly strange coming from a government committed to the indivisibility of religion and state and to enshrining the theory of rule by the Islamic jurist. In recent years, Iran has tried to turn the tables on its critics, offering implausible arguments to the effect that Rushdie was an offender under international law and that European countries were violating international law in praising and welcoming Rushdie.[54] The boldness of Khomeini's flouting of international law in issuing the Rushdie death edict was thus an exception to the more common Iranian habit of seeking ways to persuade the international community that Iran followed international law and that the accusations that Iran denied freedom of religion were baseless.[55]

The Sudan Under Islamization

Too little attention was originally paid to the Taha case, an apostasy case that presaged others that were to follow. Neither governments nor organizations concerned with human rights devoted the same energy to protesting Taha's judicial murder as they did to protesting Khomeini's call for killing Rushdie four years later. The 1985 execution of Mahmud Muhammad Taha, the leader of the Sudanese Republican movement, as a heretic and apostate from Islam proved that regimes committed to Islamization were ready to kill Muslims for supposedly heretical beliefs. Moreover, the clash between Ja'far Nimeiri and Taha exemplifies the conflict that exists between governmental invocations of Islam to justify violating international human rights and Muslims' beliefs that Islam supports the very international human rights that governments are violating in the name of Islam.

Taha had led a liberal school of thought in the Sudan known variously as the Republicans and the Republican Brothers. Republicans viewed Islam as establishing an egalitarian order that was fully compatible with human rights. Taha offered a controversial interpretation of the history and aims of the revelation of the Qur'anic verses. According to his interpretation, much of what had come to be regarded as timeless *shari'a* rules was actually legislation that had been intended only to guide the early Muslim community in Medina. In accordance with this interpretation, Taha was able to justify discarding various *shari'a* rules that violated human rights law, saying that they were never meant to be permanently binding on Muslims. Taha held that Islam, correctly interpreted, supported complete equality between men and women and Muslims and non-Muslims.[56] Taha's liberal, reformist views were anathema to many Muslim conservatives—so much so that in 1976 al-Azhar officially declared him to be an apostate.[57] His views were also attacked by the Ikhwan, or Muslim Brothers, a movement one faction of which subsequently collaborated with the Omar al-Bashir regime in spreading repression in the name of Islam.

The Republicans criticized the human rights violations that were propagated as a result of Nimeiri's Islamization campaign of 1983–1985. The Republicans brought several unsuccessful suits claiming that the imposition of the premodern *shari'a* rules violated the constitution by discriminating against non-Muslims and women.[58] Taha was arrested along with a group of his followers and tried in January 1985. He boycotted as illegal and unconstitutional his original trial for offenses against the Sudan Penal Code of 1983 and the State Security Act of 1973. The trial court's judgment, which did not address the issue of apostasy, was overridden on appeal by a ruling convicting Taha of the additional offense of apostasy from Islam and condemning him to die. Both the legal and the constitutional dimensions of this case warrant discussion, as they illustrate the deleterious impact that Islamization had on the system of justice and the rule of law.

Instead of an Islamic constitution, the Sudan still had its 1973 constitution at the time of Taha's trial and execution, which violated the operative constitutional norms. The constitution provided in Article 70 that no person could be executed for a crime that was not set forth in the law at the time when the act was committed and in Articles 47 and 48 that freedom of thought, belief, and expression were guaranteed.[59]

There was no Sudanese law in force in 1985 establishing that apostasy from Islam constituted a crime. The Nimeiri regime may have been inhibited from formally reinstating the death penalty for apostasy by the same reasons that had deterred Iran from doing so and also out of fear of a negative reaction from southern Sudanese. Even without an apostasy penalty, the Islamization program had alienated the South and led in 1983 to the renewed outbreak of the Sudan's protracted civil war. Southern Sudanese, who were largely animist and Christian, saw Islamization as a policy that relegated them to second-class status, and reviving the apostasy penalty would only have exacerbated their resentments.

Since there had been no actual trial of the apostasy issue, the appellate court had little evidence on which to base a ruling that Taha was guilty of this offense. To establish his apostasy, the court referred to an ex parte civil proceeding that had been brought in Khartoum in 1968 by private plaintiffs offended by Taha's opinions, which had resulted in a ruling that he was an apostate. The appellate court also relied on declarations by al-Azhar and the Muslim World League to the effect that Taha was an apostate.[60] Thus, Taha was convicted of a capital crime without ever having had a criminal trial establishing his guilt or innocence and in the course of proceedings lacking any semblance of due process. When the judgment calling for the execution of Taha as a heretic was referred to Nimeiri, he said that he was upholding it "on the basis of *Shari'ah* law to protect the nation from the danger of Mahmud Muhammad Taha and his slander of God and his insolence towards Him [God] and to protect this homeland from heresy."[61] In reality, of course, Nimeiri wanted him killed for criticizing the human rights abuses caused by his Islamization campaign.

Taha's followers were also declared apostates from Islam. This meant that, like the Baha'is in Iran, they incurred civil death in accordance with the premodern *shari'a* rules regarding apostasy. Among the consequences were that Republicans' marriages were dissolved, sexual intercourse between the erstwhile spouses became punishable as a capital offense under the then-prevailing Islamic criminal laws, and their children became illegitimate.

Taha was publicly hanged on January 18, 1985, in a prison courtyard in Khartoum. According to reports, he conducted himself in his last moments with the utmost dignity and calm while surrounded by a taunting mob of members of the Ikhwan and other supporters of Nimeiri, who hailed his execution as a great victory for Islam. The regime calculated that Taha's execution would bring it credit for its zealous defense of Islam. The calculation was very wrong in terms of the reaction of the average Sudanese. The revulsion over the execution of the peaceable, elderly religious leader provided a strong impetus for mobilizing the popular coalition against Nimeiri that succeeded in toppling him on April 6, 1985. Owing to the policies of Nimeiri, Islam became associated with an act of medieval barbarism, but many Muslims considered this same execution a violation of the fundamental values of their religion. Killing Taha as a heretic converted him into a martyr for the cause of freedom. Arab human rights activists selected the anniversary of Mahmud Muhammad Taha's execution as the day on which Arab Human Rights Day was to be annually commemorated—a sign that in his opposition to human rights violations perpetrated in the name of Islamization, Taha did not stand alone.

The Sudan under Bashir has been appropriately characterized as "a human rights disaster."[62] In the context of the general repression perpetrated by the Sudanese government, it is not surprising to encounter reports that the non-Muslim southern Sudanese and the non-Muslim Nuba have been forced to convert to Islam. Angry reactions to tales of such forced conversions seem to have been among the factors prompting American Christians to call for the enactment of the Freedom from Religious Persecution Act. However, it would be an invidious distinction to single out the Sudan's violations of non-Muslims' freedom of religion as particularly problematic at a time when forced Arabization is also being pursued; the devastating civil war continues; and horrors such as the slaughter of civilians, the abduction and enslavement of children, and mass rapes are commonplace.[63]

Relatively few of the Sudan's problems are direct consequences of the imposition of Islamic law, most being the outgrowth of the brutalizing effects of a protracted civil war and a corrupt and ideologically rigid governing elite resorting to intimidation and violence to try to shore up its shaky dictatorship. As one observer has characterized the Bashir government, it is a totalitarian regime with a security obsession.[64] The crushing of democratic freedoms, the collapse of the remnants of the rule of law, the routine recourse to torture, and the other manifold vices of the current system mean that members of the majority religion are exposed to severe rights deprivations.[65] As an illustration, Sadiq al-Mahdi, the deposed prime minister and the leader of one of the most powerful Islamic factions in the country, decided in December 1996 after being released from incarceration that he had to flee abroad. If a prominent Islamic leader of his stature is not safe in the Sudan, it should be obvious that simply putting a stop to violations of religious freedom, such as forced conversions to Islam, could not significantly ameliorate the grim plight of the Sudan's suffering populace. In the

Sudan, it is especially important to view the violations of religious freedom as part and parcel of a wider pattern of egregious contempt for human rights and democratic pluralism on the part of the government and its collaborators in Hassan al-Turabi's National Islamic Front.

The Cairo Declaration and the Saudi Basic Law

There is no protection for freedom of religion in the Cairo Declaration or in the Saudi Basic Law, and both documents indicate that the state should propagate Islam.

Article 10 of the Cairo Declaration provides that Islam is "the religion of unspoiled nature," prohibiting any form of compulsion or exploitation of a person's poverty or ignorance in order to convert him to another religion or to atheism. Given the pro-Islamic biases in the declaration, one assumes that all conversions from Islam would be deemed to have resulted from "compulsion" or "exploitation." In contrast, there is no ban on the use of any technique that is applied to convert people *to* Islam.

Article 23 of the Saudi Basic Law calls on the state to propagate the faith, which in context would mean Wahhabism, the puritanical strain of Sunni Islam endorsed by the Saudi monarchy. As in other Muslim countries where there is no protection for freedom of religion and where the state endorses one version of Islamic orthodoxy, both non-Muslims and Muslim minorities may be adversely affected. In Saudi Arabia, the Shi'i minority, characterized as heretical by clerics associated with the monarchy, has been persecuted, but anti-Shi'i policies may shift in the wake of the Saudi rapprochement with Iran that began in 1997.[66] As already noted in Chapter 7, analysis as to whether the mistreatment of non-Muslims is religiously motivated is complicated by the fact that non-Muslims in Saudi Arabia are almost exclusively aliens, and, as such, they are particularly vulnerable to mistreatment within the Saudi system. A further complication lies in the fact that personal vendettas may play a role in who is targeted for prosecution.

The 1996 prosecution and execution of a Syrian national, 'Abd al-Karim al-Mara'i al-Naqshabandi, illustrates how difficult it may be to establish reasons for a prosecution. The Saudi style of administering justice is not constrained by principles such as the requirement that there be a law in force defining conduct as criminal before any criminal prosecution can be brought, leaving Saudi authorities unfettered discretion in defining what conduct is criminal. Human Rights Watch concluded that this case was a prime example of how the absence of any written penal code in Saudi Arabia both encourages and disguises human rights abuses.[67]

Naqshabandi's alleged offense was witchcraft, "the practice of works of magic and spells and possession of a collection of polytheistic and superstitious books."[68] Naqshabandi was apparently unaware that his possession of amulets, horoscopes, and certain religious books could expose him to criminal prosecution for witchcraft. Once he was caught in the maw of the Saudi legal system, where modern norms of due process are disregarded, Naqshabandi was apparently isolated and severely mistreated. He was also prevented from obtaining a lawyer of his choosing to assist him in preparing a defense. In December 1996 the Saudis executed Naqshabandi, whose case had been handled in such a manner that he was, it seems, not even aware on the day that he was scheduled to be killed that he had been found guilty, much less guilty of a capital crime. That witchcraft should be treated as a capital offense in the Saudi legal system speaks volumes about the caliber of justice that that system affords.

People are exposed to persecution and prosecution on religious grounds in Saudi Arabia if they run afoul of powerful interests or provoke the ire of influential personages. Just as the accusation that Nasr Hamid Abu Zaid was an apostate seems to have been originally prompted by a personal vendetta, according to Human Rights Watch, the prosecution of Naqshabandi came about after he inadvertently provoked the ire of his mercurial and vindictive Saudi employer. Again, it seems that the inaptitude of the Saudi system of criminal justice to secure an impartial administration of justice deserves the blame for the outcome, not Islam per se.[69]

Summary

The Islamic human rights schemes under discussion here evince a general lack of sympathy for the idea of freedom of religion, which is such an important component of modern human rights law. These schemes are mostly evasive or uninformative on the question of protections for freedom of religion. Since Muslim societies have inherited a tradition of prohibiting conversion from Islam, a failure to repudiate the *shari'a* rules is strongly suggestive of an intent to retain them. The lack of an unequivocal endorsement of freedom of religion in this context indicates a lack of support for the idea that people should be free to follow the religion of their choice.

The lack of endorsement of the principle of freedom of religion in the Islamic human rights schemes is one of the factors that most sharply distinguishes them from the International Bill of Human Rights, which treats freedom of religion as an unqualified right. This reveals the enormous gap that exists between their authors' mentalities and the modern philosophy of human rights. However, this does not mean that proponents of Islamic versions of rights are generally comfortable with being seen as advocates of killing others for their religious beliefs. Astute politicians can calculate more accurately than Nimeiri and Khomeini did the political costs of openly calling for executing people for apostasy. Appreciating the usefulness of hypocrisy, they disguise their intentions to apply the *shari'a* rules on apostasy and try to deceive the international community about their infringements of freedom of religion.

Although a disturbing record of assaults on the principle of religious freedom has been accumulated by countries like Egypt, Iran, Pakistan, Saudi Arabia, and the Sudan, it would be simplistic to blame Islam per se for these outcomes. After all, these countries' policies are so inimical to religious freedom that professing Muslims may be prosecuted as heretics or blasphemers for what is actually political or theological dissent or may be arbitrarily declared apostates and executed. These outcomes have little to do with mandates of Islamic law. It seems fairer to assess the violations of religious freedom in these countries as a symptom of a pervasive lack of respect for civil and political rights. After all, Muslims who have immersed themselves in the Qur'an have come to share the international ideals of human rights and believe that scrupulous respect for religious freedom is mandated by their scripture. The real conflicts over religious freedom are therefore not so much conflicts between Islamic law and international law as conflicts waged between competing factions within Muslim societies.

CHAPTER 9

An Assessment of Islamic Human Rights Schemes

The Significance of Islamic Human Rights Schemes

Proposing Islamic human rights schemes like the ones reviewed here represents only one of the possible ways that contemporary Muslims have responded to the question of how premodern Islamic doctrine should affect the reception of human rights in contemporary Muslim societies. The attitudes and values of the authors of these Islamic human rights schemes are not more Islamic in the sense of corresponding to any definitive Islamic cultural model of rights than the attitudes and values of Muslims who enthusiastically embrace international human rights as fully compatible with their religious tradition. However, state practice and the growing influence of Islamization have augmented the practical significance of the idea that Islam requires derogations from international law.

Although the Islamic human rights schemes discussed here impose many restraints and qualifications on the rights afforded by international law, they have been presented in formats and terminology designed to lead people to assume that they constitute valid counterparts of international human rights law. This is why it makes sense to call them "schemes"—combinations of elements connected by design. The similarity in formats and terminology naturally invites comparisons, but on close inspection these inevitably reveal the deficiencies of the Islamic schemes by the standards of the international documents that they superficially emulate. Where the Islamic human rights provisions diverge, it turns out that they are designed to dilute, if not altogether eliminate, civil and political rights afforded by international law. The authors of these schemes evince little real sympathy for the ideals of individual rights and freedoms. Instead they accord priority to rationalizing governmental repression, protecting and promoting social and religious conformity, and perpetuating traditional hierarchies, which includes discriminatory treatment of women and non-Muslims. They assert the supremacy of Islamic principles in all areas relevant for the protection of human rights, but these principles are left so vague and amorphous that they can provide sweeping justifications for overriding and nullifying human rights. The very incongruities of the Islamic schemes are interesting from the standpoint of the general problem of the reception of international human rights in dissimilar cultures and, particularly, in cultures in the developing world. They demonstrate how superficial and incomplete imitation of international law can lead to results that are profoundly at variance with the philosophy of human rights.

The authors do not seem to have approached their task with methodological rigor, as the many inconsistencies and deficiencies in their work indicate. At times their rights provisions suggest that they have attained only a tentative grasp of what the concept of a human right entails. There is no evidence of any serious inquiry into the reasons why human rights principles as such were not developed in premodern Islamic legal culture or what the implications of this lack of rights concepts might be for contemporary human rights projects. The authors seem to have no interest in thinking through the jurisprudential adjustments that would be needed to accommodate human rights within an Islamic framework. They incorporate rules developed by premodern Islamic jurists and traditional values without examination of the historical context in which these arose and without critical assessment of the degree to which these may be appropriately employed in the radically different political, economic, and social circumstances of the nations of today.

These Islamic human rights schemes are something other than efforts to mine the Islamic heritage for guidance. Instead of relying exclusively on the Islamic sources, the authors have also engaged in extensive—though unacknowledged—borrowings from ideas and formulations in Western constitutions and international human rights law. In presenting human rights principles that purportedly correspond to authentic Islamic criteria, the authors in fact reach out beyond the confines of the Islamic tradition, employing a variety of terms and concepts that are patently appropriated from international and Western models. These frequent borrowings and the use of principles like "equal protection of the law" that are without precedent in the premodern *shari'a* are puzzling in terms of Islamic jurisprudence, according to which rules not established using Islamic sources and criteria should be irrelevant. One would expect professedly "Islamic" human rights schemes to rest on methods that ensure that the schemes set forth pure, undiluted Islamic principles on the subject—not awkward hybrids. The resulting hybridity, which is never acknowledged, suggests that even conservative Muslims who are ostensibly dedicated to reviving authentic Islamic teachings are disposed to borrow from Western and international models when they deal with human rights. Since the authors are not prepared to confess to borrowing from outside the Islamic tradition, they naturally fail to propose adequate theories for integrating borrowed elements with Islamic ones. Not surprisingly, the resulting admixtures of undigested principles from international law and incompatible Islamic rules show little coherence.

Viewing the incompleteness of their assimilation of international law, one could nonetheless argue that Islamic human rights do constitute a step forward. After all, they suggest that even Muslim conservatives have become persuaded that human rights can and should be integrated in Islamic culture—albeit only tentatively and superficially. For example, some drafters of documents like the Universal Islamic Declaration of Human Rights (UIDHR) or the Cairo Declaration may have believed that even if these did not measure up to international standards, their promulgation would nonetheless enhance the legitimacy of human rights in the eyes of some Muslims by associating Islam with human rights.

That is, one might see the phenomenon of Islamization of human rights as representing a temporary and transitional phase in the process of assimilating international human rights principles. Perhaps the indigenization of international human rights requires—at least for many Muslims who are still attached to aspects of traditional culture—that human rights concepts initially pass through a stage in which international human rights are disassembled and reconstructed to coincide with familiar categories and readjusted to fit conservative values and mores. The merit of such transitional rights formulations would be to introduce rights gradually and conditionally so as to avoid excessive clashes with familiar Islamic strictures.

In this connection, one might speculate that some of the obfuscation and confusion that one sees in these schemes could facilitate the reception of human rights by avoiding specifics that might reveal inherent conflicts. By expedient evasive tactics and intentionally ambiguous formulations, the authors may have intended in some cases to avoid a premature break with the heritage of premodern *shariʿa* rules and associated cultural traditions, a break that could be exploited by adamant opponents of human rights eager to show that human rights principles are incompatible with adherence to Islamic law. If one took an optimistic stance, seeing in Islamic human rights a basically benign, transitional phenomenon, one might hope that the Islamic features that have been grafted onto imported human rights precepts would be eventually discarded when further social and economic development made the international standards more palatable.

Against that, one could adopt a more pessimistic view, predicting that deficiencies of the Islamic human rights schemes that have been backed by governments and influential institutions would harm the prospects for realizing human rights, not serve as a means to facilitate their eventual reception. The presence of this vague and inadequate Islamic human rights literature could actually hinder the development of an awareness of the kinds of human rights that are guaranteed in the International Bill of Human Rights and that would be needed to enable people in the Middle East to mount effective challenges to denials of human rights and, particularly, rights violations perpetrated in the name of "Islam." Since Islamization seems likely to continue, any literature that gives governments grounds for saying that there is Islamic authority for denying the rights afforded under international law could be exploited in ways that would mean setbacks for the cause of human rights.

Once embodied in law, Islamic criteria undermining rights protections could stand in the way of the adoption of human rights principles based on the international models. For example, the incorporation of Islamic limitations on human rights in the text of the 1979 Iranian Constitution means that what were previously informal obstacles in local custom and tradition to realizing international human rights protections have been elevated to the stature of formal constitutional norms that affirm Islamic restrictions on rights. These formal limitations on rights may prove difficult for subsequent generations of Iranians to dismantle—just as the retrograde Islamization measures promulgated under Muhammad Zia ul-Haq have proved resistant to challenge after democracy was restored in Pakistan. The distinctive Islamic features of Islamic human rights schemes could be seen less as a natural transitional stage in the absorption of alien institutions than as roadblocks standing in the way of adopting international human rights law.

In evaluating the significance of Islamic human rights schemes it is helpful to examine the ways that other Western ideologies and institutions have been transformed when transplanted to developing societies with dissimilar cultures. One might consider in this regard a phenomenon like the reformulation of imported Catholicism in a host environment like Brazil's. There, for many persons who retain links to African culture and institutions, the alien precepts of Roman Catholicism are acceptable only insofar as they are presented in a syncretic version combining Catholicism with features of African tradition. Thus, in the Africanized Brazilian version of Catholicism, African priests and priestesses retain their traditional authority, African folklore has been joined with Catholic worship, and analogies are drawn between Catholic saints and African gods and goddesses.[1] The resulting syncretic religion is neither strictly Catholic nor strictly African, but a scheme blending two very dissimilar traditions that has been concocted by people who had been exposed to both and who needed to find an accommodation between the two. For African Brazilians, the syncretizing of the two makes congenial what would otherwise seem to be an alien system, one threatening to their culture and social organization.

Although their hybrid religion hardly conforms to the standards of orthodoxy of the Roman Catholic Church, a powerful institution in Brazil, it is tolerated by the Church hierarchy. Some members of the Brazilian Catholic Church may feel that it is better to accept an Africanized version of Catholicism than to resist Africanization and be left with a situation where there would be no Catholic influence on local religion. That might result were the Brazilian Catholic hierarchy to insist rigidly that no deviations from Roman norms would be tolerated. Although to an outsider this toleration might seem surprising, since elements of Catholicism and African religion appear conflicting and incompatible, to those interested in promulgating Catholicism in Brazil, the resulting hybrid may seem an acceptable compromise stage en route to converting Brazilians to a more orthodox understanding of the Catholic religion.

A comparison with the Africanized Catholicism of Brazil clarifies the significance of Islamic human rights. Certainly, the Islamic human rights schemes discussed here are syncretic in nature, combining categories and terms taken from international human rights with some elements of *shari'a* rules and associated cultural values. The combinations can, however, be distinguished from the blending of elements of Catholicism and African culture and religion in Brazil, a grassroots phenomenon, not one imposed from above. Brazilian Africans are free today to choose between African religion and Catholicism but instead opt for a hybrid blend of both traditions. Brazilian Africans' religious ideas grew organically out of a situation in which people confronted an imposed Western religion that clashed with their African tradition and sought to integrate the two.

In contrast, the Islamic and international elements in Islamic human rights schemes have been artificially conjoined by members of ruling cliques, clerical and political elites, and other religious and legal "experts." Africanized Catholicism in Brazil is a manifestation of popular culture, but popular culture did not provide the impetus for creating the diluted human rights that one finds in Islamic human rights schemes. The impetus for Islamization of human rights has emerged under the auspices of repressive regimes or with the blessings of conservative religious factions and institutions. No Islamic human rights schemes have emerged via democratic processes in open political systems that incorporated input from grassroots opinion.

One could speculate that these Islamic schemes of human rights might have broad popular appeal by virtue of their simultaneous association with both Islam and human rights. In fact, there is little evidence that the Islamic labels on the enfeebled rights protections in these Islamic rights schemes make them more attractive to the average Muslim than the stronger rights guarantees found in the International Bill of Human Rights. Muslim human rights advocates and human rights associations that have emerged in Muslim countries since the 1980s have campaigned to realize the human rights set forth in international law, not watered-down "Islamic" alternatives like the ones examined here. Awareness of what the international guarantees of rights and freedoms mean is spreading. As the world is brought closer together by modern communications, it becomes more difficult even for the most repressive regimes to block the penetration of ideas of democracy and human rights, which in the late 1980s resoundingly demonstrated their popular appeal and capacity to undermine the legitimacy of despotic governments around the globe. Precisely because Muslim countries have human rights records that range from the mediocre to the atrocious, they provide fertile soil for conversions to the ideals of international human rights, which address the problems that actually face contemporary Muslims.

Proponents of the idea that Islamic criteria should override and cancel out international human rights principles, leaving people in Muslim societies with rights inferior to those guaranteed to the rest of humanity, have not been willing to submit this proposition to the general public for a popular vote. However, when dictators imposing Islamization have been ousted and Muslims acquainted with the impact of Islamization on rights have been allowed to vote, their disenchantment has been patent. When voters had the opportunity to vote in free elections in the Sudan in 1986 and in Pakistan after 1988, the candidates most closely identified with Islamization fared dismally and those who criticized rights abuses and who were identified with commitments to democratize and expand freedoms did well. Furthermore, in 1997, when Iran loosened its strictures sufficiently to allow a cleric critical of curbs on freedom in the name of Islamization to run for president, he won in a landslide. Iran requires all candidates for public office to support its Islamic ideology, but in Pakistan and the Sudan, where voters had a chance to vote against candidates who were associated with the official Islamic ideologies espoused by the previous dictatorships, they effectively repudiated Islamization.

To identify what is at stake in the contest between Islamic and international human rights, one needs to ask who would benefit and who would lose if international human rights provisions were enacted into law and effective mechanisms to ensure their observance were set in place. The benefits of international human rights would be felt by the population as a whole, which would be spared the pervasive rights abuses that have plagued Middle Eastern societies. With international human rights in place, instead of being terrorized by brutal rulers, the population would have a chance to hold rulers accountable for their misdeeds and to build up the institutions of civil society. Instead of living in intellectual prisons, they would be free to enjoy access to cultures from around the world and could express their ideas without fear of dire consequences lest they offend some cultural commissar or reactionary cleric. Rather than being compelled to live like children under the tutelage of governments that equate morality with repression, they could live like adults, free to make their own choices regarding how to live a meaningful and rewarding life. Implementation of the international norms would lead to enhanced rights for women and religious minorities, who would be freed of the discrimination that relegates them to a vulnerable and inferior status. Muslims would no longer be menaced with punishment for heresy and apostasy if they questioned old verities or official lines on religious orthodoxy. The losers would include unpopular, tyrannical rulers and groups whose interests are closely linked to the preservation of privilege and inequality and the repression of dissident voices. Muslim men's reactions might be equivocal. They would forfeit their privileged status both within the family and, to a lesser extent, in society at large, but many might find the loss of such privileges outweighed by the benefits of an open society and an accountable government.

Islamic Particularism Versus Universality

The authors of the Islamic human rights schemes reviewed here display a remarkable ambivalence regarding international human rights law. While speaking in terms of cultural particularism and exploiting features of the Islamic heritage to make a case for derogating from international law, the authors of these schemes have striven to disguise as much as possible disparities between their Islamic rights schemes and the international standards. Their eagerness to hide the disparities between their Islamic rights and international law seems incongruous. Since the authors consistently maintain that Islamic law is superior to all secular legal principles, they might be expected to dismiss other conflicting rights principles as incorrect. Sultanhussein Tabandeh, as noted, actually did this at certain points. Tabandeh argued that Islam should be the universal model, replacing the rights set forth in international law. He asked:

> Why do we not simply put into practice our own Islamic laws? Indeed, why do we not put them forward at the United Nations Assembly and at its various Commissions and Conferences? Why do we not orientate the compasses of the nations of the world by the pole-star of Islam, and publicly glory in our possession of laws that so exactly fit the human condition? Why do we not demonstrate the value of these laws, and illustrate their excellence in our words and in our practice? Why do we not invite the United Nations to express their Conventions in the terms already laid down in the Islamic Canon?[2]

Tabandeh is exceptional in being prepared to acknowledge openly that following Islamic criteria entails departures from international law. For him, the Islamic criteria are nonetheless normative. In part because the au-

thors of these Islamic human rights schemes have complicated and ambiva-
lent relationships to the system of international law and in part because of
the authors' own political preferences, their relationship to the Islamic legal and cultural heritage is not nearly as straightforward as his.

One can see the ambivalence in the stances of countries like Iran and
Saudi Arabia, which approached the World Conference on Human Rights
of June 1993 disposed to press the case for Islamic particularism. In their
domestic policies, they consistently relied on Islam to bar the application of
international human rights norms. However, when the conference con-
vened, both presented Islamic human rights as if they were compatible
with adherence to international law. Both urged the acceptance of Islamic
versions of human rights in lieu of the international ones, but without acknowledging, as Raja'i Khorasani had previously done, that this entailed
violating international norms. Indeed, they seemed to have decided to mute
their opposition to international human rights and, rather than insisting on
cultural relativism, to advocate a kind of vague, qualified universalism.

For example, the Saudi foreign minister, in speaking at the conference,
maintained that Islamic law afforded "a comprehensive system for universal human rights." Instead of glorifying Islamic cultural particularism, he
professed to concur that the principles and objectives on which human
rights were based were "of a universal nature," merely adding the modest
caveat that in their application it was necessary to show "consideration for
the diversity of societies, taking into account their various historical, cultural, and religious backgrounds and legal systems."[3]

The head of Iran's delegation at the conference denied that rights based
on religious teachings sacrificed the value of the individual for the well-being of the community. Far from pressing for a cultural relativist approach
to human rights, he contended that human rights were universal. He also
asserted that a multidimensional approach to rights, meaning in context
one that would take into account Islamic rights, could "provide a better
background for the full realization of human rights." He argued that
"drawing from the richness and experience of all cultures, and particularly
those based on divine religions, would only logically serve to enrich human
rights concepts."[4] Thus, rather than following Iran's earlier practice and
candidly admitting that Iran's Islamic rights entailed clashes with international law—and asserting that Islamic law justified its violations of human
rights—the Iranian delegation changed tactics and spoke as if Iran's concern was using Islamic principles to enhance rights.

After debates over the universality of rights, the Vienna Declaration and
Program of Action issued at the end of the conference asserted: "The universal nature of these rights and freedoms is beyond question." However,
the declaration injected a note of ambiguity by also advising that "the significance of national and regional particularities and various historical,

cultural and religious backgrounds must be borne in mind." The ambiguity in the final declaration must have pleased Iran and Saudi Arabia, which had apparently decided that international human rights had garnered so much legitimacy that, at least when faced with international audiences, they would be imprudent to continue opposing the principle of their universality outright. Instead, they found it preferable to adopt a more nuanced stance in hopes of blurring the issue of what they meant when they called for taking Islamic culture into account.

Islamization and Cultural Nationalism

Campaigns for Islamization of law are based on the notion that the imposition of Western law was part of an imperialist plot both to undermine the independence of Muslim states and to demean the Islamic heritage. The impetus behind the campaigns to reinstate Islamic law and cast aside laws associated with the era of Western domination is as much nationalist as it is religious. Campaigns to Islamize human rights can be linked to the unease that is felt in the Muslim Middle East over the extent of the region's cultural dependency on the contemporary West. Resentment of this dependency leads Middle Easterners to strive for cultural autonomy, to defend institutions associated with their own cultural heritage against charges of backwardness, and to offer countermodels to Western ideas and institutions.[5] Some of the features of the Islamic human rights schemes discussed here are influenced by the environment in which they were produced, where resentment of Western cultural dominance is very potent. The perspectives of the authors of the human rights schemes are influenced by cultural nationalism, and the Islamic schemes are also designed to appeal to sentiments of cultural nationalism.

The thrust of these campaigns is to show that Islam and indigenous culture have institutions comparable to those in the West and that they are equally "advanced." But what is "advanced" is constantly being defined in modern, Western terms. Thus, in the course of reacting against Western law, proponents of Islamization do not necessarily achieve the goal of banishing the influence of the Western legal culture. This leads to cultural confusion in drawing up Islamic counterparts to Western legal models, because the Islamic counterparts are constructed with constant reference to the Western models that they are designed to replace. The *shari'a* is reformulated to fit borrowed Western categories, such as constitutional rights provisions. The result is an admixture of Islamic and Western elements, replicating alien formulations of human rights and constitutional principles—albeit often only in a superficial manner and without incorporating their philosophical premises.

As examples of this cultural confusion, one could cite two of the authors who most energetically condemn the West: Both Abu'l A'la Mawdudi and

Sultanhussein Tabandeh sensed that the authority of the *shariʿa* rules used to restrict human rights depends on their finding Western examples and precedents that confirm their soundness. In his book explaining why the Western model of emancipation for women is bad and should be repudiated by Muslims, Mawdudi relied extensively on the findings of Western "scientists," "experts," and "authorities" to establish that Western freedoms have led to social and moral disaster—with the corollary that *shariʿa* rules mandating female subjugation and seclusion are sound.[6] Tabandeh, despite his claiming to believe in the superiority of *shariʿa* law, found a clinching argument to support his assertion that under *shariʿa* rules women should be excluded from politics in the fact that women were denied the vote in Switzerland, "one of the most civilized and most perfect societies of the world."[7] These arguments are revealing: The criticisms they fear are those that emanate from Muslims who are familiar with Western models and approaches to rights. Therefore Mawdudi and Tabandeh have felt compelled to devise rationales for *shariʿa* rules based on Western science— or pseudoscience—and Western experience. Such Western-inspired rationales are, however, utterly irrelevant from the standpoint of Islamic jurisprudence and would play no role in any rights scheme that was actually based on Islamic sources and a more rigorous methodology.

Cultural nationalism also helps explain why authors of Islamic human rights schemes insist, despite the overwhelming historical evidence to the contrary, that human rights originated in Islam, pretending that the Western and international principles from which they are heavily borrowing are the derivative ones. Because the sources of Islamic law date from the seventh century, and all Islamic law is in theory derived from these sources, the authors seem to have concluded that human rights must be shown to have been established from the outset of Islamic legal history. Thus, Islamic human rights principles have to be projected back into the seventh century—as they are in the preamble to the Cairo Declaration, which situates them in the Revelation to the Prophet Muhammad. There is an utter failure to deal with the historical reality that, although the Islamic sources may have foreshadowed ideas that were later developed into human rights principles, the study of Islamic civilization shows that the potential of the sources as statements of human rights principles was not developed until the twentieth century.

If one bears in mind the need to avoid acknowledging an intellectual debt to Western civilization, the claims for the Islamic origins of human rights become intelligible. What one sees in these Islamic human rights schemes is a manifestation of a broader phenomenon that has been commented on by French scholars observing contemporary developments in Islamic thought. Called *concordisme* or *concordisme pieux* (harmonization or pious harmonization), the practice involves strained attempts by Muslims to project modern intellectual developments that have emerged out-side the Muslim world back into the Islamic past. The impetus behind this *concordisme* is a desire to show that Islam anticipated all valued achievements of modern civilization. It entails retroactively Islamizing these by in-venting supposed Islamic antecedents. However, in this process readings of Islam are being forced to conform to external models, at the same time that comparative intellectual history is being distorted.

A desire to establish that the West is indebted to Islam for advances that the West has wrongfully claimed as its own prompted the foreword to the UIDHR to assert that "Islam gave to mankind an ideal code of human rights fourteen centuries ago," this being calculated using the Islamic lunar calendar. In the 1980 Kuwait seminar on human rights in Islam, the con-clusion was drawn that "Islam was the first to recognize basic human rights and almost 14 centuries ago it set up guarantees and safeguards that have only recently been incorporated in universal declarations of human rights."[8] In the keynote address at the same seminar, it was claimed: "To the student of the Qur'an not one word, in the preamble or in the objec-tives of the [UN] Charter and not a single article in the text of the 'Univer-sal Declaration of Human Rights' will seem unfamiliar. . . . [T]he 'Univer-sal Declaration of Human Rights' must follow as a basic corollary, or an extension of the Qur'anic programme."[9] Attending a 1997 Sarajevo semi-nar on the Qur'an and human rights, Iran's Ayatollah Jannati insisted that Islam had best defined all aspects of human rights and that the human rights proposed by the United Nations merely recapitulated rights pro-pounded over a thousand years earlier.[10]

Tabandeh, for all of his professed disappointment with certain features of the Universal Declaration of Human Rights (UDHR), argued that Islam anticipated all the declaration's provisions and projected these back into the Islamic past, asserting that the UDHR "has not promulgated anything that was new nor inaugurated innovations. Every clause of it, indeed, every valuable regulation needed for the welfare of human society . . . already ex-isted in a better and more perfect form in Islam."[11] Despite the fact that the details of Tabandeh's commentary on the UDHR reveal a deep philosophi-cal antipathy toward the rights and freedoms that it provides, Tabandeh obviously feels that Islam will be considered deficient if it cannot be shown to have anticipated the UDHR

It is instructive to contrast the attitudes of authors of the Islamic human rights schemes reviewed here with those of the authors of the International Bill of Human Rights, which betray none of the defensiveness of the for-mer. When one considers the improbability of a drafter of an international human rights document being moved to boast that the *shari'a* had not pro-mulgated anything that constituted an innovation in relation to interna-tional human rights or to claim that the provisions in the international document were more perfect than those in the *shari'a,* one is able to appreciate the great difference in perspectives. From the standpoint of specialists in international law, there is no need to assert its superiority vis-à-vis the *shari'a* because the authority of international law is taken as a given. The idea of the potential relevance of the *shari'a*—or any other religious law— as a rival and more prestigious standard never even occurs to them. In contrast, to establish the authority of their own Islamic models, Tabandeh and others like him must try to discredit international human rights or portray them as derivative.

Mawdudi, who, as has been shown here, espoused ideas that are in fundamental conflict with international human rights law, likewise attempted to defend the thesis that human rights originated in Islam, while castigating Westerners for their presumptions to have originated human rights. In keeping with his general concern for showing that Islam and Muslim societies are wrongly accused of being culturally backward and underdeveloped, he complained that "people in the West have the habit of attributing every beneficial development in the world to themselves."[12] After presenting his ideas on human rights, Mawdudi asserted: "This is a brief sketch of those rights which 1400 years ago Islam gave to man. . . . It refreshes and strengthens our faith in Islam when we realize that even in this modern age, which makes such loud claims of progress and enlightenment, the world has not been able to produce more just and equitable laws than those given 1400 years ago. On the other hand, it is saddening to realize that Muslims nonetheless often look for guidance to the West."[13]

Mawdudi clearly meant to persuade Muslims that they should abandon all references to the allegedly derivative Western rights concepts and refer instead to the original models, which are Islamic rights.[14] His disappointment with Muslims who seek intellectual guidance in the West did not reflect the teachings of Islam, the doctrines of which are free of nationalist bias and which do not set any geographical limits on where Muslims may search for wisdom and enlightenment. His injunctions to Muslims not to look for guidance in Western rights principles instead reflected his espousal of the cause of cultural nationalism.

One sees that cultural nationalism lies behind some of the confusion in these Islamic human rights schemes. If Islam is taken as having anticipated the most influential post–World War II human rights documents, Islamic human rights and constitutional rights provisions must somehow be made to look like those in the international documents and Western constitutions. This means that instruments like the UDHR effectively set the agendas for presentations of the Islamic human rights that are designed to replace them, whence ensues the extensive borrowing from Western models and terminology. In such an endeavor, there is no room for critical examination of whether the rules and priorities of the premodern *shari'a* that the authors seek to preserve are compatible with human rights. Internal contradictions and inconsistencies are the inevitable result of the authors' casually appropriating the formulas and terminology of international human rights law without first assessing the intellectual foundations on which international human rights rest in comparison with the underpinnings of premodern Islamic jurisprudence.

Another feature of Islamic human rights that indicates the influence of cultural nationalism is the frequent reference to practice in the West (from any period in the history of Western civilization) that deviated from modern human rights standards along with a corresponding unwillingness to deal with actual rights problems in contemporary Muslim societies. Accounts of the golden age under the Prophet Muhammad and his immediate successors in the seventh century are treated as the model of how Islamic rights work in practice—as if the perfections being ascribed to *shari'a* law meant that all Muslim societies over the centuries have conformed to the ideals of the golden age of Islam. The failure to examine critically the rights situation in Muslim societies throughout history reflects this literature's apologetic, defensive function—to denigrate Western civilization and to exalt the heritage of Islamic civilization rather than to come to grips with human rights problems that contemporary Muslims actually face, as well as the historical origins of these.

Of course, historically, governments in both the West and the Muslim world have engaged in conduct that would constitute egregious violations of rights by the standards of modern human rights norms. Judged by contemporary standards, both Western and Muslim societies have over the centuries accumulated records of serious infringements of civil and political rights. However, despite many grievous lapses, Western countries since the nineteenth century have by and large been moving in the direction of affording greater protections for the human rights of their citizens and imposing limits on the abilities of governments to infringe on these rights. Today, the rights protections afforded in the law of Western democracies, although far from perfect, are nonetheless better developed than elsewhere. In contrast, in the Muslim world the current human rights situation is generally a dismal one, even worse than it was under traditional, despotic regimes. The oppressive rule of the centralized, authoritarian, or totalitarian regimes that predominate in the Middle East is stifling in its impact on freedom, because the state has greatly increased its power and a variety of social and economic changes have weakened the ability of societies to resist governmental overreaching and coercion.[15] Thus, in lieu of progress in the direction of enhancing rights, the actual trends in Middle Eastern countries have often been in the direction of diminishing individual autonomy and freedom.

The realities of oppression and rights violations by governments in the Muslim world are neglected by the authors of Islamic human rights

schemes. Naturally, they have no wish to address how Islamization programs have degraded rights. Instead, where the latter do treat real human
rights problems, they tend to focus on Western human rights violations in
an attempt to show that Western human rights protections are inadequate
and ineffectual and that Westerners who criticize human rights abuses in
the Middle East are hypocritical.[16] When one considers how improbable it
would be for people in a Western society to try to deflect criticism of their
governments' violations of human rights by pointing out that serious violations of human rights had occurred in Muslim countries, one grasps that
such tactics reveal which side feels beleaguered and defensive about its
progress in implementing human rights.

By alluding to the violations of human rights that have been perpetrated
by the West, the authors seem to think they are discrediting both the Western rights models and potential Western critics of their Islamic human
rights schemes. Thus, the record of rights violations in the West, which was
touched on in the Kuwait seminar, was somehow deemed relevant to understanding the comparative merits of Islamic human rights.[17] In contrast,
the proponents of Islamic human rights at the 1980 Kuwait seminar on Islam and human rights expressly denied that Islamic human rights could be
evaluated by reference to the historical record, saying, "It is unfair to judge
Islamic law (Shari'a) by the political systems which prevailed in various pe-
riods of Islamic history."[18]

This last statement would be unexceptionable if it meant that one should
distinguish between practice and theory and between the conduct of governments and the teachings of the Islamic religion, but it would be mis-
guided if it suggested that the efficacy of human rights guarantees could
not be evaluated by the degree to which they protect rights in practice. The
historical record of the centuries in which Islamic law was officially the
governing standard indicates that efficacious protections for rights analogous to modern human rights were virtually nonexistent.

Actual Human Rights Concerns in the Middle East

As has been noted, the Islamic human rights literature avoids dealing with
actual human rights problems in the Middle East, but many human rights
activists in the Middle East are engaged in struggles to identify the actual
causes of oppression and to devise concrete, practical solutions that offer
prospects for ending rights violations. A deep cleavage has resulted between the idealistic focus of proponents of Islamization, who tend to envisage Islamic law as the magical solution to all problems, and the focus of
Muslim human rights activists on the institutional failings and procedural
deficiencies that must be corrected in order to secure human rights protections. A recent debate between Islamists and human rights activists has

confirmed how Islamists stress the virtues of Islamic principles in the abstract, whereas Muslim human rights activists stress the need to attend to details of process and institutional frameworks.[19]

In striking contrast to the silence of Islamic human rights schemes regarding actual human rights problems, a thoughtful and exceptionally outspoken critique of the human rights situation in the Arab world was publicly issued by a group of Arab intellectuals after a meeting in Tunis in 1983. Portions of their critique, which also applies, mutatis mutandis, to many aspects of the rights predicaments in non-Arab countries in the region, will be summarized and paraphrased here to show how Middle Easterners who are not swept up in the politics of cultural nationalism and who are not engaged in apologetic enterprises vis-à-vis the West appraise the situation.

The critique asserts that under various pretexts—such as the needs of socialism, development, realization of pan-Arab unity, protecting national sovereignty, and fighting Israel—demands for democracy have been denied. It claims that freedom, aside from its social usefulness, is a value in and of itself, one that all Arabs long for and all regimes deny. Not only are Arabs prevented from free expression and from participating in the determination of their fate, but also they are constantly exposed to repression. Fear of imprisonment, murder, mass murder, and torture dominates their lives. Arab individuals are so humiliated, their spheres of personal freedom so restricted, and their voices so crushed into silence and subjugation that they become prone to despair and the incapacity to act. These repressive measures are condemned in the critique, along with institutions such as emergency courts and police-state tactics; the critique demands that trials be conducted according to law. It calls on Arab governments to respect civil rights and not to infringe personal freedoms guaranteed by the UDHR. The first priority is affirmed to be equal treatment for all citizens regardless of belief, descent, or sex. In most Arab countries, it says, authority is based on the subjugation of citizens. The consequences are confusion in values and norms and the absence of critical thought. A monolithically structured, hermetically closed system of authority dominates the scene, leaving no room for political or intellectual pluralism or for the development of genuine culture. The participants called for guarantees for certain freedoms, especially freedom of belief, freedom of opinion and expression, freedom to participate, freedom of assembly, and freedom to form political organizations and unions. They also demanded guarantees for the rights of women and minorities and an independent judiciary.[20]

This critique should be borne in mind because it proves that intellectuals who genuinely desire human rights in the Middle East are prepared to speak out to denounce the actual patterns of human rights violations by current governments and that they do not hesitate to invoke international human rights norms in their criticisms. It also confirms that the common forms of oppression by Middle Eastern regimes are not just objectionable by Western standards but are perceived by people within these societies, especially their educated members, to be impermissibly harsh in their impact on individuals and stultifying in terms of their impact on society and culture. The comments show that the kinds of justifications that are offered by government officials for patterns of repression are not necessarily accepted by the people in these societies and that the latter do not consider participatory democracy an exotic, Western luxury; instead, they attribute many of the problems afflicting their own societies to its absence.

An important study of the connections between the lack of democracy and the violations of human rights in the Arab world published in Egypt developed many of the themes discussed in the Tunis declaration.[21] It is noteworthy that a work produced by Arabs that undertakes a critical evaluation of rights problems does not bother to discuss Islamic human rights schemes; the implication is that they are irrelevant. There are many indications that the kinds of Islamic human rights schemes that are reviewed here do not impress Muslims who are sincerely committed to devising realistic formulas for ending human rights abuses and advancing democratic governance.

In significant contrast to the kinds of critiques just mentioned, the Islamic human rights schemes examined in this book insist on the absolute perfection of abstract Islamic ideals while ignoring altogether the myriad problems of institutionalizing and implementing human rights protections and democratizing closed systems in the Middle East. The schemes talk of Islamic human rights as if such rights enjoyed unquestioned authority and automatic efficaciousness by reason of their divine provenance, owing to which no government would dare to tamper with them. For example, in its Preamble, the UIDHR says of Islamic human rights that "by virtue of their Divine source and sanction these rights can neither be curtailed, abrogated or disregarded by authorities, assemblies or other institutions, nor can they be surrendered or alienated."[22] In presenting the Cairo Declaration at the 1993 World Conference on Human Rights in Vienna as the authoritative statement of Islamic rights, the Saudi foreign minister insisted that in Islamic law, human rights are not mere moral exhortations but "legislative orders," containing "all the legal texts necessary for ensuring their implementation and enforcement."[23] He thereby suggested that Islamic law and the Cairo Declaration afforded efficacious rights protections.

Supporters of such positions must ignore the grim reality of the human rights situation in the Middle East, because to admit its dimensions and the lack of respect that governments have routinely shown for the law, including Islamic law, would entail confronting the fact that the religious pedigrees of Islamic rules are not by themselves sufficient to guarantee that they will be respected in practice. Muslims who are genuinely committed to advancing human rights and who understand the prerequisites for establishing a free and democratic order realize that it is reforms in the prevailing political cultures and systemic changes, and not simple appeals to abstract Islamic ideals, that can lay the groundwork for guaranteeing the rule of law and the effective protection of human rights.

Summary

As this assessment has indicated, the Islamic human rights schemes discussed in the foregoing are products of the political contexts in which they emerged. Their Islamic pedigrees are dubious, and the principles they contain do not represent the result of rigorous, scholarly analyses of the Islamic sources or a coherent approach to Islamic jurisprudence. Instead, they seem largely shaped by their conservative authors' negative reactions to the model of freedom in Western societies and the scope of rights protections afforded by the International Bill of Human Rights. Resentment of the West and cultural nationalism have also shaped the authors' approach to human rights. Placing these reactions under an Islamic rubric does not mean that Islam is the real impetus behind the resulting rights provisions.

The Islamic human rights schemes reviewed here do not simply replicate principles stated in the Islamic sources, even though they often incorporate references to Islamic sources. The consequences of using these sources for designing schemes of rights or protorights are not self-evident, as the great diversity of Muslim opinion in this area proves. Thus, all conclusions about the implications of the Islamic sources necessarily rest on interpretations of the sources, interpretations that, depending on the philosophy of the interpreters, have led to conclusions that were in some instances favorable to human rights, and in others incompatible with respect for human rights.

In producing their Islamic human rights schemes, the authors used material from the Islamic heritage, often confused with the values found in traditional societies, in a highly selective manner, resulting in a one-sided representation of Islamic teachings relating to rights that suited the authors' conservative proclivities. Although they borrow extensively from international law, their objective is to dilute and distort it. They have been disinclined to seek a synthesis of Islamic and international human rights that could unsettle the status quo or serve the cause of curbing the actual patterns of human rights violations prevailing in Middle Eastern countries. Instead, they have repeatedly exploited Islam as if it provided a warrant for perpetuating and even exacerbating the prevailing repression and rights abuses.

These Islamic human rights schemes reflect their authors' own preferences for antirationalist, antihumanistic currents in Islamic thought. Thus, from an array of options afforded by Islamic civilization, the schemes deliberately incorporate those elements that present obstacles to the accommodation of modern human rights principles—obstacles that are then attributed to Islam. If the authors' aim had been to advance protection for human rights in Muslim milieus, they could have acknowledged that the Islamic heritage comprises rationalist and humanistic currents and that it is replete with values that complement modern human rights such as concern for human welfare, justice, tolerance, and egalitarianism. These could provide the basis for constructing a viable synthesis of Islamic principles and international human rights, as proved by the work of enlightened Muslims who have demonstrated the compatibility of Islam and human rights.

All this leads to the conclusion that the characteristics of the Islamic human rights schemes examined here should not be ascribed to peculiar features of Islam or its inherent incompatibility with human rights. Instead, these diluted rights should be seen as part of a broader phenomenon of attempts by elites—the beneficiaries of undemocratic and hierarchical systems—to legitimize their opposition to human rights by appealing to supposedly distinctive cultural traditions.

Excerpts from the Constitution of the Islamic Republic of Iran of 24 October 1979 As Amended to 28 July 1989[1]

In the Name of Allah, the Compassionate, the Merciful
We sent aforetime Our apostles with clear signs, and sent down with them
the Book and the Balance that men may uphold justice . . . (57:25)

Preamble

The Constitution of the Islamic Republic of Iran sets forth the cultural, social, political, and economic institutions of Iranian society on the basis of Islamic principles and norms, which represent the earnest aspiration of the Islamic *Ummah* [community]. . . .

The Form of Government in Islam

In the view of Islam, government does not derive from the interests of a class, nor does it serve the domination of an individual or a group. It represents rather the crystallization of the political ideal of a people who bear a common faith and common outlook, taking an organized form in order to initiate the process of intellectual and ideological evolution towards the final goal, i.e., movement towards *Allah*. Our nation, in the course of its revolutionary developments, has cleansed itself of the dust and impurities that accumulated during the *taghuti* [heathenish] past and purged itself of foreign ideological influences, returning to authentic intellectual standpoints and world-view of Islam. It now intends to establish an ideal and model society on the basis of Islamic norms. The mission of the Constitution is to realize the ideological objectives of the movement and to create conditions conducive to the development of man in accordance with the noble and universal values of Islam. . . .

Legislation setting forth regulations for the administration of society will revolve around the Qur'an and the *Sunnah*. Accordingly, the exercise of meticulous and earnest supervision by just, pious, and committed scholars of Islam (*al-fuqaha al-'udul)* is an absolute necessity. . . .

Women in the Constitution

Through the creation of Islamic social infrastructures, all the elements of humanity that hitherto served the multifaceted foreign exploitation shall regain their true identity and human rights. As part of this process, it is only natural that women should benefit from a particularly large augmentation of their rights, because of the greater oppression that they suffered under the *taghuti* regime.

The family is the fundamental unit of society and the main centre for the growth and edification of human being[s]. Compatibility with respect to belief and ideal, which provides the primary basis for man's development and growth, is the main consideration in the establishment of a family. It is the duty of the Islamic government to provide the necessary facilities for the attainment of this goal. This view of the family unit delivers woman from being regarded as an object or as an instrument in the service of promoting consumerism and exploitation. Not only does woman recover thereby her momentous and precious function of motherhood, rearing of ideologically committed human beings, she also assumes a pioneering social role and becomes the fellow struggler of man in all vital areas of life. Given the weighty responsibilities that woman thus assumes, she is accorded in Islam great value and nobility.

An Ideological Army

In the formation and equipping of the country's defence forces, due attention must be paid to faith and ideology as the basic criteria. Accordingly, the Army of the Islamic Republic of Iran and the Islamic Revolutionary Guards Corps are to be organized in conformity with this goal, and they will be responsible not only for guarding and preserving the frontiers of the country, but also for fulfilling the ideological mission of *jihad* in God's way; that is, extending the sovereignty of God's law throughout the world. . . .

General Principles

Article 1

The form of government of Iran is that of an Islamic Republic, endorsed by the people of Iran on the basis of their longstanding belief in the sovereignty of truth and Qur'anic justice, in the referendum of . . . [March 29 and 30, 1979], through the affirmative vote of a majority of 98.2% of eligible voters, held after the victorious Islamic Revolution led by the eminent *marji' al-taqlid* [source of emulation], Ayatullah al-'Uzma Imam Khumayni.

Article 2

The Islamic Republic is a system based on belief in:

1. the One God (as stated in the phrase "There is no god except Allah"), His exclusive sovereignty and the right to legislate, and the necessity of submission to His commands;
2. Divine revelation and its fundamental role in setting forth the laws;

3. the return to God in the Hereafter, and the constructive role of this belief in the course of man's ascent towards God;
4. the justice of God in creation and legislation;
5. continuous leadership *(imamah)* and perpetual guidance, and its fundamental role in ensuring the uninterrupted process of the revolution of Islam;
6. the exalted dignity and value of man, and his freedom coupled with responsibility before God; in which equity, justice, political, economic, social, and cultural independence, and national solidarity are secured by recourse to:
   A. continuous *ijtihad* [interpretation] of the *fuqaha* possessing necessary qualifications, exercised on the basis of the Qur'an and the *Sunnah* of the *Ma'sumun* [the Prophet, his daughter Fatima, the Shi'i Imams], upon all of whom be peace;
   B. sciences and arts and the most advanced results of human experience, together with the effort to advance them further;
   C. negation of all forms of oppression, both the infliction of and the submission to it, and of dominance, both its imposition and its acceptance.

Article 3

In order to attain the objectives specified in Article 2, the government of the Islamic Republic of Iran has the duty of directing all its resources to the following goals:

1. the creation of a favourable environment for the growth of moral virtues based on faith and piety and the struggle against all forms of vice and corruption;
2. raising the level of public awareness in all areas, through the proper use of the press, mass media, and other means;
3. free education and physical training for everyone at all levels, and the facilitation and expansion of higher education;
4. strengthening the spirit of inquiry, investigation, and innovation in all areas of science, technology, and culture, as well as Islamic studies, by establishing research centres and encouraging researchers;
5. the complete elimination of imperialism and the prevention of foreign influence;
6. the elimination of all forms of despotism and autocracy and all attempts to monopolize power;
7. ensuring political and social freedoms within the framework of the law;
8. the participation of the entire people in determining their political, economic, social, and cultural destiny;
9. the abolition of all forms of undesirable discrimination and the provision of equitable opportunities for all, in both the material and intellectual spheres;
10. the creation of a correct administrative system and elimination of superfluous government organizations;

11. all round strengthening of the foundations of national defence to the utmost degree by means of universal military training for the sake of safeguarding the independence, territorial integrity, and the Islamic order of the country;
12. the planning of a correct and just economic system, in accordance with Islamic criteria, in order to create welfare, eliminate poverty, and abolish all forms of deprivation with respect to food, housing, work, health care, and the provision of social insurance for all;
13. the attainment of self-sufficiency in scientific, technological, industrial, agricultural, and military domains, and other similar spheres;
14. securing the multifarious rights of all citizens, both women and men, and providing legal protection for all, as well as the equality of all before the law;
15. the expansion and strengthening of Islamic brotherhood and public cooperation among all the people;
16. framing the foreign policy of the country on the basis of Islamic criteria, fraternal commitment to all Muslims, and unsparing support to the *mustad'afun* [oppressed] of the world.

Article 4

All civil, penal, financial, economic, administrative, cultural, military, political, and other laws and regulations must be based on Islamic criteria. This principle applies absolutely and generally to all articles of the Constitution as well as to all other laws and regulations, and the *fuqaha* of the Guardian Council are judges in this matter.

Article 5

During the Occultation of the *Wali al-'Asr* [Shi'i Imam] (may God hasten his reappearance), the *wilayah* [governance] and leadership of the Ummah devolve upon the just *('adil)* and pious *(muttaqi) faqih* [jurist], who is fully aware of the circumstances of his age; courageous, resourceful, and possessed of administrative ability, [he] will assume the responsibilities of this office in accordance with Article 107.

Article 7

In the Islamic Republic of Iran, the affairs of the country must be administered on the basis of public opinion expressed by the means of elections, including the election of the President, the representatives of the Islamic Consultative Assembly, and the members of councils, or by means of referenda in matters specified in other articles of this Constitution. . . .

Article 8

In the Islamic Republic of Iran, *al-'amr bil-ma'ruf wa al-nahy 'an al-munkar* [commanding the good and forbidding the evil] is a universal and reciprocal duty that must be fulfilled by the people with respect to one another, by the government with respect to the people, and by the people with respect to the government. The conditions, limits, and nature of this duty will be specified by law. (This is in accordance with the Qur'anic verse: "The believers, men and women, are guardians of one another; they enjoin the good and forbid the evil" [9:71]). . . .

Article 9

In the Islamic Republic of Iran, the freedom, independence, unity, and territorial integrity of the country are inseparable from one another, and their preservation is the duty of the government and all individual citizens. No individual, group, or authority, has the right to infringe in the slightest way upon the political, cultural, economic, and military independence or the territorial integrity of Iran under the pretext of exercising freedom. Similarly, no authority has the right to abrogate legitimate freedoms, not even by enacting laws and regulations for that purpose, under the pretext of preserving the independence and territorial integrity of the country.

Article 10

Since the family is the fundamental unit of Islamic society, all laws, regulations, and pertinent programmes must tend to facilitate the formation of a family, and to safeguard its sanctity and the stability of family relations on the basis of the law and the ethics of Islam.

Article 12

The official religion of Iran is Islam and the Twelver Ja'fari school . . . and this principle will remain eternally immutable. Other Islamic schools, including the Hanafi, Shafi'i, Maliki, Hanbali, and Zaydi, are to be accorded full respect, and their followers are free to act in accordance with their own jurisprudence in performing their religious rites. These schools enjoy official status in matters pertaining to religious education, affairs of personal status (marriage, divorce, inheritance, and wills) and related litigation in courts of law. In regions of the country where Muslims following any one of these schools of *fiqh* [jurisprudence] constitute the majority, local regulations, within the bounds of the jurisdiction of local councils, are to be in accordance with the respective school of *fiqh*, without infringing upon the rights of the followers of other schools.

Article 13

Zoroastrian, Jewish, and Christian Iranians are the only recognized religious minorities, who, within the limits of the law, are free to perform their religious rites and ceremonies, and to act according to their own canon in matters of personal affairs and religious education.

Article 14

In accordance with the sacred verse ("God does not forbid you to deal kindly and justly with those who have not fought against you because of your religion and who have not expelled you from your homes" [60:8]), the government of the Islamic Republic of Iran and all Muslims are duty-bound to treat non-Muslims in conformity with ethical norms and the principles of Islamic justice and equity, and to respect their human rights. This principle applies to all who refrain from engaging in conspiracy or activity against Islam and the Islamic Republic of Iran. . . .

The Rights of the People

Article 19

All people of Iran, whatever the ethnic group or tribe to which they belong, enjoy equal rights; and colour, race, language, and the like, do not bestow any privilege.

Article 20

All citizens of the country, both men and women, equally enjoy the protection of the law and enjoy all human, political, economic, social, and cultural rights, in conformity with Islamic criteria.

Article 21

The government must ensure the rights of women in all respects, in conformity with Islamic criteria, and accomplish the following goals:

1. create a favourable environment for the growth of woman's personality and the restoration of her rights, both the material and intellectual;
2. the protection of mothers, particularly during pregnancy and childrearing, and the protection of children without guardians;
3. establishing competent courts to protect and preserve the family;
4. the provision of special insurance for widows, and aged women and women without support;
5. the awarding of guardianship of children to worthy mothers, in order to protect the interests of the children, in the absence of a legal guardian.

Article 22

The dignity, life, property, rights, residence, and occupation of the individual are inviolate, except in cases sanctioned by law.

Article 23

The investigation of individuals' beliefs is forbidden, and no one may be molested or taken to task simply for holding a certain belief.

Article 24

Publications and the press have freedom of expression except when it is detrimental to the fundamental principles of Islam or the rights of the public. The details of this exception will be specified by law.

Article 25

The inspection of letters and the failure to deliver them, the recording and disclosure of telephone conversations, the disclosure of telegraphic and telex communications, censorship, or the willful failure to transmit them, eavesdropping, and all forms of covert investigation are forbidden, except as provided by law.

Article 26

The formation of parties, societies, political or professional associations, as well as religious societies, whether Islamic or pertaining to one of the recognized religious minorities, is permitted provided they do not violate the principles of independence, freedom, national unity, the criteria of Islam, or the basis of the Islamic Republic. No one may be prevented from participating in the aforementioned groups, or be compelled to participate in them.

Article 27

Public gatherings and marches may be freely held, provided arms are not carried and that they are not detrimental to the fundamental principles of Islam.

Article 28

Everyone has the right to choose any occupation he wishes, if it is not contrary to Islam and the public interests, and does not infringe the rights of others. The government has the duty, with due consideration of the need of society for different kinds of work, to provide every citizen with the opportunity to work, and to create equal conditions for obtaining it. . . .

Article 32

No one may be arrested except by the order and in accordance with the procedure laid down by law. In case of arrest, charges with the reasons for accusation must, without delay, be communicated and explained to the accused in writing, and a provisional dossier must be forwarded to the competent judicial authorities within a maximum of twenty-four hours so that the preliminaries to the trial can be completed as swiftly as possible. The violation of this article will be liable to punishment in accordance with the law. . . .

Article 37

Innocence is to be presumed, and no one is to be held guilty of a charge unless his or her guilt has been established by a competent court.

Article 38

All forms of torture for the purpose of extracting confession or acquiring information are forbidden. Compulsion of individuals to testify, confess, or take an oath is not permissible; and any testimony, confession, or oath obtained under duress is devoid of value and credence. Violation of this article is liable to punishment in accordance with the law.

Article 39

All affronts to the dignity and repute of persons arrested, detained, imprisoned, or banished in accordance with the law, whatever form they may take, are forbidden and liable to punishment.

Article 40

No one is entitled to exercise his rights in a way injurious to others or detrimental to public interests. . . .

The Right of National Sovereignty and the Powers Deriving Therefrom

Article 56

Absolute sovereignty over the world and man belongs to God, and it is He Who has made man master of his own social destiny. No one can deprive man of this divine right, nor subordinate it to the vested interests of a particular individual or group. The people are to exercise this divine right in the manner specified in the following articles. . . .

Powers and Authority of the Islamic Consultative Assembly

Article 72

The Islamic Consultative Assembly cannot enact laws contrary to the *usul* and *ahkam* [sources and rules] of the official religion of the country or to the Constitution. It is the duty of the Guardian Council to determine whether a violation has occurred, in accordance with Article 96. . . .

Article 91

With a view to safeguard the Islamic ordinances and the Constitution, in order to examine the compatibility of the legislations passed by the Islamic Consultative Assembly with Islam, a council to be known as the Guardian Council is to be constituted with the following composition:

1. six *'adil fuqaha*, conscious of the present needs and the issues of the day, to be selected by the Leader, and
2. six jurists, specializing in different areas of law, to be elected by the Islamic Consultative Assembly from among the Muslim jurists nominated by the Head of the Judicial Power. . . .

Article 96

The determination of compatibility of the legislation passed by the Islamic Consultative Assembly with the laws of Islam rests with the majority vote of the *fuqaha* on the Guardian Council; and the determination of its compatibility with the Constitution rests with the majority of all the members of the Guardian Council. . . .

The Leader or Leadership Council

Article 107

After the demise of the eminent *marji al-taqlid* and great leader of the universal Islamic revolution, and founder of the Islamic Republic of Iran, Ayatullah al-Uzma

Imam Khumayni ... who was recognised and accepted as *marji'* and Leader by a decisive majority of the people, the task of appointing the Leader shall be vested with the experts elected by the people. The experts will review and consult among themselves concerning all the *fuqaha* possessing the qualifications specified in Articles 5 and 109. In the event they find one of them better versed in Islamic regulations, the subjects of the *fiqh,* or in political and social issues, or possessing general popularity or special prominence for any of the qualifications mentioned in Article 109, they shall elect him as the Leader. Otherwise, in the absence of such a superiority, they shall elect and declare one of them as the Leader. The Leader thus elected by the Assembly of Experts shall assume all the powers of the *wilayat al-amr* [command] and all the responsibilities arising therefrom.

The Leader is equal with the rest of the people of the country in the eyes of law. . . .

Article 112

Upon the order of the Leader, the Nation's Exigency Council shall meet at any time the Guardian Council judges a proposed bill of the Islamic Consultative Assembly to be against the principles of *Shari'ah* or the Constitution, and the Assembly is unable to meet the expectations of the Guardian Council. Also, the Council shall meet for consideration on any issue forwarded to it by the Leader and shall carry out any other responsibility as mentioned in this Constitution.

The permanent and changeable members of the Council shall be appointed by the Leader. The rules for the Council shall be formulated and approved by the Council members subject to the confirmation by the Leader. . . .

The Presidency

Article 115

The President must be elected from among religious and political personalities possessing the following qualifications:

Iranian origin; Iranian nationality; administrative capacity and resourcefulness; a good past record; trustworthiness and piety; convinced belief in the fundamental principles of the Islamic Republic of Iran and the official *madhhab* [school of law] of the country.

The Army and the Islamic Revolution Guard Corps

Article 144

The Army of the Islamic Republic of Iran must be an Islamic Army, i.e., committed to Islamic ideology and the people, and must recruit into its service individuals who have faith in the objectives of the Islamic Revolution and are devoted to the cause of realizing its goals.

The Cairo Declaration on Human Rights in Islam[1]

The Member States of the Organisation of the Islamic Conference,

Reaffirming the civilizing and historical role of the Islamic Ummah which God made the best nation that has given mankind a universal and well-balanced civilization in which harmony is established between this life and the hereafter and knowledge is combined with faith; and the role that this Ummah should play to guide a humanity confused by competing trends and ideologies and to provide solutions to the chronic problems of this materialistic civilization;

Wishing to contribute to the efforts of mankind to assert human rights, to protect man from exploitation and persecution, and to affirm his freedom and right to a dignified life in accordance with the Islamic Shari'ah;

Convinced that mankind which has reached an advanced stage in materialistic science is still, and shall remain, in dire need of faith to support its civilization and of a self motivating force to guard its rights;

Believing that fundamental rights and universal freedoms in Islam are an integral part of the Islamic religion and that no one as a matter of principle has the right to suspend them in whole or in part or violate or ignore them in as much as they are binding divine commandments, which are contained in the Revealed Books of God and were sent through the last of His Prophets to complete the preceding divine messages thereby making their observance an act of worship and their neglect or violation an abominable sin, and accordingly every person is individually responsible—and the Ummah collectively responsible—for their safeguard;

Proceeding from the above-mentioned principles,

Declare the following:

Article 1:

A. All human beings form one family whose members are united by submission to God and descent from Adam. All men are equal in terms of basic human dignity and basic obligations and responsibilities, without any discrimination on the grounds of race, colour, language, sex, religious belief, political affiliation, social status or other considerations. True faith is the guarantee for enhancing such dignity along the path to human perfection.

B. All human beings are God's subjects, and the most loved by Him are those who are most useful to the rest of His subjects, and no one has superiority over another except on the basis of piety and good deeds.

Article 2:

A. Life is a God-given gift and the right to life is guaranteed to every human being. It is the duty of individuals, societies and states to protect this right from any violation, and it is prohibited to take away life except for a Shari'ah prescribed reason.
B. It is forbidden to resort to such means as may result in the genocidal annihilation of mankind.
C. The preservation of human life throughout the term of time willed by God is a duty prescribed by Shari'ah.
D. Safety from bodily harm is a guaranteed right. It is the duty of the state to safeguard it, and it is prohibited to breach it without a Shari'ah-prescribed reason.

Article 3:

A. In the event of the use of force and in case of armed conflict, it is not permissible to kill non-belligerents such as old men, women and children. The wounded and the sick shall have the right to medical treatment; and prisoners of war shall have the right to be fed, sheltered and clothed. It is prohibited to mutilate dead bodies. It is a duty to exchange prisoners of war and to arrange visits or reunions of the families separated by the circumstances of war.
B. It is prohibited to fell trees, to damage crops or livestock, and to destroy the enemy's civilian buildings and installations by shelling, blasting or any other means.

Article 4:

Every human being is entitled to inviolability and the protection of his good name and honour during his life and after his death. The state and society shall protect his remains and burial place.

Article 5:

A. The family is the foundation of society, and marriage is the basis of its formation. Men and women have the right to marriage, and no restrictions stemming from race, colour or nationality shall prevent them from enjoying this right.
B. Society and the State shall remove all obstacles to marriage and shall facilitate marital procedure. They shall ensure family protection and welfare.

Article 6:

A. Woman is equal to man in human dignity, and has rights to enjoy as well as duties to perform; she has her own civil entity and financial independence, and the right to retain her name and lineage.
B. The husband is responsible for the support and welfare of the family.

Article 7:

A. As of the moment of birth, every child has rights due from the parents, society and the state to be accorded proper nursing, education and material, hygienic and moral care. Both the fetus and the mother must be protected and accorded special care.

B. Parents and those in such like capacity have the right to choose the type of education they desire for their children, provided they take into consideration the interest and future of the children in accordance with ethical values and the principles of the Shari'ah.

C. Both parents are entitled to certain rights from their children, and relatives are entitled to rights from their kin, in accordance with the tenets of the Shari'ah.

Article 8:

Every human being has the right to enjoy his legal capacity in terms of both obligation and commitment, [and] should this capacity be lost or impaired, he shall be represented by his guardian.

Article 9:

A. The question [*sic*] for knowledge is an obligation and the provision of education is a duty for society and the State. The State shall ensure the availability of ways and means to acquire education and shall guarantee educational diversity in the interest of society so as to enable man to be acquainted with the religion of Islam and the facts of the Universe for the benefit of mankind.

B. Every human being has the right to receive both religious and worldly education from the various institutions of education and guidance, including the family, the school, the university, the media, etc., and in such an integrated and balanced manner as to develop his personality, strengthen his faith in God and promote his respect for and defence of both rights and obligations.

Article 10:

Islam is the religion of unspoiled nature. It is prohibited to exercise any form of compulsion on man or to exploit his poverty or ignorance in order to convert him to another religion or to atheism.

Article 11:

A. Human beings are born free, and no one has the right to enslave, humiliate, oppress or exploit them, and there can be no subjugation but to God the Most-High.

B. Colonialism of all types being one of the most evil forms of enslavement is totally prohibited. Peoples suffering from colonialism have the full right to freedom and self-determination. It is the duty of all States and peoples to support the struggle of colonized peoples for the liquidation of all forms of colonialism and occupation, and all States and peoples have the right to preserve their independent identity and exercise control over their wealth and natural resources.

Article 12:

Every man shall have the right, within the framework of Shari'ah, to free movement and to select his place of residence whether inside or outside his country and if persecuted is entitled to seek asylum in another country. The country of refuge shall ensure his protection until he reaches safety, unless asylum is motivated by an act which Shari'ah regards as a crime.

Article 13:

Work is a right guaranteed by the State and Society for each person able to work. Everyone shall be free to choose the work that suits him best and which serves his interests and those of society. The employee shall have the right to safety and security as well as to all other social guarantees. He may neither be assigned work beyond his capacity nor be subjected to compulsion or exploited or harmed in any way. He shall be entitled—without any discrimination between males and females—to fair wages for his work without delay, as well as to the holidays allowances and promotions which he deserves. For his part, he shall be required to be dedicated and meticulous in his work. Should workers and employers disagree on any matter, the State shall intervene to settle the dispute and have the grievances redressed, the rights confirmed and justice enforced without bias.

Article 14:

Everyone shall have the right to legitimate gains without monopolization, deceit or harm to oneself or to others. Usury *(riba)* is absolutely prohibited.

Article 15:

A. Everyone shall have the right to own property acquired in a legitimate way, and shall be entitled to the rights of ownership, without prejudice to oneself, others or to society in general. Expropriation is not permissible except for the requirements of public interest and upon payment of immediate and fair compensation.

B. Confiscation and seizure of property is prohibited except for a necessity dictated by law.

Article 16:

Everyone shall have the right to enjoy the fruits of his scientific, literary, artistic or technical production and the right to protect the moral and material interests stemming therefrom, provided that such production is not contrary to the principles of Shari'ah.

Article 17:

A. Everyone shall have the right to live in a clean environment, away from vice and moral corruption, an environment that would foster his self-development and it is incumbent upon the State and society in general to afford that right.

B. Everyone shall have the right to medical and social care, and to all public amenities provided by society and the State within the limits of their available resources.

C. The State shall ensure the right of the individual to a decent living which will enable him to meet all his requirements and those of his dependents, including food, clothing, housing, education, medical care and all other basic needs.

Article 18:

A. Everyone shall have the right to live in security for himself, his religion, his dependents, his honour and his property.

B. Everyone shall have the right to privacy in the conduct of his private affairs, in his home, among his family, with regard to his property and his relationships. It is not permitted to spy on him, to place him under surveillance or to besmirch his good name. The State shall protect him from arbitrary interference.

C. A private residence is inviolable in all cases. It will not be entered without permission from its inhabitants or in any unlawful manner, nor shall it be demolished or confiscated and its dwellers evicted.

Article 19:

A. All individuals are equal before the law, without distinction between the ruler and the ruled.

B. The right to resort to justice is guaranteed to everyone.

C. Liability is in essence personal.

D. There shall be no crime or punishment except as provided for in the Shari'ah.

E. A defendant is innocent until his guilt is proven in a fair trial in which he shall be given all the guarantees of defence.

Article 20:

It is not permitted without legitimate reason to arrest an individual, or restrict his freedom, to exile or to punish him. It is not permitted to subject him to physical or psychological torture or to any form of humiliation, cruelty or indignity. Nor is it permitted to subject an individual to medical or scientific experimentation without his consent or at the risk of his health or of his life. Nor is it permitted to promulgate emergency laws that would provide executive authority for such actions.

Article 21:

Taking hostages under any form or for any purpose is expressly forbidden.

Article 22:

A. Everyone shall have the right to express his opinion freely in such manner as would not be contrary to the principles of the Shari'ah.

B. Everyone shall have the right to advocate what is right, and propagate what is good, and warn against what is wrong and evil according to the norms of Islamic Shari'ah.

C. Information is a vital necessity to society. It may not be exploited or misused in such a way as may violate sanctities and the dignity of Prophets, undermine moral and ethical values or disintegrate, corrupt or harm society or weaken its faith.

D. It is not permitted to arouse nationalistic or doctrinal hatred or to do anything that may be an incitement to any form or racial discrimination.

Article 23:

A. Authority is a trust; and abuse or malicious exploitation thereof is absolutely prohibited, so that fundamental human rights may be guaranteed.

B. Everyone shall have the right to participate, directly or indirectly in the administration of his country's public affairs. He shall also have the right to assume public office in accordance with the provisions of Shari'ah.

Article 24:

All the rights and freedoms stipulated in this Declaration are subject to the Islamic Shari'ah.

Article 25:

The Islamic Shari'ah is the only source of reference for the explanation or clarification of any of the articles of this Declaration.

Cairo, 14 Muharram 1411H
5 August 1990

Notes

Chapter 1

1. Excellent analyses of this problem can be found in the work of Bassam Tibi: *The Crisis of Modern Islam: A Preindustrial Culture in the Scientific Technological Age,* trans. Judith von Silvers (Salt Lake City: University of Utah Press, 1988); and *Islam and the Cultural Accommodation of Social Change,* trans. Clare Krojzl (Boulder: Westview Press, 1990).

2. A useful survey of human rights activity can be found in the articles assembled in *MERIP Middle East Report,* November-December 1987. See H. E. Chehabi, *Iranian Politics and Religious Modernism: The Liberation Movement of Iran Under the Shah and Khomeini* (Ithaca: Cornell University Press, 1990); Virginia Sherry, "The Human Rights Movement in the Arab World: An Active and Diverse Community of Human Rights Advocates Exists in Several Countries of the Region," *Human Rights Watch* 4, Special Middle East Watch Issue (Fall 1990), 6–7; Kevin Dwyer, *Arab Voices: The Human Rights Debate in the Middle East* (Berkeley: University of California Press, 1991); Ann Elizabeth Mayer, "Moroccans: Citizens or Subjects? A People at the Crossroads," *New York University Journal of International Law and Politics* 26 (1993), 63–105; Hanny Megally, "Amnesty International and Human Rights in the Arab World: A Summary of the Last Decade," in *Democracia y Derechos Humanos en el Mundo Árabe,* ed. Gema Martín Muñoz (Madrid: Agencia Española de Cooperación Internacional, 1993), 163–176; Susan Waltz, *Human Rights and Reform: Changing the Face of North African Politics* (Berkeley: University of California Press, 1995); and *Cairo Papers in Social Science. Human Rights: Egypt and the Arab World* 17 (Fall 1994). For cyberspace sources, see Nancy Gallagher, "Middle East and North African Human Rights Activism in Cyberspace," *Middle East Studies Association Bulletin* 31 (July 1997), 17–19.

3. See Alan Watson, *Legal Transplants: An Approach to Comparative Law* (Edinburgh: Scottish-Academic Press, 1974), 6–9.

4. The writings of Abdullahi An-Na'im are important exceptions. These include *Toward an Islamic Reformation: Civil Liberties, Human Rights and International Law* (Syracuse, N.Y.: Syracuse University Press, 1990). See also Sami Aldeeb Abu Sahlieh, "Les Droits de l'homme et l'Islam," *Revue générale de droit international public* 89 (1985), 625–716; "Liberté religieuse et apostasie dans l'Islam," *Praxis juridique et religion* 3 (1986), 43–76; and *Les Musulmans face aux droits de l'homme: Religion et droit et politique. Etude et documents* (Bochum, Germany: Verlag Dr. Dieter Winkler, 1994). Critical appraisals are also presented in Jack

Donnelly, "Human Rights and Human Dignity: An Analytic Critique of Non-Western Conception of Human Rights," *American Political Science Review* 76 (1982), 306–316; Jack Donnelly, *Universal Human Rights in Theory and Practice* (Ithaca: Cornell University Press, 1989), 50–52; Lucie Pruvost, "Déclaration universelle des droits de l'homme dans l'Islam et Charte internationale des droits de l'homme: Convergences-Divergences, *IslamoChristiana* 9 (1983), 141–157; Maurice Borrmans, "Les droits de l'homme en milieu musulman," *Studia Missionalia* 39 (1990), 254–276; Bassam Tibi, *Der Schatten Allahs: Islam und Menschenrechte* (Munich: Piper Press, 1994); and Tore Lindholm and Kari Vogt, eds., *Islamic Law Reform and Human Rights: Challenges and Rejoinders* (Copenhagen: Nordic Human Rights Publications, 1993).

5. Perverse mischaracterizations that are deployed by persons who are determined to discredit critical examinations of this topic are exemplified by the far-fetched accusations that hostile reviewers have hurled at earlier editions of this book. These include charges that the book presents Islam as a monolithic model (!), that it imagines that Islam is static and inherently opposed to rights (!), and that it argues that "contemporary Muslims do not possess the culture that entitles them to be concerned with human rights" (!). See in this connection the review by Ahmad Dallal, *Middle East Studies Association Bulletin* 26 (1992), 245–246; remarks in John Strawson, "A Western Question to the Middle East: 'Is There a Human Rights Discourse in Islam?'" *Arab Studies Quarterly* 19 (Winter 1997), 31–58; and characterizations in Ridwan al-Sayyid, "Contemporary Muslim Thought and Human Rights," *IslamoChristiana* 21 (1995), 27–41. This book may have many failings, but putting forward such stereotypes is not one of them.

6. People who tend to oppose open discussion of sensitive issues are rarely specialists in international law. Combined expertise in Islamic law and international law can provide the basis for undertaking critical comparative study of the two, as proved by the work of Abdullahi An-Na'im.

7. Edward Said, *Orientalism* (London: Routledge and Kegan Paul, 1978).

8. These comments echo remarks made in Sadiq Jalal al-'Azm, "Orientalism and Orientalism in Reverse," in *Forbidden Agendas: Intolerance and Defiance in the Middle East,* ed. Jon Rothschild (London: Al-Saqi Books, 1984), 349–381. See also "The Importance of Being Earnest about Salman Rushdie," *Die Welt des Islams* 31 (1991), 1–49, by the same author.

9. A good illustration of this position can be found in Adamantia Pollis and Peter Schwab, "Human Rights: A Western Construct with Limited Applicability," in *Human Rights: Cultural and Ideological Perspectives,* ed. Adamantia Pollis and Peter Schwab (New York: Praeger, 1979), 1–18.

10. Ibid., 14. Pollis has come to acknowledge that the state may exploit the language of cultural relativism to rationalize its own repression. See Adamantia Pollis, "Cultural Relativism Revisited: Through a State Prism," *Human Rights Quarterly* 18 (1996), 316–344. Strangely, the author argues that universalists' conceptual framework blinds them to non-Western states' violations of the values and notions of justice and humanity in their own cultures. In reality, as this book demonstrates, espousing the universality of human rights encourages inquiry into whether supposedly cultural rationales for deviating from international law may in reality be prompted by state policy and political interests that should be distinguished from the local culture(s).

11. United Nations General Assembly. Thirty-Ninth Session. Third Committee. Sixty-fifth meeting, held on Friday, December 7, 1984, at 3 p.m. New York. A/C.3/39/SR.65.

12. See Ann Elizabeth Mayer, "Universal Versus Islamic Human Rights: A Clash of Cultures or a Clash with a Construct?" *Michigan Journal of International Law* 15 (1994), 317–320, 371–377, 392.

13. Fernando Teson, "International Human Rights and Cultural Relativism," *Virginia Journal of International Law* 25 (1985), 875.

14. Donnelly, *Universal Human Rights*, 114.

15. For a critical evaluation of cultural relativists' tendency to totalize and reify Islamic culture, see Mayer, "Universal Versus Islamic Human Rights," 379–402; and Reza Afshari, "An Essay on Islamic Cultural Relativism in the Discourse on Human Rights," *Human Rights Quarterly* 16 (1994), 235–276. The need to differentiate between the ideologized Islam sponsored by Iran's national government and Islamic religion and culture as these persist in a village is shown by the observations in Reinhold Loeffler, *Islam in Practice: Religious Beliefs in a Persian Village* (Albany: State University of New York Press, 1988); and Erika Loeffler Friedl, *Women of Deh Koh: Lives in an Iranian Village* (Washington, D.C.: Smithsonian Institution, 1989).

16. John Kelsay, "Saudi Arabia, Pakistan, and the Universal Declaration of Human Rights," in *Human Rights and the Conflict of Cultures: Western and Islamic Perspectives on Religious Liberty,* ed. David Little, John Kelsay, and Abdulaziz Sachedina (Columbia: University of South Carolina Press, 1988), 35–36.

17. Ibid., 36–37.

18. I have not run across a single instance where a Muslim conversant with international human rights who felt injured by a government act in breach of internationally guaranteed human rights voluntarily acquiesced in the violation of the right on the grounds that Muslims were not entitled to claim the same rights as other human beings or that rights protections were alien to Islamic culture.

19. Regarding the Western tendency to consider it incongruous for Orientals to have modern ideas, see Rhoda E. Howard, "Cultural Absolutism and the Nostalgia for Community," *Human Rights Quarterly* 15 (1993), 315–338.

20. Teson, "International Human Rights," 895.

21. This trend has been dissected in Rhoda E. Howard, *Human Rights and the Search for Community* (Boulder: Westview Press, 1995).

22. Louis Muñoz, "The Rationality of Tradition," *Archiv für Rechts und Sozialphilosophie* 68 (1981), 212.

23. Donnelly, *Universal Human Rights*, 117.

24. Ibid., 118.

25. Jack Donnelly, "Cultural Relativism and Universal Human Rights," *Human Rights Quarterly* 6 (1984), 411.

26. Rachad Antonius, "Human Rights and Cultural Specificity: Some Reflections," in *Cairo Papers in Social Science. Human Rights: Egypt and the Arab World* 17 (Fall 1994), 22.

27. See Ann Elizabeth Mayer, "Qadhafi's Retreat from Revolutionary Legalism," in *Qadhafi's Revolution, 1969–1994,* ed. Dirk Vanderwalle (New York: St. Martin's Press, 1995), 113–137.

28. See, for example, the discussions among Islamists and human rights activists in Lawyers Committee for Human Rights, *Islam and Justice: Debating the Future of Human Rights in the Middle East and North Africa* (New York: Lawyers Committee for Human Rights, 1997), showing how Islamists seek to associate their goals with human rights. Sometimes current Islamists' programs can actually sound more like the appeals of human rights nongovernmental organizations (NGOs). See Khaled Elgindy, "The Rhetoric of Rashid Ghannouchi," *Arab Studies Quarterly* (Spring 1995), 101–119. At the same time, human rights NGOs are seeking to educate Muslims about how human rights can be harmonized with Islamic values. See the manual prepared by the Sisterhood Is Global Institute, Mahnaz Afkhami and Haleh Vaziri, *Claiming Our Rights: A Manual for Women's Human Rights Education in Muslim Societies* (Bethesda, Md.: Sisterhood Is Global Institute, 1996).

29. Abdullahi An-Na'im, "Religious Minorities Under Islamic Law and the Limits of Cultural Relativism," *Human Rights Quarterly* 9 (1987), 5.

Chapter 2

1. Updated information on ratifications can be found at <http://www.un.org/newfiles/frontboo/toc4.htm>. After some delay, the relevant information also appears in hard copy adjacent to the respective human rights treaties in the annual volumes of the United Nations publication *Multilateral Treaties Deposited with the Secretary-General.*

2. Louis Henkin, "International Human Rights as Rights," in *Human Rights: NOMOS XXIII,* ed. J. Roland Pennock and John W. Chapman (New York: New York University Press, 1981), 258–259.

3. The translation in this edition is taken from "Constitution of the Islamic Republic of Iran of 24 October 1979 as amended to 28 July 1989," *Constitutions of the Countries of the World,* Albert Blaustein and Gisbert Flanz, eds. (Dobbs Ferry: Oceana, 1992).

4. The problems of establishing constitutional government in Iran are discussed in Yann Richard, *Le Shi'isme en Iran: Imam et Révolution* (Paris: Maisonneuve, 1980); Abdul-Hadi Hairi, *Shi'ism and Constitutionalism in Iran* (Leiden: Brill, 1977); Said Arjomand, ed., *Authority and Political Culture in Shi'ism* (Albany: State University of New York Press, 1988); and Janet Afary, *The Iranian Constitutional Revolution, 1906–1911: Grassroots Democracy, Social Democracy, and the Origins of Feminism* (New York: Columbia University Press, 1996).

5. Shaul Bakhash, *The Reign of the Ayatollahs* (New York: Basic Books, 1984).

6. The amendments are discussed in Asghar Schirazi, *The Constitution of Iran: Politics and the State in the Islamic Republic,* trans. John O'Kane (London: I. B. Tauris, 1997), 95, 110–111, 234–237.

7. Both English and Arabic versions of the Cairo Declaration were submitted to the United Nations by the Organization of the Islamic Conference (OIC) prior to the World Conference on Human Rights in Vienna. See UN GAOR, World Conference on Human Rights, 4th Session, Agenda Item 5, UN Doc. A/CONF.157/PC/62/Add.18 (1993).

8. Ann Elizabeth Mayer, "Universal Versus Islamic Human Rights: A Clash of Cultures or a Clash with a Construct?" *Michigan Journal of International Law* 15 (1994), 375.

9. Ibid., 371–379.

10. See Isabelle Vichniac, "La Commission internationale de juristes dénonce un project de 'déclaration des droits de l'homme en Islam,'" *Le Monde,* February 13, 1992. In response to a subsequent critical report by the International Commission of Jurists on the rule of law in Iraq, Iraq argued for a cultural relativist approach, defending its political order by asserting that democracy was affected by the "social, religious, and local characteristics of a nation" and that liberal democracy succeeded in the West because it suited the characteristics of Western societies—implying that it was unsuitable for Iraq. See International Commission of Jurists, *Iraq and the Rule of Law. Draft. A Study by the International Commission of Jurists* (February 1994).

11. "Closing Session of Teheran's Islamic Summit Delayed," *Deutsche Presse-Agentur,* December 11, 1997, available in LEXIS, Nexis Library, ALLWLD File.

12. An English translation of the Saudi Basic Law can be found in "Saudi Arabia: The New Constitution," *Arab Law Quarterly* 8 (1993), 258–270. The reforms are discussed in Rashed Aba-Namay, "The Recent Constitutional Reforms in Saudi Arabia," *International and Comparative Law Quarterly* 42 (1993), 295–331.

13. Article 7 of the law said that the government derived its power from the Islamic sources, the Qur'an and the custom of the Prophet, which constituted law superior to the Basic Law and other laws, and Article 1 asserted that Saudi Arabia was an Islamic state.

14. Even some ideologues of Islamization have conceded that Islam does not afford a comprehensive system of guidance. While pretending to govern Iran according to a putative Islamic model, Iran's postrevolutionary leaders have had to recognize the insufficiency of the Islamic legal corpus as a blueprint for running a contemporary government. See Schirazi, *The Constitution of Iran.*

15. For examples of how Muslims are meshing human rights ideas with the Islamic tradition, see Abdullahi An-Na'im, *Toward an Islamic Reformation: Civil Liberties, Human Rights and International Law* (Syracuse, N.Y.: Syracuse University Press, 1990); Abdullahi El-Naiem [An-Na'im], "A Modern Approach to Human Rights in Islam: Foundations and Implications for Africa," in *Human Rights and Development in Africa,* ed. Claude Welch Jr. and Ronald Meltzer (Albany: State University of New York Press, 1984), 75–89; and Abdullahi An-Na'im, "Religious Freedom in Egypt: Under the Shadow of the Islamic *Dhimma* System," in *Religious Liberty and Human Rights in Nations and Religions,* ed. Leonard Swidler (Philadelphia: Ecumenical Press, 1986), 43–59. See also Subhi Mahmassani, *Arkan huquq al-insan* (Beirut: Dar al-'ilm li'l-malayin, 1979); H. E. Chehabi, *Iranian Politics and Religious Modernism: The Liberation Movement of Iran under the Shah and Khomeini* (Ithaca: Cornell University Press, 1990); Tore Lindholm and Kari Vogt, eds., *Islamic Law Reform and Human Rights: Challenges and Rejoinders* (Copenhagen: Nordic Human Rights Publications, 1993); Fatima Mernissi, *Islam and Democracy: Fear of the Modern World,* trans. Mary Jo Lakeland (Reading, Mass.: Addison-Wesley, 1992); and Lawyers Committee for Human Rights, *Islam and Justice: Debating the Future of Human Rights in the Middle East and North*

Africa (New York: Lawyers Committee for Human Rights, 1997). The rethinking by contemporary Muslim feminists of the premodern norms of *shari'a* law affecting women, which is discussed in Chapter 6, is another example of the trend toward harmonization of Islamic precepts with international rights.

16. "Sudan Moslem Prayer Leaders Criticise Government," *Agence France Presse,* November 22, 1997, available in LEXIS, Nexis Library, ALLWLD File.

17. Suroosh Irfani, *Revolutionary Islam in Iran: Popular Liberation or Religious Dictatorship?* (London: Zed Books, 1983) (on unnumbered page preceding the dedication page).

18. See his speeches in Mohammad Khatami, *Hope and Challenge: The Iranian President Speaks* (Binghamton, N.Y.: Institute of Global Cultural Studies, Binghamton University, 1997). He argues: "When confronting the opponent in the name of rejecting the West and defending religion, if we step on freedom we will have caused a great catastrophe" (17). However, he concedes: "A system like ours, based as it is on Islamic utopian ideology, is bound to restrict some individual liberties" (49).

19. How cynically Iranian women have been reacting to clerical sermons about Islamic morality is suggested by the interviews in Haleh Esfandiari, *Reconstructed Lives: Women and Iran's Islamic Revolution* (Baltimore: Johns Hopkins University Press, 1997).

20. "Protest Demonstration Against Khamenei Opponents in Iran," *Deutsche Presse-Agentur,* November 19, 1997, available in LEXIS, Nexis Library, ALLWLD File.

21. Quoted by Edward Mortimer, "Islam and Human Rights," *Index on Censorship* 12 (October 1983), 5.

22. Bashir's military clique, which overthrew the elected government and seized power in Sudan in 1989, had a different perspective from Nimeiri's. By the time Bashir came to power, the Sudanese had already become disenchanted with Nimeiri's Islamization program, and Islamization had forfeited its mystique. Thus, rather than catering to popular sentiment favoring Islamization, the Bashir regime was simply following its own ideological inclinations in disregard of the democratically expressed will of the voters, only a minority of whom had supported candidates committed to Islamization in the preceding democratic interlude.

23. See Lawyers Committee for Human Rights, *The Justice System of the Islamic Republic of Iran* (May 1993), 47–50; and Africa Watch, *Sudan: Sudanese Human Rights Organizations* (November 4, 1991), 2–5.

24. The reports reviewing the human rights situations in these countries have burgeoned to the point that it is impractical to attempt a comprehensive listing, but various individual reports will be referred to throughout. For specific assessments, consult the relevant country chapters in *Amnesty International Report, Human Rights Watch World Report,* and *U.S. State Department Country Reports on Human Rights Practices,* all issued annually. See also topical reports prepared by the Africa, Asia, and Middle East regional sections of Human Rights Watch and also by Amnesty International, the Lawyers Committee for Human Rights, the International Commission of Jurists, and the Fédération Internationale des Droits de l'Homme. Reports prepared for the UN Commission on Human Rights are often informative. Excellent reports have been produced by local human rights groups,

but one must be very careful to distinguish independent human rights groups from local organizations set up to disseminate pro-government propaganda. Relevant documentation can also be found in publications like *Index on Censorship* and *Human Rights Quarterly*. See also Ann Elizabeth Mayer, "The Fundamentalist Impact on Law, Politics, and Constitutions in Iran, Pakistan, and the Sudan," in *Fundamentalisms and the State: Remaking Polities, Economics, and Militance,* ed. Martin Marty and Scott Appleby (Chicago: University of Chicago Press, 1993), 110–151.

25. See the comments of Ali Oumlil in Lawyers Committee for Human Rights, *Islam and Justice,* 72.

26. Human Rights Watch/Middle East, Iran: Power Versus Choice. Human Rights and Parliamentary Elections in the Islamic Republic of Iran, vol. 8, no.1 (E) (March 1996).

27. "Ayatollah Yazdi Denounces 'Conspiracy' Aimed at Undermining Country," *BBC Summary of World Broadcasts,* November 24, 1997, available in LEXIS, Nexis Library, ALLWLD File.

28. An English text of the declaration can be found in the British Broadcasting Company Summary of World Broadcasts, Part 4, "The Middle East, Africa and Latin America." See *BBC Summary of World Broadcasts,* May 1, 1984, ME/7631/A/2.

29. Ibid., ME/7631/A/9.

30. *BBC Summary of World Broadcasts,* September 25, 1984, ME/7757/A/6.

31. *BBC Summary of World Broadcasts,* May 1, 1984, ME/7631/A/8.

32. Ibid., ME/7631/A/9.

33. "The Transitional Constitution of the Republic of the Sudan, 1985," in Albert Blaustein and Gisbert Flanz, eds., *Constitutions of the Countries of the World* (Dobbs Ferry, N.Y.: Oceana, 1989). Article 3 made constitutional principles supreme so that they would prevail over other laws; Article 5 said that the state shall strive to "eradicate racial and religious fanaticism"; Article 11, that the state and each person "shall be subject to the rule of law as applied by the courts"; and Article 17, that all persons would be equal before the law.

34. Useful background is provided in J. Millard Burr and Robert O. Collins, *Requiem for the Sudan: War, Drought, and Disaster on the Nile* (Boulder: Westview Press, 1995); Human Rights Watch/Africa, *Civilian Devastation: Abuses by All Parties in the War in Southern Sudan* (New York: Human Rights Watch, 1994); and Ann Lesch, *The Sudan: Contested National Identities* (Bloomington: Indiana University Press, forthcoming).

35. Regarding rights violations in Sudan, see Africa Watch, *Denying "the Honor of Living." Sudan: A Human Rights Disaster* (March 1990). Other Africa Watch reports include *Sudan: Destruction of the Independent Secular Judiciary. Military Government Clamps Down on Press Freedom* (September 25, 1989); *Threat to Women's Status from Fundamentalist Regime* (March 1990); *Sudan: Sudanese Human Rights Organizations* (November 4, 1991); *New Islamic Penal Code Violates Basic Human Rights (April 1991); Inside al-Bashir's Prisons* (February 1991); *The Ghosts Remain: One Year After an Amnesty is Declared, Detention and Torture Continue Unabated* (February 1991); and *Eradicating the Nuba* (September 1992). On recent developments, see Amnesty International, *Sudan: What Future for Human Rights?* AI Index, AFR/54/01/95; Human Rights Watch/Africa, *Behind the*

Red Line: Political Repression in Sudan (New York: Human Rights Watch, 1996); and Lawyers Committee for Human Rights, *Beset by Contradictions: Islamization, Legal Reform and Human Rights in the Sudan* (July 1996).

36. Africa Watch, *Sudan: Sudanese Human Rights Organizations.*

37. "Transitional National Assembly Committee Completes Study of Draft Human Rights Document," *BBC Summary of World Broadcasts,* May 10, 1993, available in LEXIS, Nexis Library, ALLWLD File.

38. "Sudan Politics: Army Fears Losing Power to Supreme Court," *Inter Press Service,* August 5, 1997, available in LEXIS, Nexis Library, ALLWLD File. On the various pseudoconstitutionalist initiatives taken by Bashir's government, see Peter Nyot Kok, "Codifying Islamic Absolutism in the Sudan: A Study in Constitution-Making under al-Bashir," *Orient* 36 (1995), 673–706.

39. "Sudan Says UN Human Rights Text Offends Islam," *Agence France Presse,* February 23, 1994, available in LEXIS, Nexis Library, ALLWLD File.

40. "Sudan Calls UN Official a Blasphemer," *International Herald Tribune,* March 9, 1994, available in LEXIS, Nexis Library, ALLWLD File.

41. As noted, President Zia was allied with groups like Mawdudi's Jama'at-i-Islami. "Emir" is the term Mawdudi advocated for the leader of an Islamic government, which does not seem a coincidence in this context.

42. "Political Plan Announced, Seventh Session of Federal Council. Address by President General Muhammad Zia ul-Haq, Islamabad, August 12, 1983. Supplement to the Constitution of the Islamic Republic of Pakistan," in Blaustein and Flanz, *Constitutions,* 182.

43. See Rubya Mehdi, *The Islamization of the Law in Pakistan* (Chippenham, England: Nordic Institute of Asian Studies, 1994).

44. Relevant analyses include Valentine Moghadam, "Revolution, Islamist Reaction, and Women in Afghanistan," in *Women and Revolution in Africa, Asia, and the New World,* ed. Mary Ann Tetreault (Columbia: University of South Carolina Press, 1994), 211–235; and Olivier Roy, *Afghanistan: From Holy War to Civil War* (Princeton: Darwin Press, 1995).

45. "Taleban Change Afghanistan's Official Name," *BBC Summary of World Broadcasts,* October 28, 1997, available in LEXIS, Nexis Library, ALLWLD File.

46. Amnesty International, *Afghanistan: Grave Abuses in the Name of Religion,* AI Index, ASA 11/12/96 (November 18, 1996), 1.

47. This topic is discussed in Aba-Namay, "Recent Constitutional Reforms," 295–331, and is critically evaluated in Middle East Watch, *Empty Reforms: Saudi Arabia's New Basic Laws* (May 1992).

48. For discussions of the petitions that had preceded the Basic Law, see Middle East Watch, *Empty Reforms,* 59–62.

49. See, for example, the chapter on Saudi Arabia in U.S. State Department Country Reports on Human Rights Practices for 1993, December 27, 1993, available in LEXIS, Nexis Library, ALLWLD File.

50. Middle East Watch, *Empty Reforms,* 2.

51. The statement of the committee can be found in FBIS-NES-93-092, May 17, 1993, 38. See also "Opinion: Saudi 'Human Rights Committee' a Tool for Religious Extremists," *Arab Times,* May 15, 1993, available in LEXIS, Nexis Library, ALLWLD File; Mamoun Fandy, "New Crackdown on Rights Must Stop," *Chris-*

tian Science Monitor, May 21, 1993, available in LEXIS, Nexis Library, ALLWLD File; and "Saudi Rights Group Says It Is Not Out to Stir Trouble," *Reuter Library Report,* June 14, 1993, available in LEXIS, Nexis Library, ALLWLD File.

52. "Saudi Clergy Condemns Debut of Human Rights Group," United Press International, May 13, 1993, available in LEXIS, Nexis Library, ALLWLD File.

53. CDLR, *The Committee for the Defense of Legitimate Rights: Yearbook '94–95* (London: CDLR, 1995).

54. "Interior Minister on Yemen, Human Rights, Other Issues," *BBC Summary of World Broadcasts,* January 9, 1995, available in LEXIS, Nexis Library, ALLWLD File.

Chapter 3

1. Leo Strauss, *Natural Right and History* (Chicago: University of Chicago Press, 1953), 181–182.

2. J. Roland Pennock, "Rights, Natural Rights, and Human Rights: A General View," in *Human Rights: NOMOS XXIII,* ed. J. Roland Pennock and John W. Chapman (New York: New York University Press, 1981), 1.

3. This provocative interpretation has been put forward in Tore Lindholm, "Prospects for Research on the Cultural Legitimacy of Human Rights: The Cases of Liberalism and Marx," in *Human Rights in Cross-Cultural Perspectives: A Quest for Consensus,* ed. Abdullahi An-Na'im (Philadelphia: University of Pennsylvania Press, 1992), 397.

4. Ibid., 396–397.

5. For a general account, see A. J. Arberry, *Sufism: An Account of the Mystics of Islam* (New York: Macmillan, 1950). Notwithstanding Sufis' concentration on dissolving the individual and achieving spiritual oneness with God, their focus on the perfection of the individual soul and their common disregard for Islamic law and ritual does tend to link them with currents of thought that would challenge authority.

6. The ideas of the Mu'tazila are discussed in George Hourani, *Islamic Rationalism: The Ethics of 'Abd al-Jabbar* (Oxford: Clarendon Press, 1971); Majid Khadduri, *The Islamic Conception of Justice* (Baltimore: Johns Hopkins University Press, 1984), 41–53; and Chikh Bouamrane, *Le problème de la liberté humaine dans la pensée musulmane: Solution mu'tazilite* (Paris: J. Vrin, 1978).

7. Bouamrane, *Le problème de la liberté humaine,* 344–345.

8. For an introduction to his ideas, see Valla Vakili, "Debating Religion and Politics in Iran: The Political Thought of Abdolkarim Sorush," Council on Foreign Relations, Occasional Paper Series, no. 2 (New York: Council on Foreign Relations, 1996).

9. He discussed his views on this topic at a public forum held at American University in Washington, D.C., in March 1997. On another occasion, a proposed lecture by Sorush in Tehran was angrily denounced by a student group that accused him of seeking freedom from what has been created by God, the kind of charge one would expect Iranian conservatives to hurl at reform-minded, rationalist intellectuals. "Basij Students Protest Against Planned Public Lecture By Sorush," *BBC Summary of World Broadcasts,* November 18, 1997, available in LEXIS, Nexis Library, ALLWLD File.

10. Many samples of the exchanges between Sorush and his enemies among Iranian officialdom and its minions can be found in LEXIS, Nexis Library, ALLWLD File. See, for example, "Iran Ayatollah Slams Moslem Reformers As Traitors," *Reuters North American Wire,* October 27, 1995; "Hezbollah Gang Threatens to Hang Deviant University Students," *BBC Summary of World Broadcasts,* May 14, 1996; "Academic Responds to Foreign Minister Velayati's Comments," *BBC Summary of World Broadcasts,* January 16, 1996; "Islamic Students Say Islamic Thinker Sorush Wants to Topple System," *BBC Summary of World Broadcasts,* June 2, 1996; and "Cry for Help By Iranian Thinker," *The Guardian,* June 7, 1996.

11. Khadduri, *The Islamic Conception of Justice,* 78–105.

12. The struggles between proponents of reason and Revelation in Islamic intellectual history are described in A. J. Arberry, *Revelation and Reason in Islam* (London: Allen and Unwin, 1957); Khadduri, *The Islamic Conception of Justice,* 39–58, 64–70; and Mohamed El-Shakankiri, "Loi divine et loi humaine et droit dans l'histoire juridique de l'Islam," *Studia Islamica* 59 (1981), 161–182.

13. Khomeini's views are presented in Farhang Rajaee, *Islamic Values and World View: Khomeyni on Man, the State, and International Politics* (Lanham, Md.: University Press of America, 1983), 42–45.

14. These points are made in Noel Coulson, "The State and the Individual in Islamic Law," *International and Comparative Law Quarterly* 6 (1957), 49–60.

15. In this, Islamic legal thought resembles aspects of the natural law approach to rights in Western civilization. See Myres McDougal, Harold Lasswell, and Lung-chu Chen, *Human Rights and World Order: The Basic Policies of an International Law of Dignity* (New Haven: Yale University Press, 1980), 68–71.

16. Background on this is offered in Erwin J. Rosenthal, *Political Thought in Medieval Islam: An Introductory Outline* (Cambridge: Cambridge University Press, 1962).

17. Coulson, "The State and the Individual," 50.

18. Examples of works that document the humanism that was and continues to be part of the Islamic tradition are Mohammed Arkoun, *L'humanisme Arabe au ive/ve siècle: Miskawayh, philosophe et historien* (Paris: J. Vrin, 1970) and *Rethinking Islam: Common Questions, Uncommon Answers* (Boulder: Westview Press, 1994); Marcel Boisard, *L'humanisme de l'Islam* (Paris: Albin Michel, 1979); Hisham Djait, *La Personnalité et le devenir arabo-islamiques* (Paris: Albin Michel, 1974); Joel Kraemer, *Humanism in the Renaissance of Islam: The Cultural Revival During the Buyid Age* (Leiden: Brill, 1986); Fazlur Rahman, *Islam and Modernity: Transformation of an Intellectual Tradition* (Chicago: University of Chicago Press, 1982); and Roy Mottahedeh, "Toward an Islamic Theology of Toleration," in *Islamic Law Reform and Human Rights: Challenges and Rejoinders,* ed. Tore Lindholm and Kari Vogt (Copenhagen: Nordic Human Rights Publications, 1993), 25–36.

19. Some examples are given in Franz Rosenthal, *The Muslim Concept of Freedom Prior to the Nineteenth Century* (Leiden: Brill, 1960), 100–101, 105, 144.

20. Elie Adib Salem, *Political Theory and Institutions of the Khawarij* (Baltimore: Johns Hopkins University Press, 1965); Khadduri, *The Islamic Conception of Justice,* 20–23.

21. The general ignorance of Kharijite doctrines is partly linked to the fact that the remnants of the original community fled under persecution to remote parts of the Muslim world. Thus, one finds them in places like Oman and in the mountains or isolated settlements in Algeria. Because so much of the writing by Kharijites was destroyed by their foes, the source materials on their ideas are quite limited.

22. Hani Shukrallah, "Human Rights in Egypt: The Cause, the Movement and the Dilemma," *Cairo Papers in Social Science. Human Rights: Egypt and the Arab World. Fourth Annual Symposium*, 17 (Fall 1994), 55. For a discussion of the tensions between these value systems as they are embodied in the current political struggles in Morocco, see Fatima Mernissi, *Islam and Democracy: Fear of the Modern World*, trans. Mary Jo Lakeland (Reading, Mass.: Addison-Wesley, 1992); and Ann Elizabeth Mayer, "Moroccans: Citizens or Subjects? A People at the Crossroads," *New York University Journal of International Law and Politics* 26 (1993), 63–105.

23. For background see Said Amir Arjomand, "Constitutions and the Struggle for Political Order: A Study in the Modernization of Political Traditions," *European Journal of Sociology* 33 (1992), 39–82.

24. For an examination of the case of Egypt, see Farhat Ziadeh, *Lawyers, the Rule of Law, and Liberalism in Modern Egypt* (Stanford: Hoover Institution, 1968).

25. A classic account of the changing political views of the Arab elite at the time that constitutionalist ideas were percolating through Muslim societies is in Albert Hourani, *Arabic Thought in the Liberal Age, 1798–1939* (Oxford: Oxford University Press, 1967).

26. Examples can be found in Abdol Karim Lahidji, "Constitutionalism and Clerical Authority," in *Authority and Political Culture in Shi'ism*, ed. Said Arjomand (Albany: State University of New York Press, 1988), 133–158; and Abdul-Hadi Hairi, *Shi'ism and Constitutionalism in Iran* (Leiden: Brill, 1977).

27. Ann Elizabeth Mayer, "Religious Legitimacy and Constitutionalism: The 1992 Saudi Basic Law and the 1992 Moroccan Constitution Compared," *McGill Studies in Religion: Religion, Pluralism and Law* 5 (forthcoming).

28. An example of the uncertain status of constitutionalism is the fact that, to avoid offending Muslims who believe that constitutions are un-Islamic, the 1992 Saudi Basic Law in its own text disavows any intention to be a constitution. Instead, it modestly calls itself *al-nizam al-asasi li'l-hukm*, or "basic regulation for government." Article 1 of the Basic Law reaffirms the primacy of the Islamic sources, maintaining that the country's "constitution," or *dustur*, is the Qur'an and the *sunna* of the Prophet Muhammad.

29. Examples of Professor An-Na'im's work can be found in his "A Modern Approach to Human Rights in Islam: Foundations and Implications for Africa," in *Human Rights and Development in Africa*, ed. Claude Welch Jr. and Ronald Meltzer (Albany: State University of New York Press, 1984), 75–89; his study of the religious reformer Mahmud Muhammad Taha, along with the translation of Taha's major work, *The Second Message of Islam* (Syracuse, N.Y.: Syracuse University Press, 1987); and his *Toward an Islamic Reformation: Civil Liberties, Human Rights and International Law* (Syracuse, N.Y.: Syracuse University Press, 1990).

30. Arkoun, *Rethinking Islam*.

31. Sadiq Jalal al-'Azm, *Naqd al-fikr al-dini* (Beirut: Dar al-tali'a, 1972).

32. See, for example, Abu'l A'la Mawdudi, *Human Rights in Islam* (Leicester, England: Islamic Foundation, 1980), 39; Sultanhussein Tabandeh, *A Muslim Commentary on the Universal Declaration of Human Rights,* trans. F. J. Goulding (Guildford, England: F. J. Goulding, 1970), 1, 85; and the first page of the English-language pamphlet version of the Universal Islamic Declaration of Human Rights (UIDHR).

33. This is particularly true in the case of the UIDHR, Tabandeh, and Mawdudi. They cite sources without attempting to show how the rights they purport to see in the text have been derived. Examples will be offered subsequently.

34. The writings of Mawdudi epitomize these characteristics.

35. A. K. Brohi, "The Nature of Islamic Law and the Concept of Human Rights," in International Commission of Jurists, Kuwait University, and Union of Arab Lawyers, *Human Rights in Islam: Report of a Seminar Held in Kuwait, December 1980* (International Commission of Jurists, 1982), 43–60.

36. A. K. Brohi, "Islam and Human Rights," *PLD Lahore* 28 (1976), 148–160.

37. A. K. Brohi, "The Nature of Islamic Law and the Concept of Human Rights," *PLD Journal* (1983), 143–176.

38. Brohi, "The Nature of Islamic Law" (Kuwait seminar), 48.

39. Brohi, "Islam and Human Rights," 150.

40. Ibid., 151.

41. Ibid., 152.

42. Ibid., 159.

43. For similar perspectives, see Abdul Aziz Said, "Precept and Practice of Human Rights in Islam," *Universal Human Rights* 1 (1979), 73–74, 77; M. F. al-Nabhan, "The Learned Academy of Islamic Jurisprudence," *Arab Law Quarterly* 1 (1986), 391–392; Taymour Kamel, "The Principle of Legality and Its Application in Islamic Criminal Justice," in *The Islamic Criminal Justice System,* ed. Cherif Bassiouni (New York: Praeger, 1982), 169; and Cherif Bassiouni, "Sources of Islamic Law and the Protection of Human Rights," in *The Islamic Criminal Justice System,* ed. Cherif Bassiouni (New York: Praeger, 1982), 13–14, 23.

44. This failure to accord significance to the question of the rights of the individual vis-à-vis the state has a counterpart in the *shari'a* classification of rights in only two categories, the rights of God (to obedience from Muslims), *huquq Allah,* and the rights of the slaves (of God), *huquq 'ibad.* The latter are the rights that give individuals legal claims against other individuals. Coulson, "The State and the Individual," 50.

45. Abu'l A'la Mawdudi, *The Islamic Law and Constitution* (Lahore: Islamic Publications, 1980), 252. The original, in a more accurate translation, reads: "Hearing and obeying are the duty of a Muslim man both regarding what he likes and what he dislikes." Ibn al-Farra' al-Baghawi, *Mishkat Al-Masabih,* vol. 2, trans. James Tobson (Lahore: Muhammad Ashraf, 1963), 780.

46. Jack Donnelly, "Human Rights as Natural Rights," *Human Rights Quarterly* 4 (1982), 391.

47. Mawdudi, *Human Rights,* 24.

48. Ibid., 24–25.

49. Ibid., 36.

50. Ibid., 37.

51. It is not unheard of, but highly unusual, to claim that the dead have human rights. If one adopted the view, based on a coherent philosophical approach, that the dead have human rights, one would be likely to propose other rights for the dead as well. See Raymond Belliotti, "Do Dead Human Beings Have Rights?" *Personalist* 60 (1979), 201–210.

52. Universal Islamic Declaration of Human Rights (UIDHR), Article 1.b.

53. Mawdudi, *Human Rights,* 18.

54. Because so many of the harms that women suffer are at the hands of private actors, in the 1990s efforts have been made to expand international human rights law to cover conduct in the private sphere, such as violence against women in the family. See, e.g., Celina Romany, "State Responsibility Goes Private: A Feminist Critique of the Public/Private Distinction in International Human Rights Law," in *Human Rights of Women: National and International Perspectives,* ed. Rebecca J. Cook (Philadelphia: University of Pennsylvania Press, 1994), 85–115. Given the way that they treat women's rights and their largely negative responses to the Convention on the Elimination of All Forms of Discrimination Against Women (CEDAW), discussed in Chapter 6, the authors of the Islamic human rights schemes reviewed here would not seem to be envisaging such a shift or to be likely to welcome such expansion of women's international human rights.

55. Mawdudi, *Human Rights,* 36.

56. Ibid., 17.

57. Ibid., 18.

58. UIDHR, Article 20.e.

59. Mawdudi, *Human Rights,* 38.

60. Ibid., 22.

61. UIDHR, Arabic version, Article 14.

Chapter 4

1. Rosalyn Higgins, "Derogations Under Human Rights Treaties," *British Yearbook of International Law* 48 (1976–1977), 281.

2. Myres McDougal, Harold Lasswell, and Lung-chu Chen, "The Aggregate Interest in Shared Respect and Human Rights: The Harmonization of Public Order and Civic Order," *New York Law School Law Review* 23 (1977–1978), 183.

3. Ibid., 201–202.

4. Ibid., 202.

5. Universal Declaration of Human Rights (UDHR), Articles 1, 7, 10, and 16, respectively.

6. UDHR, Article 17, and International Covenant on Civil and Political Rights (ICCPR), Article 18.

7. UDHR, Article 23, and International Covenant on Economic, Social, and Cultural Rights (ICESCR), Article 6.

8. Johannes Morsink, "The Philosophy of the Universal Declaration," *Human Rights Quarterly* 6 (1984), 318.

9. UDHR, Articles 19, 20, and 21, respectively.

10. ICCPR, Articles 19, 21, 22, and 25, respectively.

11. ICCPR, Articles 6 and 9, respectively.

12. Ebow Bondzie-Simpson, "A Critique of the African Charter on Human and Peoples' Rights," *Howard Law Journal* 31 (1988), 660–661.

13. See Courtney W. Howland, "The Challenge of Religious Fundamentalism to the Liberty and Equality Rights of Women: An Analysis Under the United Nations Charter," *Columbia Journal of Transnational Law* 35 (1997), 327–331.

14. Yves Linant de Bellefonds, *Traité de droit musulman comparé*, vol. 1, *Théorie de l'acte juridique* (Paris: Mouton, 1965), 18–50; and Noel Coulson, *A History of Islamic Law* (Edinburgh: Edinburgh University Press, 1964), 21–119. There is a large literature on this subject written by Islamic jurists from a very early period in Islamic legal history on.

15. The results of Islamic reformist thought are assessed in many studies, including Malcolm Kerr, *Islamic Reform* (Berkeley: University of California Press, 1966); Charles Adams, *Islam and Modernism in Egypt: A Study of the Modern Reform Movement Inaugurated by Muhammad Abduh* (New York: Russell and Russell, 1968); and Aziz Ahmad, *Islamic Modernism in India and Pakistan, 1857–1964* (London: Oxford University Press, 1967).

16. See Abdul-Hadi Hairi, *Shi'ism and Constitutionalism in Iran* (Leiden: Brill, 1977), which gives many examples of the objections raised by the ulama to the proposed constitution.

17. One eyewitness to a religious demonstration against the proposed constitution reported that religious students chanted "We do not want liberty" and "We do not want a constitution," while a mullah proclaimed that merciful Allah could pardon drinking wine, gambling, adultery, murder, and every form of crime, but constitutionalists were to be killed in as great numbers as possible, egging on his followers to beat two constitutionalists to death. The naked mangled bodies of the constitutionalists were then displayed. Ibid., 218.

18. The phenomenon of the ulama misconstruing the purport of Western freedoms is examined in many parts of Hairi's book. A good example is the explanation that one religious scholar gave for his support of freedom of speech and freedom of the press. He seems to have understood this freedom to mean that writers and religious orators would be allowed to familiarize people with the truth regarding freedom in accordance with the *sunna* and the Qur'anic verse 16:125: "Call unto the way of thy Lord with wisdom and fair exhortation and reason with them in the better way." Ibid., 219.

19. Article 15 allowed persons to be dispossessed of property in cases where religious law authorized it. Although this could be read as a religious restriction on the right of private ownership, the traditional clerical interpretations of the *shari'a* afforded great protections for private property. Here, the "Islamic" grounds for interfering with the right would have been interpreted very narrowly, probably more narrowly than in many secular legal systems.

20. Abid Al-Marayati, *Middle Eastern Constitutions and Electoral Laws* (New York: Praeger, 1968), 17–20.

21. Shaul Bakhash, *The Reign of the Ayatollahs* (New York: Basic Books, 1984), 77.

22. Ibid., 78.

23. Ibid.

24. This and the following translations are taken from "Constitution of the Islamic Republic of Iran of 24 October 1979 As Amended to 28 July 1989," in Albert Blaustein and Gisbert Flanz, eds., *Constitutions of the Countries of the World* (Dobbs Ferry, N.Y.: Oceana, 1992).

25. *Qavanin* (pl. of *qanun*) would normally refer to secular laws. However, with the modifications by the adjective "Islamic," as here, *qavanin* seems to mean "Islamic principles." This application of the term contrasts with the use of *qavanin* in Article 4, where the reference can only be to secular law, since there it is stated that laws, *qavanin*, should be based on (and qualified by) "Islamic principles," *mavazin-e eslami*. In the context of Article 4, *qavanin* must logically refer to secular laws, since interpreting *qavanin* in that article to refer to Islamic law would result in the provision saying that Islamic principles should be based on Islamic principles.

26. The arbitrariness of the censorship process is documented in Middle East Watch, *Guardians of Thought: Limits on Freedom of Expression in Iran* (New York: Human Rights Watch, August 1993).

27. For a review of the deficiencies of Iran's courts, see Lawyers Committee for Human Rights, *The Justice System of the Islamic Republic of Iran* (New York: Lawyers Committee for Human Rights, 1993).

28. "President Khatami Announces Establishing of New Constitution Supervision Body," *BBC Summary of World Broadcasts,* December 2, 1997, available in LEXIS, Nexis Library, ALLWLD File.

29. "Let's Talk Not Fight, Iran's Khatami Demands," *Deutsche Presse-Agentur,* November 17, 1997, available in LEXIS, Nexis Library, ALLWLD File.

30. Amnesty International, *Iran: Human Rights Violations Against Shi'i Religious Leaders and Their Followers,* AI Index, MDE/13/18/97.

31. "Iranian Leader Orders Prosecution of Dissident Cleric" and "Iranian Dissident Cleric Could Be Tried for Plotting Against Regime," *Agence France Presse,* November 26, 1997, available in LEXIS, Nexis Library, ALLWLD File.

32. "Campaign Against Khomeini's Former Successor Gets Violent" and "Several Policemen Injured in Clashes with Protesters in Iran," *Agence France Presse,* November 19, 1997, available in LEXIS, Nexis Library, ALLWLD File; and "Montazeri: Once Second Most Powerful Man in Iran Turns Dissident," *Agence France Presse,* November 25, 1997, available in LEXIS, Nexis Library, ALLWLD File.

33. "Protest Demonstration Against Khamenei Opponents in Iran," *Deutsche Presse-Agentur,* November 19, 1997, available in LEXIS, Nexis Library, ALLWLD File.

34. "Political Infighting in Iran Spreads to Holy City," *Agence France Presse,* November 20, 1997, available in LEXIS, Nexis Library, ALLWLD File.

35. For an introduction to Sorush's ideas, see Valla Vakili, "Debating Religion and Politics in Iran: The Political Thought of Abdolkarim Sorush," Council on Foreign Relations, Studies Department, Occasional Paper Series, no. 2 (New York: Council on Foreign Relations, 1996).

36. How under Khomeini calculations of political interests could override any concern for fidelity to *shari'a* law can be seen in the regime's support of the storming of the U.S. embassy in Tehran and the taking of diplomats as hostages, measures in flagrant contravention of Shi'i law. See Roy Mottahedeh, "Iran's Foreign

Devils," *Foreign Affairs* 38 (1980), 19–34. How *raison d'état* ranked above Islamic law was also shown in Ayatollah Khomeini's assertion on January 7, 1988, that his government was free to undertake any actions that it deemed in the interests of Islam. He claimed that Iran's Islamic government was among the most important divine institutions and had priority over such secondary institutions as prayers, fasting, and the pilgrimage—even though the latter are conventionally seen as fundamental pillars of the Islamic faith. See Asghar Schirazi, *The Constitution of Iran: Politics and the State in the Islamic Republic,* trans. John O'Kane (London: I. B. Tauris, 1997), 229–231. Khomeini's command on February 14, 1989, that Salman Rushdie, a British citizen living in Great Britain, be executed for apostasy without trial or an opportunity to defend himself showed a similar disregard for *shari'a* standards of legality. The death edict has never won the endorsement of any distinguished independent Islamic jurists, and, now proffering a far more sophisticated line on human rights, the Iranian regime has gone to some pains to try to distance itself from the ruling, which even Iran's clerical leaders seem to have come to realize is indefensible. See Ann Elizabeth Mayer, "Islamic Rights or Human Rights: An Iranian Dilemma," *Iranian Studies* 29 (Summer-Fall 1996), 290–292.

37. Space does not allow discussion of the council here, but it is examined in Schirazi, *The Constitution of Iran,* 64–65, 66, 77, 92, 95–96, 102, 108, 110–111, 132, 165, 172, 184, 187, 196, 213–214, 219–220, 234–237, 251, 296–298.

38. Examples of the problems of translating the UIDHR can be seen in two attempts to provide literal translations of the Arabic version into English and French, which have resulted in inconsistent interpretations of important passages. See *IslamoChristiana* 9 (1983), 103–120 (English) and 121–140 (French).

39. In the English-language pamphlet version of the UIDHR published by the Islamic Council, these notes are placed on page 16 after the rights provisions.

40. It will be recalled that the Islamic qualifications included in Iranian constitutional rights provisions were similarly vague and open-ended.

41. In the Arabic counterpart of this article, one discovers that it actually offers a "right" to propagate Islam.

42. *Al-intiqal* in the Arabic, but translated into English as "transfer."

43. See, for example, Abu'l A'la Mawdudi, *Purdah and the Status of Women in Islam* (Lahore: Islamic Publications, 1979), 145–147, 200–209.

44. Sultanhussein Tabandeh, *A Muslim Commentary on the Universal Declaration of Human Rights,* trans. F. J. Goulding (Guildford, England: F. J. Goulding, 1970), 20.

45. This position correlates with standards set in anti-Ahmadi legislation enacted in 1984 by the Zia government in Pakistan. The treatment of Pakistan's Ahmadi minority will be discussed in Chapter 8.

46. Tabandeh, *A Muslim Commentary,* 73.

47. Abu'l A'la Mawdudi, *Human Rights in Islam* (Leicester, England: Islamic Foundation, 1980), 28–29.

48. See "Transitional National Assembly Approves Document on Human Rights," *BBC Summary of World Broadcasts,* July 20, 1993, available in LEXIS, Nexis Library, ALLWLD File.

49. *Zaheeruddin v. State,* 26 S.C.M.R. (S.Ct.) 1718 (1993) (Pak.), 1773–1774.

50. Ibid., 1775.

51. Kilian Bälz, "Submitting Faith to Judicial Scrutiny Through the Family Trial: The Abu Zayd Case," *Die Welt des Islams* 37 (1997), 149.

Chapter 5

1. A valuable introduction to these two aspects of the Islamic heritage is Louise Marlow, *Hierarchy and Egalitarianism in Islamic Thought* (Cambridge: Cambridge University Press, 1997).

2. A summary of the rules on personal status can be found in Joseph Schacht, *Introduction to Islamic Law* (Oxford: Clarendon Press, 1964), 24–33. A survey of sources dealing with inequality can be found in Ann Elizabeth Mayer, "Stratification, Authority and Justice in the Law of the Islamic Middle East," *BRISMES Bulletin* 4 (1977), 82–91; and 5 (1978), 3–19.

3. An example would be the condemnation of the principle of equality in the supplement to the first Iranian Constitution, signed by a number of prominent Shi'i clerics. See Abdul-Hadi Hairi, *Shi'ism and Constitutionalism in Iran* (Leiden: Brill, 1977), 221–222, 232–233.

4. Abu'l A'la Mawdudi, *Human Rights in Islam* (Leicester, England: Islamic Foundation, 1980), 28–29.

5. Ibid., 21.

6. Ibid., 32.

7. The translation is taken from "Constitution of the Islamic Republic of Iran of 24 October 1979 As Amended to 28 July 1989," in Albert Blaustein and Gisbert Flanz, eds., *Constitutions of the Countries of the World* (Dobbs Ferry, N.Y.: Oceana, 1992).

8. The texts cited are 3:64, "None of us shall take others for lords besides Allah," and 49:13, "We have created you male and female." These are not texts that were historically interpreted to mandate full legal equality—nor does Tabandeh, in his critique of the UDHR, interpret them to establish an Islamic principle of nondiscriminatory treatment of women and non-Muslims.

9. Sultanhussein Tabandeh, *A Muslim Commentary on the Universal Declaration of Human Rights,* trans. F. J. Goulding (Guildford, England: F. J. Goulding, 1970), 15.

10. Ibid., 19.

11. Ibid., 20.

12. Jacobus Ten Broek, *The Antislavery Origins of the Fourteenth Amendment* (Berkeley: University of California Press, 1951).

13. For a discussion of this, see Oscar Garibaldi, "General Limitations on Human Rights: The Principle of Legality," *Harvard International Law Journal* 17 (1976), 525–526.

14. Illuminating descriptions of some aspects of early Muslim reactions to and interpretations of the principle of equality and equality before the law are in Hairi, *Shi'ism and Constitutionalism,* 224–234.

15. This was the interpretation of Mirza Muhammad Hussain Na'ini, a leading Shi'i cleric, who supported the Iranian constitutionalist movement and endeavored to show that constitutional rights accorded with Islam. Ibid., 224.

16. Relevant analysis is provided in Courtney W. Howland, "The Challenge of Religious Fundamentalism to the Liberty and Equality Rights of Women: An Analysis Under the United Nations Charter," *Columbia Journal of Transnational Law* 35 (1997), 329–330.

17. For example, the Prophet is quoted as saying that there can be no superiority of the Arab over the non-Arab, of the red (meaning "white" in contemporary American usage) over the black, or of the black over the red save in piety; the Prophet is further quoted as saying that if his own daughter stole, her hand would be cut off like that of any other thief.

18. Because the Arabic and English categories of grounds on the basis of which it is impermissible to discriminate do not correspond and because the English translation is obviously only a very rough approximation of the Arabic, the English cannot be used to clarify the meaning of the particularly ambiguous terms *jins* and *'irq*, which potentially have overlapping meanings. At best, one could presume that in order to avoid redundancy, if *'irq* is taken to mean "race," *jins* should be taken to have some other meaning. The antidiscrimination language in the Preamble of the UIDHR is also not helpful in deciphering the precise meanings of the terms because of a lack of parallelism between the language it uses and that of Article 3.b. For example, the Preamble states that there can be no discrimination based on *asl* (origin or descent), *'unsur* (origin, race, or ethnic status), *jins* (the ambiguity of which has just been noted), color, language, or religion. Because other provisions of the UIDHR mandate sex-based discrimination, reading *jins* in Article 3.b to mean "sex," which would ordinarily be perfectly natural, entails internal inconsistencies in the document. To avoid such internal inconsistencies, one would tend to assume that *jins* should be assigned a meaning other than "sex." However, when one takes into account the frequent inconsistencies in the Islamic human rights literature, one cannot be sure that the authors of the UIDHR would have been troubled by including some provisions barring sex-based discrimination and others mandating such discrimination.

19. *Ansar Burney v. Federation of Pakistan*, PLD FSC, 1983, 73.

20. Ibid., 93.

21. It is interesting to contrast the result of this Pakistani case with the law enforced in Iran after the Islamic Revolution excluding women from the judiciary. This will be discussed in relation to the overall status of women (Chapter 6), but it is mentioned here as yet another illustration of the differences among contemporary Muslims about how Islamic law affects women's rights.

22. This same Qur'anic command is included in Article 6 of the Azhar draft constitution and Article 8 of the Iranian Constitution, but without any connection being made between it and a right of association.

23. It does not seem accidental that the Western reader, who in most cases will not be able to translate the Arabic, is being given a very dissimilar version of the article, one that makes it look much more like a familiar international human rights concept. One sees in this provision yet another example of a pervasive pattern of discrepancies between the Arabic and English versions of the UIDHR where issues of equality are involved.

24. Nuri was active in organizing the revolutionary committees and the Revolutionary Guards, in the debates over the postrevolutionary constitution, and in the

Majles after the revolution. This information was kindly provided by Professor Hamid Algar.

25. Yahya Noori [Nuri], "The Islamic Concept of State," *Hamdard Islamicus* 3 (1980), 78.

26. Ibid., 83.

27. Ibid., 70–80.

28. One should not assume that cultural differences make Orwell's ideas inaccessible to Iranians or Muslims generally, or that Iranians do not grasp the inconsistencies and contradictions in Islamic rights formulations. A particularly interesting indication of the fact that Iranians perceive the relevance of Orwell's work to their current circumstances is the enormous popularity that Orwell has enjoyed in Iran since the revolution. By 1984 a Persian translation of *Animal Farm* had become one of Iran's best-selling books and George Orwell Iran's best-selling author. "Book Boom in Tehran," *Index on Censorship* (October 1984), 9.

Chapter 6

1. Fazlur Rahman, "The Status of Women in the Qur'an," in *Women and Revolution in Iran,* ed. Guity Nashat (Boulder: Westview Press, 1983), 38.

2. Naila Minai, *Women in Islam: Tradition and Transition in the Middle East* (New York: Seaview, 1981), 1–24; and Jane Smith, "Women, Religion, and Social Change in Early Islam," in *Women, Religion, and Social Change,* ed. Yvonne Haddad and Ellison Findley (Albany: State University of New York Press, 1985), 19–35.

3. Rahman, "The Status of Women," 37.

4. See the examination of disparities between the original sources and later interpretations in Barbara Stowasser, "The Status of Women in Early Islam," in *Muslim Women,* ed. Freda Hussain (New York: St. Martin's Press, 1984), 11–43; Bouthaina Shaaban, "The Muted Voices of Women Interpreters," in *Faith and Freedom: Women's Human Rights in the Muslim World,* ed. Mahnaz Afkhami (London: I. B. Tauris, 1995), 61–77; Fatima Mernissi, *The Veil and the Male Elite: A Feminist Interpretation of Women's Rights in Islam* (Reading, Mass.: Addison-Wesley, 1991); and Leila Ahmad, *Women and Gender in Islam: Historical Roots of a Modern Debate* (New Haven: Yale University Press, 1992). Mernissi argues that Islam elevated the status of women and that women under the leadership of the Prophet and his early successors played active roles, only later to be relegated to the status that they had prior to Islam under the rule of the Umayyad caliphs. Ahmad offers a similar interpretation, although arguing that it was changes under the Abbasid caliphs that precipitated the decline in women's status. The approaches of these two authors are critically appraised in Reza Afshari, "Egalitarian Islam and Misogynist Islamic Tradition: A Critique of the Feminist Reinterpretation of Islamic History and Heritage," *Critique: Journal of Critical Studies of Iran and the Middle East* 4 (Spring 1994), 13–34.

5. Introductions to aspects of women's status in the *shari'a* can be found in Joseph Schacht, *Introduction to Islamic Law* (Oxford: Clarendon Press, 1964), 126–127; Yves Linant de Bellefonds, *Traité de droit musulman comparé,* vol. 2, *Le Mariage: La Dissolution du mariage* (Paris: Mouton, 1965); Noel Coulson, *Succession in the*

Muslim Family (Cambridge: Cambridge University Press, 1971); and Ghassan Ascha, *Du Statut inférieur de la femme en Islam* (Paris: L'Harmattan, 1987).

6. A summary of these changes can be found in J. N. D. Anderson, *Law Reform in the Muslim World* (London: Athlone, 1976). See also Tahir Mahmood, *Personal Law in Islamic Countries* (New Delhi: Academy of Law and Religions, 1987).

7. A perfect embodiment of this response can be found in Abu'l A'la Mawdudi, *Purdah and the Status of Women in Islam* (Lahore: Islamic Publications, 1979). Many aspects of this literature are reviewed by Ascha, *Du Statut inférieur.*

8. See Abdullahi El-Naiem [An-Na'im], "A Modern Approach to Human Rights in Islam: Foundations and Implications for Africa," in *Human Rights and Development in Africa,* ed. Claude Welch Jr. and Ronald Meltzer (Albany: State University of New York Press, 1984), 82; and Mernissi, *The Veil and the Male Elite.*

9. The feminist literature is currently burgeoning. Samples of what is currently being written can be seen in Freda Hussain and Kamelia Radwan, "The Islamic Revolution and Women: The Quest for the Qur'anic Model," in *Muslim Women,* ed. Freda Hussain (New York: St. Martin's Press, 1984), 44–70; Fatna Sabbah [pseud.], *Women in the Muslim Unconscious* (New York: Pergamon, 1984); Farah Azari, *Women of Iran: The Conflict with Fundamentalist Islam* (London: Ithaca Press, 1983); Rashida Patel, *Women and the Law in Pakistan* (Karachi: Faiza Publications, 1979); Guity Nashat, ed., *Women and Revolution in Iran* (Boulder: Westview Press, 1983); Fatima Mernissi, *Islam and Democracy: Fear of the Modern World,* trans. Mary Jo Lakeland (Reading, Mass.: Addison-Wesley, 1991), and *The Veil and the Male Elite;* Ahmad, *Women and Gender in Islam;* Khawar Mumtaz and Farida Shaheed, *Women of Pakistan: Two Steps Forward, One Step Back?* (London: Zed Books, 1987); Riffat Hassan, "Feminist Theology: The Challenges for Muslim Women," *Critique: Journal for Critical Studies of the Middle East* (Fall 1996), 53–66; Mahnaz Afkhami, ed., *Faith and Freedom: Women's Human Rights in the Muslim World* (London: I. B. Tauris, 1995); Ziba Mir-Hosseini, "Stretching the Limits: A Feminist Reading of the Shari'a in Post-Khomeini Iran," *Women Living Under Muslim Laws: Dossier* 17 (June 1997), 31–61; Ayesha M. Imam, "The Muslim Religious Right ("Fundamentalists") and Sexuality," *Women Living Under Muslim Laws: Dossier* 17 (June 1997), 7–25; and Mahnaz Afkhami and Erika Friedl, eds., *Muslim Women and the Politics of Participation: Implementing the Beijing Platform* (Syracuse, N.Y.: Syracuse University Press, 1997).

10. This is a consistent theme of Mawdudi's writings. For an example of his arguments, see Mawdudi, *Purdah and the Status of Women,* 21–24.

11. Ibid., 73–74.

12. Ibid., 24.

13. One sign of this might be seen in the actual patterns of personal status law reform and constitutional guarantees of women's rights in Muslim countries. In most Muslim countries the choice has been to compromise, keeping some elements of the *shari'a* system of personal status but including many reforms improving the rights of women. See Anderson, *Law Reform in the Muslim World.*

14. Sultanhussein Tabandeh, *A Muslim Commentary on the Universal Declaration of Human Rights,* trans. F. J. Goulding (Guildford, England: F. J. Goulding, 1970), 1.

15. See, for example, his comments on Article 16 of the UDHR. Ibid., 41–45.

16. Ibid., 35.

17. Ibid., 41–45.

18. Ibid., 37–38.

19. Ibid., 38–39.

20. Ibid., 40.

21. Ibid., 58.

22. Ibid., 51.

23. Ibid., 57. The alliteration here, it should be recalled, is that of Tabandeh's translator.

24. Ibid., 52.

25. Abu'l A'la Mawdudi, *The Islamic Law and Constitution* (Lahore: Islamic Publications, 1980), 262–263; and *Purdah and the Status of Women,* passim, and on divorce, 151.

26. Mawdudi, *Purdah and the Status of Women,* 12.

27. Ibid., 12–15, 26–71.

28. Ibid., 15.

29. Ibid., 73.

30. Abu'l A'la Mawdudi, *Human Rights in Islam* (Leicester, England: Islamic Foundation, 1980), 18.

31. The systematic rapes of women during the strife in Bosnia have heightened the awareness of the need for international law to address such campaigns as violations of human rights and as war crimes. See Donna Sullivan, "Women's Human Rights and the 1993 World Conference on Human Rights," *American Journal of International Law* 88 (1994), 155–156; and Theodor Meron, "Rape as a Crime Under International Humanitarian Law," *American Journal of International Law* 87 (1993), 424–428.

32. Mawdudi, *Human Rights,* 18.

33. Indeed, restrictions on women's testimony in the *shari'a* rules of evidence can make it especially difficult for a woman to prove such an offense and obtain the conviction of the offender because in the cases of *hadd* crimes (those for which the penalty is set or implied in the text of the Qur'an), the testimony of women witnesses may be barred altogether.

34. Naturally, the sordid details of these incidents were publicized in India, Pakistan's enemy. See, for example, Amita Malik, *The Year of the Vulture* (New Delhi: Orient Longman, 1972). Mawdudi and his followers backed the efforts of the Pakistani government to crush the movement to establish an independent Bangladesh. The mass rapes of Bengali women, carried out by an army dominated by Punjabis and following a policy aimed at humiliating, degrading, and terrifying the Bengali ethnic group, constituted the kinds of rapes that particularly concern international law. However, far from being moved to condemn these rapes, Mawdudi was trying to deny that they had ever occurred.

35. According to the preface, Mawdudi's human rights pamphlet is translated from a speech delivered on November 16, 1975, at the Civil Rights and Liberties Forum in the Flatties Hotel in Lahore. Mawdudi, *Human Rights,* 7. Mawdudi and his audience in Lahore, capital of the Punjab, which has traditionally supplied most of Pakistan's military manpower, must have been aware of the Bengali rapes and how they had tarnished Pakistan's image when he made his 1975 speech.

36. See Shahla Haeri, "The Politics of Dishonor: Rape and Power in Pakistan," in *Faith and Freedom: Women's Human Rights in the Muslim World*, ed. Mahnaz Afkhami (London: I. B. Tauris, 1995), 161–174; and Rubya Mehdi, "The Offence of Rape in the Islamic Law of Pakistan," *Women Living Under Muslim Laws: Dossier* 18 (July 1997), 98–108. The sexism of the Pakistani laws on rape in the wake of Islamization is dissected in Asifa Quraishi, "Her Honor: An Islamic Critique of the Rape Laws of Pakistan from a Woman-Sensitive Perspective," *Michigan Journal of International Law* 18 (1997), 287–320. From the standpoint of a Muslim feminist, the kinds of laws that Mawdudi vaunts are profoundly problematic.

37. This is because according to the choice-of-law rules in Islam and in the law of Muslim countries, Islamic criteria are used to judge the validity of a mixed marriage. The fact that the religious law of the husband allows such a marriage is treated as irrelevant. Relevant Islamic choice-of-law rules are discussed in Klaus Wähler, *Interreligiöses Kollisionsrecht im Bereich privatrechtlicher Rechtsbeziehungen* (Cologne: Carl Heymanns Verlag, 1978), 157–158. Muslim conservatives today share the view that the validity of a mixed marriage is to be judged under *shari'a* rules. See Mawdudi, *The Islamic Law and Constitution*, 287. This principle is applied as public policy in Muslim countries where the law does not specifically ban such marriages.

38. Examples of such rules are discussed in Mahmood, *Personal Law*, 275–276.

39. These references appear on p. 19 of the English version.

40. For example, see Mawdudi's invocation of this verse; Mawdudi, *Purdah and the Status of Women*, 149.

41. Yves Linant de Bellefonds, *Traité de droit musulman comparé*, vol. 3, *Filiation: Incapacités, liberalités entre vifs* (Paris: Mouton, 1965), 81–142.

42. In theory, the guardian could also marry off a male ward without his consent, but because of the ease with which a Muslim man could terminate an unwanted marriage, this had little practical effect or significance.

43. This has been a sensitive issue. The difficulties a Muslim feminist experienced in maintaining an open discussion of women's reactions to forced marriages are a topic in Fadela M'Rabet, *La Femme Algérienne suivi de les Algériennes* (Paris: Maspero, 1969), 143–165.

44. "The Couple Who Vowed to Take On Tradition," *South China Morning Post*, July 5, 1997, available in LEXIS, Nexis Library, ALLWLD File. The ruling upholding the validity of their marriage under the existing laws prompted demands that Pakistan's laws should be changed to allow the enforcement of parental authority. "Pakistan: Marriage Judgment May Threaten Women's Rights," *Inter Press Service*, March 17, 1997, available in LEXIS, Nexis Library, ALLWLD File. See also Ann Elizabeth Mayer, "Aberrant 'Islams' and Errant Daughters: The Turbulent Legacy of Beijing in Muslim Societies," in *Muslim Women and the Politics of Participation: Implementing the Beijing Platform*, ed. Mahnaz Afkhami and Erika Friedl (Syracuse, N.Y.: Syracuse University Press, 1997), 32–33.

45. Anderson, *Law Reform in the Muslim World*, 102–105.

46. See, for example, Mawdudi, *Purdah and the Status of Women*, 144–155.

47. Noel Coulson, *Succession in the Muslim Family* (Cambridge: Cambridge University Press, 1971), 214.

48. Linant de Bellefonds, *Traité de droit musulman comparé*, vol. 2, 451–470.

49. The translation is from "Constitution of the Islamic Republic of Iran of 24 October 1979 As Amended to 28 July 1989," in Albert Blaustein and Gisbert Flanz, eds., *Constitutions of the Countries of the World* (Dobbs Ferry, N.Y.: Oceana, 1992).

50. Doreen Hinchcliffe, "The Iranian Family Protection Act," *International and Comparative Law Quarterly* 17 (1968), 516–521; and Eliz Sanasarian, *The Women's Rights Movement in Iran: Mutiny, Appeasement, and Repression from 1990 to Khomeini* (New York: Praeger, 1982), 94–97. The situation of women in the aftermath of the abrogation of the Family Protection Act is examined in Ziba Mir-Hosseini, *Marriage on Trial: A Study of Islamic Family Law. Iran and Morocco Compared* (New York: I. B. Tauris, 1993).

51. Sanasarian, *The Women's Rights Movement in Iran*, 136–137.

52. Shahla Haeri, "The Institution of Mut'a Marriage in Iran: A Formal and Historical Perspective," in *Women and Revolution in Iran*, ed. Guity Nashat (Boulder: Westview Press, 1983), 231–252; and *Law of Desire: Temporary Marriage in Iran* (London: I. B. Tauris, 1989).

53. Valentine M. Moghadam, *Modernizing Women: Gender and Social Change in the Middle East* (Boulder: Lynne Rienner, 1993), 171–206.

54. Relevant works include Nashat, *Women and Revolution in Iran;* Azar Tabari and Nahid Yeganeh, eds., *In the Shadow of Islam: The Women's Movement in Iran* (London: Zed Books, 1982); Sanasarian, *The Women's Rights Movement in Iran;* Azari, *Women of Iran;* Val Moghadam, "Women, Work, and Ideology in the Islamic Republic," *International Journal of Middle East Studies* 20 (1988), 221–243; Mahnaz Afkhami and Erika Friedl, eds., *In the Eye of the Storm: Women in Post-Revolutionary Iran* (Syracuse, N.Y.: Syracuse University Press, 1994); and Haleh Esfandiari, *Reconstructed Lives: Women and Iran's Islamic Revolution* (Baltimore: Johns Hopkins University Press, 1997).

55. The incident described here was reported in the world's press, including *The Herald* (Harare) and the *New York Times* on January 22, 1986.

56. See Ann Elizabeth Mayer, "Islamic Rights or Human Rights: An Iranian Dilemma," *Iranian Studies* 29 (Summer-Fall 1996), 284–288.

57. "Iranian Team Set for Atlanta Despite Visa Bother," *Deutsche Presse-Agentur,* July 9, 1996, available in LEXIS, Nexis Library, ALLWLD File.

58. Reports on conflicting trends can be seen in "Iranian Women Disrespecting Islamic Dress Code to Face Imprisonment," *Deutsche Presse-Agentur,* July 30, 1996, available in LEXIS, Nexis Library, ALLWLD File; "Iran Passes Law on Women's Alimony," Xinhua New Agency, July 20, 1997, available in LEXIS, Nexis Library, ALLWLD File; and "Iran to Raise Moslem Women's Rights at Islamic Summit," *Deutsche Presse-Agentur,* November 26, 1997, available in LEXIS, Nexis Library, ALLWLD File.

59. See "President Rafsanjani's Daughter Interviewed on Women's Issues, Society," *BBC Summary of World Broadcasts,* October 26, 1996, available in LEXIS, Nexis Library, ALLWLD File.

60. Human Rights Watch/Middle East, *Iran: Leaving Human Rights Behind. The Context of the Presidential Elections,* vol. 9, no. 2 (E) (May 1997), 3.

61. "Iranian Leader Warns Women Against Copying Western Feminist Trends," *Agence France Presse,* October 22, 1997, available in LEXIS, Nexis Library, ALLWLD File.

62. "Iranian Cleric Blasts Taleban for Defaming Islam," *Reuters North American Wire,* October 4, 1996, available in LEXIS, Nexis Library, ALLWLD File.

63. "Sudan: Threat to Women's Status from Fundamentalist Regime," *News from Africa Watch,* April 9, 1990.

64. Ibid.; "Sudan's Capital Bans Mixing of Sexes in Public," *New York Times,* October 27, 1996, 6; Sondra Hale, "Gender Politics and Islamization in the Sudan," *Women Living Under Muslim Laws: Dossier* 18 (July 1997), 51–80; and Sondra Hale, "Legal Aid, New Laws and Violence Against Women in the Sudan," *Women Living Under Muslim Laws: Dossier* 18 (July 1997), 81–92.

65. *The Meaning of the Glorious Koran,* trans. Marmaduke Pickthall (Albany: State University of New York Press, 1976).

66. See, for example, Tabandeh, *A Muslim Commentary,* 51–52; and Mawdudi, *Purdah and the Status of Women,* 185–201.

67. Aspects of the traditional Arab concept of female honor, or *'ird,* and its manipulation to secure male dominance have been studied in the anthropological literature on the Middle East. See, for example, Peter Dodd, "Family Honor and the Forces of Change in Arab Society," *International Journal of Middle East Studies* 4 (1973), 40–54. A critique of mechanisms of oppression in Arab society that analyzes how the concept of *'ird* has been used to deny women their humanity and basic rights can be found in Nawal El-Saadawi, *The Hidden Face of Eve: Women in the Arab World* (Boston: Beacon Press, 1981), 7–90.

68. As of early 1998, the only other countries to do so were Pakistan and the United Arab Emirates.

69. See Valentine Moghadam, "Revolution, Islamist Reaction, and Women in Afghanistan," in *Women and Revolution in Africa, Asia, and the New World,* ed. Mary Ann Tetreault (Columbia: University of South Carolina Press, 1994), 211–235.

70. Amnesty International, *Women in Afghanistan: A Human Rights Catastrophe,* AI Index: ASA 11/03/95.

71. "Equal in Death Only Men Keep Afghan Women Out of Sight," *Toronto Sun,* November 27, 1997, available in LEXIS, Nexis Library, ALLWLD File.

72. Amnesty International, *Afghanistan: Grave Abuses in the Name of Religion,* AI Index: ASA 11/12/96; and "Afghanistan: The Taliban Regime and Its Impact on Afghan Women and Society. Statements from Afghan Women, Reports and International Action," *Women Living Under Muslim Laws: Dossier* 17 (June 1997), 93–113.

73. "WHO to Investigate Afghan Women Health Care Risks," *Agence France Presse,* October 24, 1997, available in LEXIS, Nexis Library, ALLWLD File; and "Afghanistan: The Taliban Regime," *Dossier,* 93–113.

74. "Iranian Radio Carries Tashkent Anti-Taleban Embassy Statement," *BBC Summary of World Broadcasts,* November 22, 1997, available in LEXIS, Nexis Library, ALLWLD File.

75. "Battalion of Women to Tackle Taliban," *Daily Telegraph,* November 19, 1997, available in LEXIS, Nexis Library, ALLWLD File.

76. John Burns, "Sex and the Afghani Woman: Islam's Straightjacket," *New York Times*, August 29, 1997, A4.

77. "Islamic Rule Weighs Heavily for Afghans," *New York Times,* September 24, 1997, A6.

78. See Belinda Clark, "The Vienna Convention Reservations Regime and the Convention on Discrimination Against Women," *American Journal of International Law* 85 (1991), 281–321; and Jane Connors, "The Women's Convention in the Muslim World," in *Human Rights As General Norms and a State's Right to Opt Out: Reservations and Objections to Human Rights Conventions,* ed. J. P. Gardner (London: British Institute of International and Comparative Law, 1997), 85–103.

79. Ann Elizabeth Mayer, "Rhetorical Strategies and Official Policies on Women's Rights: The Merits and Drawbacks of the New World Hypocrisy," in *Faith and Freedom: Women's Human Rights in the Muslim World,* ed. Mahnaz Afkhami (London: I. B. Tauris, 1995), 105–119.

80. Tabandeh, *A Muslim Commentary,* 39.

81. Ibid., 41.

82. Ibid., 51.

83. Ibid., 52.

84. Mawdudi, *Purdah and the Status of Women in Islam,* 113–122.

85. Ibid., 120.

86. Ibid., 121–122.

87. Javad Bahonar, "Islam and Women's Rights," *al-Tawhid* 1 (1984), 160.

88. Ibid., 161.

89. Ibid., 165.

90. Ibid., 161.

91. Ibid., 164. Of course, since he was trying to show the Islamic treatment of women in a positive light, Bahonar neglected to mention that women in the Islamic inheritance scheme receive only one-half the share of a male inheriting in the same capacity.

92. See Ann Elizabeth Mayer, "Islam and Human Rights: Different Issues, Different Contexts. Lessons from Comparisons," in *Islamic Law Reform and Human Rights: Challenges and Rejoinders,* ed. Tore Lindholm and Kari Vogt (Oslo: Nordic Human Rights Publications, 1993), 121–125.

93. Mary Daly, *The Church and the Second Sex* (Boston: Beacon Press, 1985), 85.

94. Ibid., 88.

95. Ibid., 154.

96. Ibid., 115.

97. Ibid.

98. Ibid., 164.

99. Ibid., 87.

100. "Egypt: Population Conference Ends in Compromise," *Middle East Economic Digest,* September 19, 1994, available in LEXIS, Nexis Library, ALLWLD File.

101. John Hooper, "Big Issues Slip Past Religious Filibusters," *The Guardian,* September 14, 1994, available in LEXIS, Nexis Library, ALLWLD File.

102. "Head of Iranian Delegation to ICPD Comments on Its Resolutions, Iran's Role," *BBC Summary of World Broadcasts,* September 16, 1994, available in LEXIS, Nexis Library, ALLWLD File.

103. Amnesty International, *Afghanistan: Grave Abuses in the Name of Religion,* 11.

104. "UN Conference on Women: Saudi Boycott Unveils Islamic Debate," *Financial Times,* September 13, 1995, available in LEXIS, Nexis Library, ALLWLD File.

105. Valerie A. Dormady, "Women's Rights in International Law: A Prediction Concerning the Legal Impact of the United Nations' Fourth World Conference on Women," *Vanderbilt Journal of Transnational Law* 97 (1997) 105.

106. Ibid., 127.

107. "'Religious Values' Will Determine Our Women's Programme—Iran," *Agence France Press,* September 11, 1995, available in LEXIS, Nexis Library, ALLWLD File.

108. "UN: Head of Iran's Delegation Speaks About Situation of Iranian Women," *BBC Summary of World Broadcasts,* September 14, 1995, available in LEXIS, Nexis Library, ALLWLD File.

109. Hale, "Legal Aid," 90.

Chapter 7

1. Bernard Lewis, *The Emergence of Modern Turkey* (London: Oxford University Press, 1961), 104–106, 113–115, 131.

2. For background, see Peter Holt, *Egypt and the Fertile Crescent* (Ithaca: Cornell University Press, 1966); Bernard Lewis, *The Middle East and the West* (New York: Harper, 1964), and the sources cited therein; and Elizabeth Monroe, *Britain's Moment in the Middle East, 1914–56* (Baltimore: Johns Hopkins University Press, 1981).

3. The theme that European rule was needed to ensure impartial, fair government and administration of justice and to protect minorities from oppression permeates the thinking in Lord Cromer [Evelyn Baring], *Modern Egypt,* 2 vols. (New York: Macmillan, 1908), especially vol. 2, 123–259.

4. These attitudes are exemplified in Ayatollah Khomeini's writings and speeches. See Imam [Ruhollah] Khomeini, *Islam and Revolution: Writings and Declarations of Imam Khomeini,* trans. Hamid Algar (Berkeley: Mizan Press, 1981).

5. "Freedom of Religions," *Washington Post,* September 11, 1997, A14.

6. Lee Romney, "Battle Urged Against Religious Persecution," *Los Angeles Times,* October 20, 1997, 1; "Christian Right Urges Sanctions on Persecutors," *Financial Times,* August 27, 1997, available in LEXIS, Nexis Library, ALLWLD File.

7. The circumstances of the early Islamic community are described in W. Montgomery Watt, *Muhammad, Prophet and Statesman* (Oxford: Oxford University Press, 1971).

8. The law of jihad is discussed in Rudolph Peters, *Jihad in Classical and Modern Islam* (Princeton: Markus Wiener, 1996), 1–54.

9. For the evolution of jihad doctrine see ibid., 55–159; and Ann Elizabeth Mayer, "War and Peace in the Islamic Tradition and in International Law," in *Just War and Jihad: War, Peace, and Statecraft in the Western and Islamic Traditions,* ed. James Johnson and John Kelsay (Westport, Conn.: Greenwood Press, 1991), 195–226.

10. For background see A. S. Tritton, *The Caliphs and Their Non-Muslim Subjects: A Critical Study of the Covenant of Umar* (London: Cass, 1970); and Antoine Fattal, *Le Statut légal des non-musulmans en pays d'Islam* (Beirut: Imprimerie Catholique, 1958).

11. Zoroastrians and Sabeans are sometimes also included in this category.

12. A useful review of the rules pertaining to the status of *dhimmis* is in Fattal, *Le Statut légal des non-musulmans.*

13. Joseph Schacht, *Introduction to Islamic Law* (Oxford: Clarendon Press, 1964), 130–131.

14. For a survey of how the Muslim community interacted with non-Muslims on the subcontinent, see Ishtiaq Husain Qureshi, *The Muslim Community of the Indo-Pakistan Subcontinent, 610–1947: A Brief Historical Analysis* (Delhi: Renaissance Publishing House, 1985).

15. See, for example, the studies in Benjamin Braude and Bernard Lewis, eds., *Christians and Jews in the Ottoman Empire,* 2 vols. (New York: Holmes and Meier, 1982).

16. On the treatment of Jews, see Bernard Lewis, *The Jews of Islam* (Princeton: Princeton University Press, 1984).

17. Introductions to some of the changes in attitudes brought about by nationalism can be found in Albert Hourani, *Arabic Thought in the Liberal Age, 1798–1939* (London: Oxford University Press, 1962); and Lewis, *The Emergence of Modern Turkey.*

18. The implications of Islamization programs for religious minorities are emphasized in P. J. Vatikiotis, *Islam and the State* (London: Croom Helm, 1987). See also Ishtiaq Ahmad, *The Concept of an Islamic State: An Analysis of the Ideological Controversy in Pakistan* (New York: St. Martin's Press, 1987).

19. "Egypt Cracks Down on Muslim Brotherhood," *Asia Times,* April 17, 1997, available in LEXIS, Nexis Library, ALLWLD File.

20. Subhi Mahmassani, *Arkan huquq al-insan* (Beirut: Dar al-ʿilm liʾl-malayin, 1979), 260–264, 281.

21. Ibid., 260–264.

22. This approach is characteristic of chapters in S. M. Haider, ed., *Islamic Concept of Human Rights* (Lahore: Book House, 1978). In his chapter in this work, "Equality Before Law and Equal Protection of Laws As Legal Doctrines for the Prevention of Discrimination and Protection of Minorities" (213–237), Haider unequivocally endorses the principle of full equality for all citizens regardless of religion.

23. Al-Bishri's ideas are discussed in detail in Leonard Binder, *Islamic Liberalism* (Chicago: University of Chicago Press, 1988), 246–292.

24. Ibid., 287–288.

25. Abdullahi El-Naiem [An-Naʿim], "A Modern Approach to Human Rights in Islam: Foundations and Implications for Africa," in *Human Rights and Development in Africa,* ed. Claude Welch Jr. and Ronald Meltzer (Albany: State University of New York Press, 1984), 85.

26. Abdullahi An-Naʿim applied his Islamic human rights norms to critique the treatment of non-Muslims in Egypt in "Religious Freedom in Egypt: Under the Shadow of the Islamic *Dhimma* System," in *Religious Liberty and Human Rights*

in Nations and Religions, ed. Leonard Swidler (Philadelphia: Ecumenical Press, 1986), 43–59.

27. Courtney W. Howland, "The Challenge of Religious Fundamentalism to the Liberty and Equality Rights of Women: An Analysis under the United Nations Charter," *Columbia Journal of Transnational Law* 35 (1997), 329–330.

28. Ibid., 18.

29. Ibid., 15.

30. Ibid., 17.

31. Ibid., 36.

32. Ibid.

33. Ibid., 37.

34. Ibid.

35. Ibid., 70.

36. Ibid., 71.

37. Abu'l A'la Mawdudi, *Human Rights in Islam* (Leicester, England: Islamic Foundation, 1980), 30. He was not inhibited from attacking the "heretical" Ahmadis, even though their "heretical" views should have qualified them as non-Muslims, whose feelings, Mawdudi said, must be respected.

38. Without such standards it would, for example, be difficult to tell whether the Iranian government's harsh denunciations of Baha'is would be deemed in violation of Article 12.e.

39. The translation is taken from "Constitution of the Islamic Republic of Iran of 24 October 1979 As Amended to 28 July 1989," in Albert Blaustein and Gisbert Flanz, eds., *Constitutions of the Countries of the World* (Dobbs Ferry, N.Y.: Oceana, 1992).

40. See, for example, Shaul Bakhash, *The Reign of the Ayatollahs* (New York: Basic Books, 1984), 226.

41. Abu'l A'la Mawdudi, *The Islamic Law and Constitution* (Lahore: Islamic Publications, 1980), 188–189, 274–276.

42. Human Rights Watch/Middle East, *Iran: Religious and Ethnic Minorities. Discrimination in Law and Practice,* vol. 9, no. 7 (September 1997).

43. Human Rights Commission of Pakistan, *State of Human Rights in Pakistan 1993* (Lahore: Human Rights Commission of Pakistan, n.d.), 45–48.

44. This conclusion is further strengthened by a reading of the section of the Preamble that deals with the army. It provides that the goal of the army is "accomplishing an ideological mission, that is, the 'Jihad' for the sake of God, as well as for struggling to open the way for the sovereignty of the Word of God throughout the world." This is an army with the mission to engage in combat on behalf of the Islamic cause.

45. Roger Cooper, *The Baha'is of Iran,* Minority Rights Group Report 51 (London: Minority Rights Group, 1982), 7–8, 10.

46. Ibid., 11.

47. Cooper, *The Baha'is of Iran;* Douglas Martin, "The Persecution of the Baha'is of Iran, 1844–1984," *Baha'i Studies* 12-13 (1984); and Economic and Social Council Commission on Human Rights, *Report on the Human Rights Situation in the Islamic Republic of Iran by the Special Representative of the Commission, Mr. Reynaldo Galindo Pohl, Appointed Pursuant to Resolution 1986/41,* E/CN.4/1987/23. See also the Amnesty International annual reports.

48. Iran has attempted various public relations initiatives in this connection. Iran's Armenians made a statement, which in context appears to have been engineered by the regime, rejecting charges that they were being discriminated against. "Iranian Armenians Reject US Rights Reports As Biased," *BBC Summary of World Broadcasts*, October 7, 1997, available in LEXIS, Nexis Library, ALLWLD File. In addition, Ayatollah Khamene'i boasted to a visiting Armenian dignitary about Iran's good treatment of religious minorities. "Khamene'i Meets Armenian Delegation," *BBC Summary of World Broadcasts*, July 23, 1997, available in LEXIS, Nexis Library, ALLWLD File. Ayatollah Jannati of the Council of Guardians went to Armenia for a human rights seminar, where a judge in Armenia's constitutional court was reported as observing that Iran had consistently respected human rights, a principle rooted in Islamic law. "Guardian Council Secretary Visits Armenia for Human Rights Seminar," *BBC Summary of World Broadcasts*, October 21, 1997, available in LEXIS, Nexis Library, ALLWLD File. In this domain as in others, Iran seems to be belatedly struggling to convey the message that its treatment of religious minorities is enlightened.

49. Mawdudi, *Human Rights*, 21–22.

50. Mawdudi, *The Islamic Law and Constitution*, 288–291.

51. Ibid., 191–193.

52. Ibid., 297–298.

53. Ibid., 276.

54. Ibid., 287.

55. A fascinating record of materials on the 1953 disturbances and the theological, ideological, and political views of both the Ahmadis and their opponents, including Mawdudi and his Jama'at, can be seen in *Report of the Court of Inquiry Constituted Under Punjab Act II of 1954 to Enquire into the Punjab Disturbances of 1953* (Lahore: Superintendent, Government Printing, Punjab, 1954).

56. The ordinance and the human rights violations that ensued pursuant to the demotion of Ahmadis to the status of impostors wrongfully claiming to be Muslims are discussed in "Pakistan Ordinance XX of 1984: International Implications on Human Rights," *Loyola of Los Angeles International and Comparative Law Journal* 9 (1987), 661–692. See also Rashida Patel, *Islamisation of Laws in Pakistan?* (Karachi: Faiza Publications, 1986), 126–127; Amnesty International, *Pakistan: Violations of Human Rights*, April 1985, 6–7; and "Prepared Testimony of Patricia Gossman Before the Senate Foreign Relations Committee," *Federal News Service*, March 6, 1996, available in LEXIS, Nexis Library, ALLWLD File. See also the sources cited below regarding the issues raised by the *Zaheeruddin* case.

57. This case is critically evaluated in Nadeem Ahmad Siddiq, "Enforced Apostasy: Zaheeruddin v. State and the Official Persecution of the Ahmadiyya Community in Pakistan," *Law and Inequality* 14 (1995), 275–338; and Tayyab Mahmud, "Freedom of Religion and Religious Minorities in Pakistan: A Study of Judicial Practice," *Fordham International Law Journal* 19 (1995), 40–100.

58. For the text of the 1991 bill, see Rubya Mehdi, *The Islamization of the Law in Pakistan* (Richmond, England: Curzon Press, 1994), 324–329.

59. *Zaheeruddin v. State*, 26 S.C.M.R. (S.Ct.) 1718 (1993) (Pak.), 1773–1774.

60. Amnesty International, *Saudi Arabia: Religious Intolerance. The Arrest, Detention and Torture of Christian Worshippers and Shi'a Muslims* (New York: Amnesty International,1993).

61. Amnesty International, *Behind Closed Doors: Unfair Trials in Saudi Arabia,* AI Index, MDE 23/08/97.

62. "Saudi Interior Minister on 'Tendentious Campaign' By Western Media," *BBC Summary of World Broadcasts,* November 25, 1997, available in LEXIS, Nexis Library, ALWLD File. The foreign minister insisted that the Saudis were very committed to human rights. "Foreign Minister Dismisses Report Criticizing Human Rights Record," *BBC Summary of World Broadcasts,* November 26, 1997, available in LEXIS, Nexis Library, ALLWLD File.

Chapter 8

1. Sami Aldeeb Abu Sahlieh, "Les Droits de l'homme et l'Islam," *Revue générale de droit international public* 89 (1985), 636–637.

2. John Kelsay, "Saudi Arabia, Pakistan, and the Universal Declaration of Human Rights," in *Human Rights and the Conflict of Cultures: Western and Islamic Perspectives on Religious Liberty,* ed. David Little, John Kelsay, and Abdulaziz Sachedina (Columbia: University of South Carolina Press, 1988), 35–37.

3. Aldeeb Abu Sahlieh, "Les Droits de l'homme et l'Islam," 637.

4. The most recent information on CRC reservations can be found at <http://www.un.org/Depts/Treaty/final/ts2/newfiles/frontboo/toc4.htm>.

5. These patterns are surveyed in Ann Elizabeth Mayer, "Law and Religion in the Muslim Middle East," *American Journal of Comparative Law* 35 (1987), 143–147.

6. Sultanhussein Tabandeh, *A Muslim Commentary on the Universal Declaration of Human Rights,* trans. F. J. Goulding (Guildford, England: F. J. Goulding, 1970), 71.

7. Ibid., 59.

8. The author's translation of a French translation from the Arabic offered in Sami Aldeeb Abu Sahlieh, "Liberté religieuse et apostasie dans l'Islam," *Praxis juridique et religion* 23 (1986), 53.

9. Human Rights Watch/Middle East, *Iran: Religious and Ethnic Minorities. Discrimination in Law and Practice,* vol. 9, no. 7 (September 1997), 10. The official claims that Iran did not punish apostates was belied by actual facts, such as the confirmation of death sentences for two Baha'is by Iran's Supreme Court in 1997. See "Human Rights Abuses in Iran Have Ottawa On Alert," *Toronto Star,* May 25, 1997, available in LEXIS, Nexis Library, ALLWLD File.

10. Aldeeb Abu Sahlieh, "Liberté religieuse," 61–66.

11. Sources on this infamous affair include "Shari'a or Civil Code? Egypt's Parallel Legal Systems: An Interview with Ahmad Sayf al-Islam," *Middle East Report* (November-December 1995), 25–27; Nasr Abu Zaid, "The Case of Abu Zaid: Academic Freedom in Egypt," *Index on Censorship* 4 (1996), 30–39; Navid Kermani, "Die Affäre Abu Zayd: Eine Kritik am religiösen Diskurs und ihre Folgen," *Orient* 35 (1994), 25–49; "L'affaire Abu Zayd, universitaire poursuivi pour apostasie," *Monde arabe: Maghreb Machrek,* no. 151 (January-March 1996), 18; Baudouin Dupret, "Le procès: l'argumentation des tribunaux," *Monde arabe: Maghreb Machrek,* no. 151 (January-March 1996), 19–22; and Kilian Bälz, "Submitting Faith to Judicial Scrutiny Through the Family Trial: The Abu Zayd Case,"

Die Welt des Islams 37 (1997), 135–155. More details are available at <http://www.chrla.org/releases/zayd.htm>.

12. Bälz, "Submitting Faith to Judicial Scrutiny," 149.

13. Bjazet [pseud.], "La tradition? . . . Quelle tradition?" *Monde arabe: Maghreb Machrek,* no. 151 (January-March 1996), 23–31; and Kermani, "Die Affäre Abu Zayd," 29.

14. Kermani, "Die Affäre Abu Zayd," 29.

15. Ibid., 35.

16. Ibid., 33–34.

17. Ibid., 39–40.

18. Bälz, "Submitting Faith to Judicial Scrutiny," 149.

19. Kermani, "Die Affäre Abu Zaid," 48.

20. See, e.g., Mohamed Talbi, "Religious Liberty: A Muslim Perspective," in *Religious Liberty and Human Rights in Nations and Religions,* ed. Leonard Swidler (Philadelphia: Ecumenical Press, 1986), 175–188.

21. Abdulaziz Sachedina, "Freedom of Conscience and Religion in the Qur'an," in *Human Rights and the Conflict of Cultures: Western and Islamic Perspectives on Religious Liberty,* ed. David Little, John Kelsay, and Abdulaziz Sachedina (Columbia: University of South Carolina Press, 1988), 53–90.

22. Subhi Mahmassani, *Arkan huquq al-insan* (Beirut: Dar al-'ilm li'l-malayin, 1979), 123–124.

23. Talbi, "Religious Liberty," 205.

24. Tabandeh, *A Muslim Commentary,* 70.

25. Ibid., 71.

26. Ibid., 70–71.

27. Ibid., 71.

28. Ibid.

29. Ibid., 71–72. One can find similar defenses being offered by an Egyptian author for the application of the death penalty for apostasy. These are discussed in Aldeeb Abu Sahlieh, "Les Droits de l'homme et l'Islam," 643–644.

30. Tabandeh, *A Muslim Commentary,* 72.

31. Ibid., 72–73.

32. Ibid., 59.

33. Ibid., 72.

34. It should be recalled that Tabandeh's intended audience consisted of persons attending an international human rights conference in Iran.

35. J. Roland Pennock, "Rights, Natural Rights, and Human Rights: A General View," in *Human Rights: NOMOS XXIII,* ed. J. Roland Pennock and John W. Chapman (New York: New York University Press, 1981), 14.

36. The meaning of the phrase *takhdhil li'l-umma* is obscure. A related verb with the same root occurs in the Qur'an (3:160) in the sense of "forsake." However, the verbal noun *takhdhil* seems to mean something like incitement to neglect to aid companions or to be cowardly and weakhearted. Although one can predict that the prohibited speech targeted here involves ideas and beliefs that are deemed harmful to the Islamic community, just what constitutes this *takhdhil* is open to speculation.

37. How confusing this provision can be is illustrated by the protest made by the International Commission of Jurists (ICJ) over the execution of Mahmud Muham-

mad Taha, discussed in this chapter. The ICJ invoked the UIDHR provision granting freedom of religion in its protest. *Human Rights Internet Reporter* 10 (January-April 1985). Apparently, the ICJ imagined that the UIDHR prohibited executions for apostasy. In fact, it has been drafted to allow Muslims to be executed for apostasy.

38. *The Meaning of the Glorious Koran,* trans. Marmaduke Pickthall (Albany: State University of New York Press, 1976).

39. *Report of the Court of Inquiry Constituted Under Punjab Act II of 1954 to Enquire into the Punjab Disturbances of 1953* (Lahore: Superintendent, Government Printing, Punjab, 1954), 218.

40. "Prepared Testimony of Patricia Gossman Before the Senate Foreign Relations Committee," *Federal News Service,* March 6, 1996, available in LEXIS, Nexis Library, ALLWLD File.

41. Ibid.

42. "Lawyers Observe Strike Against Pakistani Judge's Murder," *Agence France Presse,* October 13, 1997, available in LEXIS, Nexis Library, ALLWLD File.

43. Paula R. Newberg, "Economic, Political Pressures Strain Pakistan's Civil Society," *Los Angeles Times,* November 16, 1997, available in LEXIS, Nexis Library, ALLWLD File.

44. Roger Cooper, *The Baha'is of Iran,* Minority Rights Group Report 51 (London: Minority Rights Group, 1982), 13–15; Douglas Martin, "The Persecution of the Baha'is of Iran, 1844–1984," *Baha'i Studies* 12-13 (1984), 49, 54–56, 58, 65; and Human Rights Watch/Middle East, *Iran: Religious and Ethnic Minorities. Discrimination in Law and Practice,* vol. 9, no. 7 (September 1997), 10–15.

45. Martin, "The Persecution of the Baha'is," 54.

46. Cooper, *The Baha'is of Iran,* 13–14; Economic and Social Council, *Report on the Human Rights Situation in the Islamic Republic of Iran,* E/CN.4/1987/20 (January 28, 1987), 20.

47. Economic and Social Council, *Report on the Human Rights Situation,* 21.

48. This translation is taken from "Constitution of the Islamic Republic of Iran of 24 October 1979 As Amended to 28 July 1989," in Albert Blaustein and Gisbert Flanz, eds., *Constitutions of the Countries of the World* (Dobbs Ferry, N.Y.: Oceana, 1992).

49. A useful source on the Rushdie death edict and subsequent controversy is Anthony Chase, "Legal Guardians: Islamic Law, International Law, Human Rights and the Salman Rushdie Affair," *American University Journal of International Law and Policy* 11 (1996), 375–435.

50. Various representative reactions and comments, largely from Muslims, can be found in *Index on Censorship* (May 1989), 7–18. Responses to the order to kill Rushdie are also discussed in Lisa Appignanesi and Sara Maitland, eds., *The Rushdie File* (Syracuse, N.Y.: Syracuse University Press, 1990).

51. See, for example, the book *For Rushdie: Essays by Arab and Muslim Writers in Defense of Free Speech* (New York: Braziller, 1994). The volume includes contributions from many of the cultural luminaries of the Muslim world and a copy of a petition on Rushdie's behalf that had been signed by 127 Iranian writers, despite the danger involved.

52. "Iranian Political Factions in Row Over Rushdie Affair," *Agence France Presse,* April 21, 1997, available in LEXIS, Nexis Library, ALLWLD File.

53. "Palestinian Affairs: Iranian Envoy Calls UN Draft Resolution on Human Rights Baseless, Irrelevant," *BBC Summary of World Broadcasts,* December 15, 1995, available in LEXIS, Nexis Library, ALLWLD File.

54. "UN Condemns Iran on Human Rights," *Agence France Presse,* March 8, 1995, available in LEXIS, Nexis Library, ALLWLD File.

55. See Ann Elizabeth Mayer, "Islamic Rights or Human Rights: An Iranian Dilemma," *Iranian Studies* 29 (Summer-Fall 1996), 290–292.

56. His views are set forth in a book that was recently translated by Abdullahi Ahmed An-Na'im, *The Second Message of Islam by Ustadh Mahmoud Mohamed Taha* (Syracuse, N.Y.: Syracuse University Press, 1987).

57. Aldeeb Abu Sahlieh, "Liberté religieuse," 51.

58. Abdullahi An-Na'im, "The Islamic Law of Apostasy and Its Modern Applicability: A Case from the Sudan," *Religion* 16 (1986), 207.

59. Ibid., 197.

60. Ibid., 209. It is significant for purposes of this study to note that the Muslim World League is the parent organization of the Islamic Council, which sponsored and published the UIDHR. According to one account, the Muslim World League actually congratulated Nimeiri for executing Taha. Aldeeb Abu Sahlieh, "Les Droits de l'homme et l'Islam," 707.

61. Ibid.

62. Africa Watch, *Denying "the Honor of Living." Sudan: A Human Rights Disaster* (March 1990).

63. See the accounts in J. Millard Burr and Robert O. Collins, *Requiem for the Sudan: War, Drought, and Disaster Relief on the Nile* (Boulder: Westview Press, 1995); and Human Rights Watch/Africa, *Civilian Devastation: Abuses by All Sides in the War in Southern Sudan* (New York: Human Rights Watch, 1994). A recent protest letter catalogues the extreme misery of the Nuba people, besieged and abused by the Bashir regime and its local militias. Forced conversions to Islam and executions of alleged apostates figure side by side with slave traffic in women and children, forced labor, orchestrated famines, pauperization, murder, rape, and genocide. Africa Policy Information Center, "Sudan: Women's Group Reports 'Genocidal Abuses' in Sudan," *Africa News,* October 26, 1997, available in LEXIS, Nexis Library, ALLWLD File. In such circumstances, focusing exclusively on religious freedom issues offers little prospect for alleviating the agony of the Nuba or ending the policies that are bringing this people close to extinction. See also Africa Watch, *Eradicating the Nuba* (September 1992).

64. Haydar Ibrahim Ali, "Le Front national islamique," *Politique Africaine* 66 (June 1997), 20.

65. Human Rights Watch/Africa, *Behind the Red Line: Political Repression in the Sudan* (New York: Human Rights Watch, 1996).

66. See Amnesty International, *Saudi Arabia: An Upsurge in Public Executions* (May 15, 1993), 6; and Amnesty International, *Religious Intolerance: The Arrest, Detention and Torture of Christian Worshippers and Shi'a Muslims* (1993), 12, 15–17. In February 1998, even as Saudi-Iranian relations were warming, a Saudi sheikh roundly denounced Shi'ism in the presence of former president Rafsanjani during his goodwill visit to the kingdom, provoking Iranian outrage. "Iranian Official Leads Pilgrims to Saudi Arabia with Warm Words on Ties," *Agence France Presse,* March 17, 1998, available in LEXIS, Nexis Library, ALLWLD File.

67. Ibid., 7–8.

68. Human Rights Watch/Middle East, *Saudi Arabia: Flawed Justice. The Execution of 'Abd al-Karim Mara'i al Naqshabandi*, vol. 9, no. 9 (E) (October 1997).

69. On these systemic problems, see Amnesty International, *Behind Closed Doors: Unfair Trials in Saudi Arabia*, AI Index, MDE 23/08/97.

Chapter 9

1. See the thorough examination of this phenomenon in Roger Bastide, *The African Religions of Brazil: Toward a Sociology of the Interpretation of Civilizations*, trans. Helen Sabba (Baltimore: Johns Hopkins University Press, 1978).

2. Sultanhussein Tabandeh, *A Muslim Commentary on the Universal Declaration of Human Rights*, trans. F. J. Goulding (Guildford, England: F. J. Goulding, 1970), 57. This position was echoed in comments by Ayatollah Khomeini. After denouncing Muslims who wanted to Westernize everything and after condemning Western human rights advocates for their hypocrisy, Khomeini railed against the idea that Muslims should measure Islam "in accordance with Western criteria." Instead, he argued, Muslims should be loyal to Islam. Imam [Ruhollah] Khomeini, *Islam and Revolution: Writings and Declarations of Imam Khomeini*, trans. Hamid Algar (Berkeley: Mizan Press, 1981), 270–272.

3. "Islam Guarantees Rights, Says Saud," *Riyadh Daily*, June 17, 1993, available in LEXIS, Nexis Library, ALLWLD File.

4. Press release of Iran's permanent mission to the United Nations entitled "Statement by H. E. Dr. Mohammad-Javad Zarif, Deputy Foreign Minister and Head of Delegation of the Islamic Republic of Iran Before the World Conference on Human Rights, Vienna, 18 June 1993."

5. The issues discussed here are not, of course, unique to the Muslim world. They relate to the search for cultural identity that is occurring in many Third World societies. A valuable analysis of the problems of establishing cultural identity in dependent countries is Borhan Ghalioun, "Identité, culture et politique culturelle dans les pays dépendants," *Peuples Méditerranéens* 16 (1981), 31–50.

6. Abu'l A'la Mawdudi, in *Purdah and the Status of Women in Islam* (Lahore: Islamic Publications, 1979), cited figures such as "Judge Ben Lindsey, President of the Juvenile Court of Denver" (59), "Dr. Kraft Ebing [sic]" (116), and "Wester Marck [sic]" (127), to show that there is a scientific justification for *shari'a* rules. Even statements in the popular U.S. monthly *Reader's Digest* are deemed worthy of citation to establish that *shari'a* rules are correct. See 45.

7. Tabandeh, *A Muslim Commentary*, 51.

8. International Commission of Jurists, Kuwait University, and Union of Arab Lawyers, *Human Rights in Islam: Report of a Seminar Held in Kuwait, December 1980* (International Commission of Jurists, 1982), 9. See also remarks on pages 11 and 34.

9. A. K. Brohi, "The Nature of Islamic Law and the Concept of Human Rights," in ibid., 54.

10. "Islam a Champion of Human Rights, Official Says," *Compass Newswire*, October 28, 1997, available in LEXIS, Nexis Library, ALLWLD File.

11. Tabandeh, *A Muslim Commentary*, 85.

12. Abu'l A'la Mawdudi, *Human Rights in Islam* (Leicester, England: Islamic Foundation, 1980), 15.

13. Ibid., 39.

14. Presumably, these are meant to resemble the ones in the scheme of drastically circumscribed and watered-down rights that he set forth in his human rights pamphlet.

15. Iraq is an excellent example of how a single brutal dictator can now entirely dominate a country. A thoughtful analysis of the level of oppression that Saddam Hussain has been able to achieve in Iraq can be found in Samir al-Khalil, *Republic of Fear: The Inside Story of Saddam's Iraq* (New York: Pantheon Books, 1989).

16. For example, see Mawdudi, *Human Rights,* 15, 17–22.

17. International Commission of Jurists, *Human Rights in Islam,* 7.

18. Ibid., 49–55.

19. Lawyers Committee for Human Rights, *Islam and Justice: Debating the Future of Human Rights in the Middle East and North Africa* (New York: Lawyers Committee for Human Rights, 1997).

20. The declaration from the meeting is presented in German translation in Bassam Tibi, "Bericht über das Kolloquium arabischer Wissenschaftler und Schriftsteller: *Multaqa Tunis al-thaqafi 'an al-hurriyat al-dimuqratiya fi al-'alam al-'arabi*/Das kulturelle Tunis-Kolloquium über die demokratischen Freiheiten in der arabischen Welt im Centre Culturel de Hammamet," April 1–3, 1983, *Orient* 24 (1983), 398–399.

21. Ali Hilal [Dassuqi], ed., *Al-Dimuqratiya wa huquq al-insan fi 'l-watan al-'arabi* (Cairo: Markaz dirasat al-wahda al-'arabiya, 1983).

22. Mawdudi made a very similar assertion, claiming, "When we speak of human rights in Islam we mean those rights granted by God. Rights granted by kings or legislative assemblies can be withdrawn as easily as they are conferred; but no individual and no institution has the authority to withdraw the rights conferred by God." Mawdudi, *Human Rights,* 15.

23. "Islam Guarantees Rights, Says Saud," *Riyadh Daily,* June 17, 1993, available in LEXIS, Nexis Library, Saudi File.

Appendix A

1. Taken from Albert Blaustein and Gisbert Flanz, eds., *Constitutions of the Countries of the World* (Dobbs Ferry, N.Y.: Oceana, 1992). Various passages corresponding to Arabic quotations in the Persian original have been omitted.

Appendix B

1. United Nations General Assembly. A/CONF.157/PC/62/Add.18, June 9, 1993. Submitted to the World Conference on Human Rights. Preparatory Committee. Fourth session. Geneva, April 19–May 7 1993. Item 5 on the provisional agenda. Annex to res. no. 49/19-P.

Index